Education for Sustainabilit

Volume 6

Education and sustainability remain two of the most important topics at this inflection point in human history. As multiple intertwined crises challenge the creation of a sustainable, just, peaceful future, education for sustainability remains ever more critical. This series builds on a variety of international efforts. As part of the United Nations Sustainable Development Goals (SDGs 2015-2030) and as echoed by the Aichi-Nagoya Declaration on Education for Sustainable Development (2014), education must speak to climate change, biodiversity, sustainable consumption and production, and the urgency of the civilizational crisis we face. Supporting this aim, there is a call for research and coordinated actions with an emphasis on the principles of human rights, gender equality, democracy, and social and environmental justice. There is also a great need for attention to the importance and relevance of traditional knowledge and indigenous wisdom in all geographical, socio-cultural, and educational contexts. While the Decade of Education for Sustainable Development (DESD) (2005-2014) has been completed, the status and advocacy of education for sustainable development remains prominent. The United Nations goals of Education for All (2000) and the Millennium Development Goals (MDGs 2000-2015) were complementary and provided a rationale for the critical importance of environmental education and education for sustainable development. The United Nations Educational, Scientific and Cultural Organization's (UNESCO) Muscat Agreement in 2014 advocated seven global education targets, one of which was to cultivate skills for global citizenship and environmental sustainability. Many of these lofty aims remained unrealized and are ever more urgent as the predicted social and environmental crises of the twenty-first century unfold dramatically before our students' eyes.

With this background, and in light of UNESCO's Education 2030 Agenda (2017) and their world-wide consultations on Futures of Education: Learning to Become (2019), this Education for Sustainability Book Series was launched. Its purpose is to echo and enhance the global importance of education for a sustainable future as an educational vision. We hope the Series will provide insights on a broad range of issues related to the intersection of, and interaction between, sustainability and education. The Series will showcase innovative practice, discusses salient theoretical topics, and use cases as examples.

For further information on this important book series, to become involved, or to propose a manuscript, please contact any of the co-editors. We are interested in new approaches; humanistic, socially-critical, and radical perspectives; examples that tell a larger story; and manuscripts that speak to the crisis and challenges we face in education and in sustainability.

John Chi-Kin Lee
The Education University of Hong Kong
Hong Kong SAR, China
Rupert Maclean
RMIT University
Melbourne, Australia
Peter Blaze Corcoran
Florida Gulf Coast University
Fort Myers, FL, USA

Fumiko Noguchi

Rethinking Education for Sustainable Development in a Local Community Context

Springer

Fumiko Noguchi
Institute for the Advanced Study
of Sustainability
United Nations University
Tokyo, Japan

ISSN 2367-1769 ISSN 2367-1777 (electronic)
Education for Sustainability
ISBN 978-981-16-9466-0 ISBN 978-981-16-9464-6 (eBook)
https://doi.org/10.1007/978-981-16-9464-6

This Springer imprint is published by the registered company Springer Nature Singapore Pte Ltd.
The registered company address is: 152 Beach Road, #21-01/04 Gateway East, Singapore 189721, Singapore

Series Editors' Introduction

This ground-breaking volume, *Rethinking Education for Sustainable Development in a Local Community Context*, by Fumiko Noguchi, who works at the United Nations University in Tokyo, is an important contribution to the Springer Book Series 'Education for Sustainability'. It is the 6th volume to be published to date in this book series.

Through its detailed and comprehensive case study of the perception of one Ainu fisherman, in Japan, concerning Education for Sustainable Development (ESD), the research study reported on in this book examines, and illustrates, how Education for Sustainable Development (ESD) aims to develop the capacity of all individuals to be socially critical, and to take social and political actions to achieve sustainable development, through all forms of education, whether this be formal, non-formal or informal education.

Fumiko Noguchi argues that schooling in the formal education system has dominated ESD policy and research. A result has been that the experiences, actions and struggles of practitioners and communities, particularly the socially marginalised, have been largely silenced, despite its value in advancing socially-critical ESD.

The contents of this highly innovative book report on research undertaken concerning a critical ethnographic study of the Mopet Sanctuary Network (MSN) in Hokkaido Japan. MSN was established in 2010 by both indigenous Ainu and on-Ainu people, to achieve sustainable community development, based on indigenous fishing rights claim initiated by the local Ainu elder fisherman, Hatakeyama. Through Noguchi's engagement with MSN, in her capacity as an environmental educator, she has attempted to integrate critical Environmental Education (EE) into the planned ESD activities.

The research reports on a praxis framework for ESD, in a community development context. This recognises the theory and practice of ESD within communities, with a particular focus on the socially marginalised, and identifies the valuable role of the educator in contributing to environmental learning and empowerment for all.

We are delighted to publish this particular title in the Springer 'Education for Sustainability' Book Series. The purpose of the book series is to echo and enhance the global importance of education for a sustainable future, as an educational vision.

We hope the Series will provide insights on a broad range of issues related to the intersection of, and interaction between, sustainability and education. The series showcases innovative practice, discusses salient theoretical topics and uses case studies as examples.

The Series adopts international, environmental education and lifelong learning perspectives and explores connections with the agenda of education for sustainable development. The intended audience includes university academics and students in educational studies, environmental education, climate change education, geography education, science education, curriculum studies, comparative education, educational leadership and teacher education; the staff of international agencies with responsibilities for education; and schoolteachers in primary and secondary schools.

Supported by the expertise of a distinguished and diverse International Advisory Board, this Series features authoritative and comprehensive global coverage, as well as diversified local, regional, national and international perspectives. As a complement to the 'Schooling for Sustainable Development' Book Series, it explores issues that go beyond primary and secondary schooling into university, vocational and community education settings. These educational issues involve multiple stakeholders ranging from international agencies, governmental and non-governmental organisations, education and business leaders to teachers, parents and, critically, students and youth. Research topics covered include global themes related to environment, such as climate change prevention, mitigation and adaptation; disaster prevention and risk reduction; biodiversity education and ecological education. They also include human ecological issues such as global citizenship, peace education, childhood development, arts education, intergenerational equity, women's and gender studies, and human rights education. Further, they include society-orientated issues such as governance, green skills for sustainable development, and patterns of applied learning and leadership for a sustainable future.

The authors of books in the Series are responsible for the choice and presentation of information and views contained in their particular volume, and for the opinions expressed therein, which are not necessarily those of UNESCO, the Education University of Hong Kong or the United Nations University in Tokyo, where the author of this particular book is employed, and so do not commit these respective organisations.

In terms of the Springer Book Series in which this volume is published, the various topics dealt with in the series are wide ranging and varied in coverage, with an emphasis on cutting edge developments, best practices and education innovations for development. More information about this book series is available at (Springer to insert web address).

We believe this book series makes a useful contribution to knowledge sharing about Education and Sustainability. Any readers of this or other volumes in the Series who have an idea for writing or editing their own book on any aspect of Education for Sustainability are encouraged to approach the Series Editors either directly or through Springer to discuss publishing their own volume in the series. The Series

Editors are always willing to assist perspective authors to shape their manuscripts in ways that make them suitable for publication in this Series.

February 2022

John Chi-Kin Lee
The Education University of Hong Kong
Hong Kong SAR, China

Rupert Maclean
RMIT University
Melbourne, Australia

University of Tasmania
Hobart, Australia

Peter Blaze Corcoran
Florida Gulf Coast University
Fort Myers, FL, USA

Foreword

As we move into the third decade of the twenty-first century, the human community has made little progress in addressing the challenges of biodiversity loss and climate change, intolerance and prejudice, poverty and inequality, rising cultural and political tensions, and the many other challenges to peace, well-being and security, which we faced at the beginning of the new Millennium. Of course, improvements have been made, but these have been scattered and localised and prone to lapses. This is due to the overwhelming focus in local, national and world affairs on addressing the symptoms of the challenges rather than their root causes and the interlinkages and dependencies among them.

This is despite our having many 'United Nations International Years of …' designed to promote and mobilise action in support of a better world. 2021 alone was the International Year of Peace and Trust as well as the International Year for the Elimination of Child Labour. It is also despite all the concerted action during United Nations Decades for A Culture of Peace and Non-violence for the Children of the World (2001–2010), on Education for All (2003–2012), on Biodiversity (2011–2020), on Nutrition (2016–2025), on Water for Sustainable Development (2018–2028) and for Peace (2019–2028). There have even been three United Nations Decades for The Eradication of Poverty (1997–2006, 2008–2017 and 2018–2027) and we are now in the fourth UN International Decade for the Eradication of Colonialism (1990–2000, 2001–2010, 2011–2020 and 2021–2030). It is perhaps not surprising that progress on all these fronts has been slow. This could reflect the single topic and symptom-focused nature of many of these different themes and the ineffectiveness of so many United Nations agencies, which, in itself, is a reflection of the systemic or structural rootedness of the very problems that the United Nations was established to address.

However, there was one United Nations Decade that was cross-sectoral and sought to address the structural causes of poverty, inequality, conflict, biodiversity loss, climate change and so on. The medium for this was a special form of education, known as Education for Sustainable Development, which was the focus of the 2005–2014 United Nations Decade of Education for Sustainable Development (UNDESD).

I was chosen by UNESCO, the United Nations agency charged with managing the UNDESD, to write the original think pieces and draft action plans to establish the rationale and scope of the Decade. It was an honour to do this with the support of colleagues around the world and it was interesting to observe the way compromises were made in the wording and, more subtly, the intent of the Decade. Yet, as Fumiko Noguchi reports in this book, the aim of Education for Sustainable Development remained using educational means to develop the capacities of everyone to be socially critical in outlook or, Freirean terms, 'conscientised', to look to root causes not symptoms, and to be willing and skilled to act—socially, economically, environmentally and politically—to help achieve sustainable development.

A UNESCO conference in Aichi-Nagoya, Japan, at the end of the UNDESD in 2014, described the UNDESD as 'successful' as it had both infused the concept of sustainable development into education and the processes of education into sustainable development. Fumiko Noguchi recognises these achievements in this book but delves beneath the surface of trends and events to ask three very important questions. Her answers form the substance of this book.

The first question concerned who did the many actors in the UNDESD had in mind when they were planning and undertaking education for sustainable development projects? This question investigates the intended audiences, which were found to be, predominantly, learners in the formal education settings schools and colleges. Fumiko Noguchi argues that this is necessary, but, unfortunately, insufficient scope for education if the important transformations needed in the world are to be achieved. And she is, of course, correct in this. It is a contradiction to use the critical nature of the world's many problems of sustainability and to advocate for reforms in school education to address them—and, then, to wait for a decade or more for school education for students to grow up and have developed the knowledge, values and skills people need to do so.

Instead, she calls for a much more comprehensive range of audiences to be catered for by proponents of educators for sustainable development. This is in line with the original conception of four audiences for Education for Sustainable Development: students, yes; but also the general public so that *everyone* can benefit from learning the knowledge, values and skills to live sustainably, workers so that they can apply sustainability values and processes in their jobs and policymakers so that they can better create a supportive context for achieving sustainable development. In this marvellous book, Fumiko Noguchi makes a strong case for Education for Sustainable Development for everyone—even an Indigenous fisherman called Hatakeyama who lives in Mombetsu on the northern coast of Hokkaido, Japan's most northerly island, across the Sea of Okhotsk from Russia.

In retelling and analysing Hatakeyama's story, Fumiko Noguchi shows that even those perceived as 'the least of us' are important parts of the 'everyone' of Education for Sustainable Development.

After establishing this point, Fumiko Noguchi asks two follow-up questions. What are the systems and processes of unsustainability that have shaped Hatakeyama's lifeworlds and those of his Indigenous Ainu community? And what processes of education can Hatakeyama (and his community) use to achieve conscientisation appropriate to make their communities safer, fairer and more sustainable places in which to live?

These are questions of how lifeworlds are shaped and how people can develop the knowledge, skills and values to successfully reshape them. In answering the first part, Fumiko Noguchi allows Hatakeyama to tell stories of Ainu and personal oppression as the minority Indigenous people of Japan, how colonialism displaced to them to the semi-Arctic far north, their current precarious living conditions, the threats to cultural and language survival, and the powerless they faced. Hatakeyama also tells of the frustrations and powerlessness he experiences in two decades of trial and error living a life of 'lonely resistance':

> I tried every method that seemed an effective way to change the policy. I learnt from fishermen and contractors and copied their way of getting close to the politicians. I approached potential politicians and paid to lobby them. I do not know how much money I wasted in 20 years. I looked for anyone who could support him [*sic* – me], including fishermen friends and various researchers. Whenever I found a relationship with supporters that were inconsistent or unsuccessful, I turned away from them. Many came and left me over the twenty years.

At first, Fumiko Noguchi felt that she was unable to sufficiently appreciate Hatakeyama's story and identify strategies for Education for Sustainable Development appropriate to it. So she listened, and listened, empathised, asked questions and, over many months, came to understand the structural forces at work in Ainu fishing communities, their hopes and aspirations, cares and frustrations, and above all, the strengths they find in their Ainu culture and Indigenous ways of viewing the world and learning. Fumiko Noguchi found that critical social workers in many countries were working on similar challenges. Working from a framework comprising elements of human rights advocacy, critical social theory and strengths (or asset)-based community development, critical social workers guide marginalised families and communities towards emancipatory goals of their choosing. This is what Fumiko Noguchi found herself doing in her educational work with Hatakeyama and his community in Mombetsu.

However, she also found that few critical social workers recognised that what they do in their work is *education*, let alone Education for Sustainable Development. Similarly, she found that very few sustainable development educators saw themselves practising critical community development. In seeing the parallels between the two fields of Education for Sustainable Development and critical community development, in this book Fumiko Noguchi shows the potential of both not only to learn from each other and operate in mutually beneficial partnerships, but also the true relevance and power of Education for Sustainable Development.

Fumiko Noguchi's book,
Rethinking Education for Sustainable Development in a Local Community Context
to modernist traditions in the world today or, at least to the neo-liberal and managerial forces that characterises so much education, community development (and sustainable development) policy and practices. Her story of the emancipatory power of Education for Sustainable Development in the lives of Hatakeyama and his community shows us that Education for Sustainable Development can be relevant to *everyone*

and that working from the perspective of critical community development can indeed contribute to change for a peaceful, just and sustainable future. In so doing, Fumiko Noguchi shows us that the features of effective Education for Sustainable Development include:

- Working with people of all ages in cross-cohort and cross-sectoral partnerships;
- Promoting anti-discriminatory analyses that reach from local to global, identifying the ways in which personal stories are political;
- Teaches people to question their 'reality' through partnering in practical local projects with other people in the community;
- Generating knowledge- and theory-in-action based upon experiences of structural analysis and social learning.

Rethinking Education for Sustainable Development in a Local Community Context has the power to revolutionise Education for Sustainable Development if only those with vested interests in maintaining a school focus see the value of the adopting the decolonial and critical community development processes that Fumiko Noguchi and Hatakeyama practised and lived in the course of their UNDESD project in Mombetsu.

December 2021

John Fien
RMIT University
Melbourne, Australia

Outline

Education for Sustainable Development (ESD) aims to develop the capacity of all individuals to be socially critical and take social and political action to achieve sustainable development through all forms of education. However, schooling and the formal education system have dominated ESD policy, research and implementation. Consequently, ESD has tended to overlook the non-formal and informal education processes within community development, which encompasses the empowerment of local people to contribute to sustainable community development. As a result, the experiences, actions and struggles of practitioners and community members, particularly the socially marginalised, have been silenced, despite its value in advancing socially-critical ESD.

This research aimed to bridge this gap between ESD and community development and examined the contributions of critical environmental education (EE) to the policy, research and practice of ESD. Hence, this research (i) investigated the relevance of critical EE to socially-critical approaches to ESD in a community development context and (ii) developed a praxis framework so that both fields would be mutually supportive to strengthen the practices.

To address these questions, the research conducted a critical ethnographic study of Mopet Sanctuary Network (MSN) in Hokkaido Japan. MSN was established in 2010 by both the indigenous Ainu and non-Ainu people to achieve sustainable community development based on the indigenous fishing rights claim initiated by the local Ainu elder fisherman, Hatakeyama. Through my engagement with MSN as an educator, I attempted to integrate critical EE into the planned ESD activities. The resulting research can be divided into two parts. Each part was guided by a different methodology and produced contrasting results.

Part I was described as *within* socially-critical ESD, to mean that as the educators we were working within the framework of critical EE. The practice of ESD, as conducted by MSN, resulted in 'patchy empowerment', whereby a few MSN members were observed to have been disempowered, while the majority were empowered to challenge the current development policies. The disempowerment of the few manifested through Hatakeyama's irrational behaviour during the process where two groups within MSN conflicted each other over the strategies for Hatakeyama's rights claim. This was symbolically represented as 'swing' of a pendulum. Furthermore, the cause of the patchy empowerment could not be explained using critical theory. These findings motivated me to go *beyond* the current theoretical and methodological frameworks for the research in Part II.

Part II applied a decoloniality approach to understanding the meaning of knowledge creation and experience learning of the local community from the perspective of the few MSN members who were disempowered, in particular, Hatakeyama. In this attempt, I gained valuable insight into how the power difference between modern knowledge and 'embodied local/indigenous knowledge' can significantly influence outcomes, even within inclusive and participatory processes.

The concepts of 'place', 'language' and 'knowledge' that made possible the inclusive and participatory process of MSN actually oppressed Hatakeyama and his embodied local/indigenous knowledge, by linking with Hatakeyama's 'feeling of inferiority'. Through ESD activities, a part of Hatakeyama's embodied local/indigenous knowledge was taken out from his local context, translated into modern Japanese (the language of the coloniser) and made to fit into modern knowledge used by the majority of members. During this process, Hatakeyama was compelled to 'swing', because none of the conflicted groups represented his knowledge and ways of learning. Thus, patchy empowerment emerged.

This research produced four key findings. Firstly, critical theory, which supports critical EE, has epistemological limitations. Secondly, critical EE, which continues to be dominated by a focus on 'schooling', further enhances the epistemological problem of critical theory. Thirdly, this epistemological limitation suggested the necessity to look beyond the perspective of modern knowledge, by taking a decoloniality approach. Fourthly, taking a decoloniality approach helped to establish the epistemology of the marginalised people from their own perspective.

Finally, this research proposed a praxis framework for ESD in a community development context. This framework recognised the theory and practice of ESD within communities, with a particular focus on the socially marginalised, and identified the valuable role of the educator in contributing to learning and empowerment for all.

Contents

Abbreviations

AAH	Hokkaido Ainu Association
AAH-MC	Hokkaido Ainu Association Mombetsu Chapter
ACCU	Asia-Pacific Cultural Centre for UNESCO
AR	Action Research
CLC	Community Learning Centres
COP10	The Tenth Meeting of the Conference of the Parties
CPA	Ainu Cultural Promotion Act (In Full—Act for the Promotion of Ainu Culture, and the Dissemination of Knowledge and Education concerning Ainu Traditions)
EE	Environmental Education
EFA	Education for All
EfS	Education for Sustainability
ESD	Education for Sustainable Development
ESD-J	Japan Council on Education for Sustainable Development (Former Japan Council on the UN Decade of Education for Sustainable Development)
GAP	Global Action Plan (On ESD)
GCED	Global Citizenship Education
HEDCC	Hokkaido Environmental Dispute Coordination Commission
HPG	Hokkaido Prefectural Government
IIS	International Implementation Scheme
IWC	International Whaling Council
MCG	Mombetsu City Government
MDCAC	Minamata Disease Certification Applicants' Council
MDGs	Millennium Development Goals
MSN	Mopet Sanctuary Network
NGO	Non-Governmental Organisation
SDGs	Sustainable Development Goals
SFSY	Sapporo Fee School 'Yu'

UNCED	United Nations Conference on Environment and Development
UNCSD	UN Commission on Sustainable Development
UNDESD	UN Decade of Education for Sustainable Development
UNDRIP	UN Declaration on the Rights of Indigenous People
UNEP	United Nations Environment Programme
UNESCO	United Nations Educational, Scientific and Cultural Organisation
UNGA	UN General Assembly
UNHRC	UN Human Rights Council
UNU-IAS	United Nations University Institute of Advance Studies
WCED	World Commission on Environment and Development
WSSD	World Summit on Sustainable Development
WWII	World War II

Important Japanese and Ainu Words Used in This Book[1]

Ainu	Indigenous People who live in greater Hokkaido area of Japan (Ainu)
Ainu Mosir	The Ainu's land or the quiet land where humans live (Ainu)
Amimoto	The head of fishermen's group (Japanese)
Chisé	A house (Ainu)
Dogai Ainu	The Ainu who left their original homeland of Hokkaido and live elsewhere in Japan and overseas (Japanese)
Ekashi	Ainu elder or a grandfather (Ainu)
Ezochi	Foreigners' land, expressing the place where the Ainu live before Hokkaido colonisation (Japanese)
Fuchi	Female elder or grandmother (Ainu)
Hokkaido kaitakusi	Hokkaido Development and Colonial Agency (Japanese)
Kamuy	Spiritual being (Ainu)
Kamuy Chep-Nomi	Ainu autumn ceremony to welcome their sacred fish, salmon for their returning to their original river (Ainu)
Kotan	Village (Ainu)
Sensei	Teacher but people also use this title to address someone in authority and to give respect to the person (Japanese)
Shamo	Japanese People (slightly disparaging expression) (Ainu)
Sui-ten	Meeting point (Sui means gathering and ten means point in Japanese) (Japanese)
Yakuza	Transnational organised crime syndicates, or mafia, originating in Japan (Japanese)
Yamato minzoku	The dominant Japanese people (Japanese)
Wajin-chi	Old expression of the place for the Japanese people, that was used for Ezochi policy under Tokugawa Shogunate (Japanese)
Wajin	The dominant native ethnic group of Japan, especially used in contrast with Ainu (Japanese)

[1] All translations that appear in this book from Japanese to English have been made by the researcher.

List of Figures

List of Tables

Chapter 1
Introduction

This book began with the life story of Satoshi Hatakeyama in Mombetsu, Hokkaido, who was the indigenous Ainu elder fisherman.[1] Indigenous rights recovery of Ainu people is the key element in the search for sustainable development in Hokkaido, the northernmost island of Japan. Through his rights claim activism, he searched for the path to achieve a sustainable society where both Ainu and non-Ainu people could live together overcoming the long-lasting colonial problems. Through Hatakeyama's life struggles and his efforts for the indigenous rights claim in Mombetsu, the socially-critical and transformative nature of Education for Sustainable Development (ESD) came under the question.

Setting the Scene

Born in an Ainu Fishing Village

I am Satoshi Hatakeyama.[2] I was born in *Kotan* (village in Ainu) in Moto-Mombetsu, where the Okhotsk Sea Ice Museum is now located, in Mombetsu City, Hokkaido. In that area, there were about 17 houses and eight to nine Ainu families were living. It was where the seawater came at the front of the houses when the sea was rough. That bridge, now called Imaryuhyo *hashi* (bridge in Japanese), used to be called Kotan hashi.

Mombetsu is a small fishing rural town. Across the Okhotsk Sea is Russia (Fig. 1.1). It is named after the main river that runs through Mombetsu and originated from the Ainu word, *mo* (quiet) and *pet* (river) (Ito, 2006, p. 183). Of the official population of 24,500 individuals in Mombetsu, many engaged in fishing, forestry and agricultural industries. We catch salmon, cod, sole and trout from the coastal waters. Food processing industries using marine products were also active.

[1] Hatakeyama's life story is written based on the interviews to Hatakeyama and the key members of Mopet Sanctuary Network (MSN) from September 2011 to 2013.

[2] Hatakeyama's life story is written based on the interviews to Hatakeyama and the key members of Mopet Sanctuary Network (MSN) from September 2011 to 2013.

F. Noguchi, *Rethinking Education for Sustainable Development in a Local Community Context*, Education for Sustainability 6,
https://doi.org/10.1007/978-981-16-9464-6_1

Fig. 1.1 Map of Japan (*Source* Maps of World, 2012. *Note* Locations depicted within red circle denote key areas of this book)

The rich natural environment of the Okhotsk Sea resulted from the deposition of rich soil from the Amur River basin (Shiraiwa, 2011).

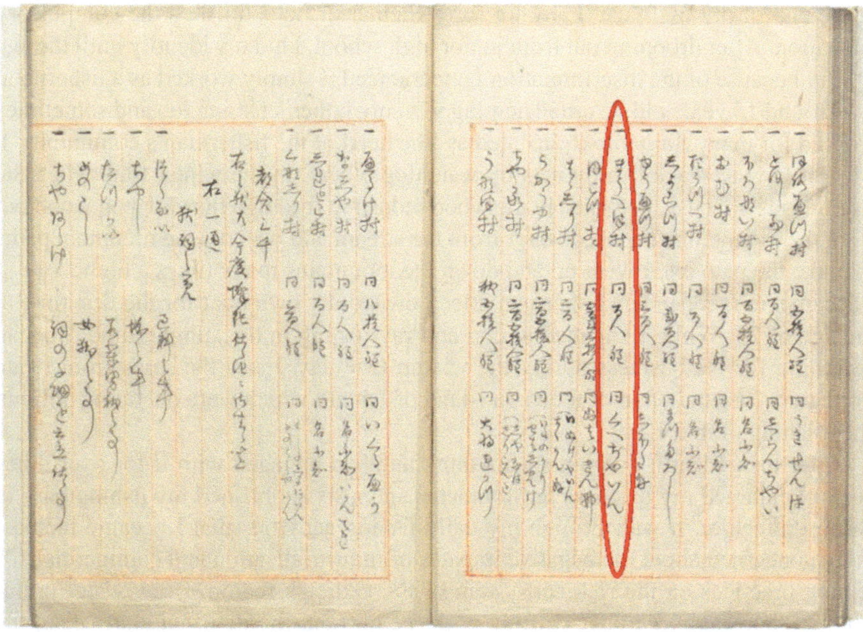

Fig. 1.2 Record of the elder, Kuhechain, in Mombetsu (*Source* Hokkaido Prefectural Library, 1731. *Note* Circled in red by the author)

The oldest record referring to the Ainu people in Mombetsu is found in a history book written by Tsugaru han,[3] which records 'There are about 100 Ainu residents in Mombetsu in the 1600s and the elder was called Kuhechain' (Ito, 2006, p. 183) (Fig. 1.2). I am his descendant. As there is no reliable demographic data about the Ainu people in Mombetsu, the Hokkaido Prefectural Government counted 355 in Okhotsk region (five cities including Mombetsu) (Center for Ainu & Indigenous Studies, 2014), while I estimate approximately only 400–500 individuals in Mombetsu. Many Ainu individuals, including most of my relatives, are hiding Ainu identity or may not even be aware of their ethnic background.

As I grew up with seven other brothers and sisters, I was always hungry. I ate the grass for the cows and even frog eggs around this area. The house where I was living was a poorly built, and the thin wooden roof was easily damaged. I saw the moon and sky from the holes in the roof when I was lying on the futon mat and saw snow on my blanket when I woke up. Bullying towards me became severe when I was in year eight and I eventually stop going to school. Wajin children at school chased me and threw rocks at me, swearing 'Ah, Inu!' [a dog in Japanese] or 'Ice cream'. I went to the local junior high school which had about 1200 students. The bullying started

[3] Tsugaru *han* (domain under Edo Shogunate governmental system) documented 250 years history of the greater Tsugaru area, including Ezo-chi. This was compiled in '*Tsugaru Ittoshi* (Compilation of Tsugaru History)' in 1731.

at the end of my first year. I am not sure whether or not I finished the compulsory education. After dropping out from junior high school, I hid my identity until the age of fifty because of the discrimination I experienced. I simply worked as a fisherman.

Around 15 years old, I started helping with my father's fishing job and sometimes worked for many *Amimoto* (translated as 'the head of the fisherman's community'). I learnt how to make fishing nets by watching others. In the winter time when the fishing was not busy, I worked in the wood industry. To sleigh the chopped wood out from the mountains, I carried water from the stream and watered the mountain paths to make the path icy. I went up and down the mountains many times a night.

I became an independent fisherman after I owned my own boat for the first time at the age of 25. While I engaged in cod and ray fishing in the summertime, I began searching for the business during the winter. One day, I saw the ships from Iwate Prefecture (northern part of the main island of Japan), which were operating dolphin spearfishing (Table 1.1).

After this, I learnt dolphin spearfishing and had engaged with it for over thirty years. I enlarged my business in Mombetsu and also established my fishing base in Iwate Prefecture. It was through my daily fishing activities that I became increasingly concerned about the negative impacts of industrialisation and commercialised fishing practices on the rich ecosystem of the Okhotsk region. I saw water pollution, an increase in garbage drifting with the current, the deformation of fish, the destruction of the sea bottom ecosystem by large trawl-boats and decreasing sea ice each year caused by climate change.[4] I thought those problems related to the growth of industrial activities and to people's lives that contributed to this environmental degradation. Eventually, I made the connection between local ecological problems and my concerns about indigenous rights issues.

When I was fishing off the coast of Mombetsu in the 1980s, I saw big trawlers from Honshu, the main island of Japan, conducting mass fishing. All of a sudden, I could not resist thinking, 'This is my sea, our sea, Ainu's sea. Why are those *Wajin* (Japanese in Ainu language) outsiders catching fish here? These are our resources. They are even destroying our sea'. At the same time, all the painful memories and emotions, and memories of my *fuchi* (female elder or grandmother in Ainu) that I had kept within myself, were rushing into my mind. While watching the fishing trawler in front of me, my emotions and memories were all mixed up. I felt furious and became unable to contain myself.

Before, I hated to talk to or even look at Ainu, despite my Ainu blood. I was very reluctant when I took over my father's role as *ekashi*, the elder, as well as the president of Ainu Association of Hokkaido, Mombetsu Chapter (AAH-MC). However, these experiences slowly changed me. I began learning about traditional ceremonies by visiting twenty Ainu communities in Hokkaido with my late brother,

[4] Drifting sea ice in Okhotsk contributes to enriched marine biodiversity. Sea ice normally drifts from Russia towards the northern coastline of Hokkaido between February and March. Sea ice enhances rich planktonic activity underneath and drifting sea ice carries the nutritious plankton across the Okhotsk Sea. The amount of sea ice has decreased and the period of sea ice has shortened due to climate change (Shiraiwa, 2011).

Table 1.1 Ainu key events and Hatakeyama's key life events

Year	Ainu key events	Year	Hatakeyama's key life events
1855	Ainu land separation between Russia and Japan began (–1872)		
1869	Hokkaido Development and Colonial Agency established		
1899	Hokkaido Ex-Aborigines Protection Act (Assimilation policy) enacted		
1901	Ex-Aboriginal Children Education Regulation developed		
1920s	Local Ainu organisations established at various places in Hokkaido (-1930)		
1931	Ainu Association of Hokkaido (AAH) established (closed during the WWII)		
		1941	Born in Mombetsu
1946	AAH re-established		
		1955	Dropped out of junior secondary school and started to help father's fishing jobs
		1966	Owned his first fishing boat
		1967	Married
1984	AAH drafted the New Ainu Law and proposed it to the government	Mid-1980s	Concerns began about marine environmental issues and Ainu rights
1992	Giichi Nomura made the statement to claim the Ainu indigenous rights at the UN General Assembly	1988	'Reluctantly' took over AAH-MC president position from his late father
1994	Shigeru Kayano became the first National Diet member as an Ainu who claimed the indigenous recognition at the Diet	1990s	Began studying Ainu ceremonies with late brother, Mineo
1997	Ex-Aboriginal Act abolished Official 'ethnic minority' status recognition by the government Ainu Cultural Promotion Act (CPA) enacted	1997	Began indigenous whaling claim with Mineo
		1999	Mineo died Publically identified as an Ainu person Began Ancestor memorial ceremony
		2001	Began *Kamuy Chep Nomi* (Salmon ceremony) in Mobetsu River

(continued)

Table 1.1 (continued)

		2005	Mombetsu City Government (MCG) proposed the industrial waste management plant construction on the Ainu secret area
2007	Adoption of the UN Declaration on Rights of Indigenous People (UNDRIP)	2007	Hokkaido Government granted permission to MCG for the plant's construction Began lobbying to the government
2008	Official indigenous recognition of Ainu people by the government G8 Summit held in Hokkaido	2008	Hatakeyama met Sapporo Free School 'Yu' Staff in Sapporo
		2010	MSN established Wife died Attended CBD-COP10 in Nagoya, Japan Made policy proposal at Fishery Agency of Japan
		2011	Daughter, son-in-laws and grandson died from the Great East Japan earthquake tsunami
		2012	House burnt down in fire Re-married
		2015	Son died

Mineo Hatakeyama. I also joined his activism on the indigenous whaling rights claim since 1997.

I Want to Live as an Ainu Fisherman

After Mineo's passing, I totally lost my interest in Ainu rights claim. I did not feel like getting involved into the indigenous whaling rights claim activism anymore and was thinking to give up the ekashi position.

On one night, Mineo appeared in my dream. He was standing looking angry and glaring at me, as if he were blaming my denial of being an Ainu. After this dream, I decided to live as an Ainu thoroughly. This dream catalysed myself to proclaim publicly that I was an Ainu person and wanted to live as the Ainu people. I decided to commit myself to being the ekashi and AAH-MC president. After this dream, I began to make a linkage between social, economic and environmental problems in Mombetsu and my Ainu rights claim in Japan.

What I mean by the indigenous rights recovery is 'substantive rights' recovery based on a holistic understanding of Ainu culture. 'Substantive' includes four meanings. Firstly, the rights have to be sought in a real-life context (in this case, his livelihood of fishing), not only as words in legal documents. Secondly, the rights have to link with economic sufficiency. Thirdly, the rights should be based on Ainu values, not Japanese values. Lastly, the rights should be something to support the social transformation of Japan. That is, recovering rights could transform the Japanese society from the one with nature's depletion to the one to see human as a part of nature, which is consistent with Ainu values of human-nature relationships.

My substantive rights claim was founded in my criticism against the Japanese government's policies for Ainu people. Ainu policies depict Ainu culture narrowly as only encompassing music, art, dance and craft. I am a fisherman; I cannot dance or do embroidery. These policies for Ainu cultural promotion are determined by the Japanese, not the Ainu people. I want to live as an Ainu fisherman.

I am not happy with the rights protection policy for the Ainu people of Japan (see Chapter 2.1). It encourages Ainu to engage with craft making and art activities that I believe are only part of the whole practice of living or even based on manipulated by the Japanese people.

Indigenous Salmon Fishing Rights

Currently, I am looking at Salmon and Whale for our 'substantive' indigenous rights claim. With regard to the salmon fishing rights, I revived *kamuy chep nomi* in Mobetsu River in 2001. This is the indigenous ceremony (nomi) to welcome the return of their god (kamuy) fish (chep) (salmon) to the original river in autumn. Ainu traditionally believed in salmon as one of our gods, as well as valuing it as our staple food. The assimilation policy banned us from hosting Kamuy chep nomi, and the development policy prohibited all Japanese residents, including the Ainu, from fishing for salmon in the rivers, to protect the commercial fishing industry.[5]

For me, reviving the kamuy chep nomi was only the entry point of the indigenous substantive rights that I want to claim. This included the right to access the local natural resources for the Ainu people's livelihood, in particular, salmon and whale, in which the Japanese government had significant economic and political interests. I lobbied the Japanese government, including the Fisheries Agency of Japan, Hokkaido Municipal Government (HMG) and Mombetsu City Government (MCG), negotiating the indigenous fishing rights on these resources for over twenty years.

Indigenous Whaling Rights

The indigenous whaling rights claim is more difficult and complicated than the ones for salmon. There are strong political pressures around whaling inside/outside Japan. I wanted to claim the indigenous whaling rights with regard to minke whale, which would allow the Ainu people to hunt a certain number of whales and sell their products for the commercial purpose of creating economic and employment opportunities for the Ainu people. There were two frameworks that were related to my indigenous whaling rights claim. One was the Aboriginal Substance Whaling framework under the International Whaling Commission (IWC). The other framework was to hunt

[5] Catching salmon in the river is strictly regulated under the Inland Waters Fishing Field Management Regulations, as part of the Fishing Law in 1949 (The Government of Japan, 1949).

whales through coastal community-based whaling. In both ways, I had to compromise my rights claim.

The Aboriginal Substance Whaling framework allows indigenous groups to hunt a certain number of whales but not for commercial purposes. In addition to this, the Japanese government's disinterest in supporting my application. With this framework, the indigenous peoples have to apply for it through the national government where they live. I had already negotiated the possibility of it with the Japanese government in the previous twenty years. The government explained to me that the application would require an enormous amount of preparatory work, and it would be hard to obtain at least 3 out of 4 votes at the IWC AGM without a clear rationale. Those words sounded me an 'excuse', as I saw that IWC had previously permitted whaling rights to the indigenous people.

The government, instead, suggested me go to the second option, Coastal Community-based Whaling. This framework allows the Japanese fishermen to hunt whales which are not protected under the IWC and in the Japanese territorial sea where the IWC is not applicable. The government limited their whaling rights to non-IWC regulated whales, such as beaked whales and fin whales. These whales were not traditionally consumed by neither *Wajin* (non-Ainu people) nor Ainu people. These are not what humans eat. Their oil is indigestible and causes diarrhoea. I also do not want to join them. For me, this is almost like digging my hands into the other's rice storage and stealing their rice. I was not interested in this suggestion, not only because I had to catch whales I did not want, but also because I did not want them to mix up Ainu whaling rights claim and the whaling claim made by *Wajin* (non-Ainu Japanese people).

I am also resentful about the government's stealthy approach to commercial whaling under the name of scientific research. I knew this had been a source of huge profit for the Japanese government. The government outlawed the sale of whale meat under the name of 'scientific research',[6] while they claimed their 'traditional' rights, to preserve the Japanese food culture in the Antarctic Ocean.[7]

The government established a public corporation under the Fishery Agency, which gave the posts to retired governmental officials.[8] All the profit from the trade also

[6] The Japanese government began their 'scientific research' on whaling in the Antarctic Ocean, because of the International Whaling Committee's (IWC) decision on the moratorium on commercial whaling (International Whaling Commission, n.d.).

[7] Greenpeace Japan (2017) contends that the whaling in the Antarctic Ocean as the Japanese tradition is not Japanese tradition, so that they have shown the opposition against the Japanese government's claim on the whaling rights in this area. According to Greenpeace Japan, the whaling in the Antarctic Ocean began for the purpose of whale oil in 1930s by importing the whaling technic from Norway. In the post-World War II time, they resumed the whaling in this area to resolve the malnutrition in Japan, by the instruction of General Douglas MacArthur under the US Occupation.

[8] There are three corporations under the Fishery Agency, which are involved in 'scientific research'. Institute of Cetacean Research conducts the research (Institute of Cetacean Research, 2017). Kyodo Senpaku Co. Ltd. operates the vessel and deals with the 'sub-product' whale meat from the research (Kyodo Senpaku Co., n.d.). Japan Whaling Association does the public relations for scientific research and whaling (Japan Whaling Association, 2017). About 250 ex-officials of the Fishery Agency are employed by these corporations (MSN, 2012). Terachi argued in a MSN meeting that

flowed to these 'public' corporations. While monopolising the whaling rights of minke whales, the government strictly regulated whaling by coastal fishermen, who hunted whales traditionally. The challenge is the Fisheries Agency of Japan, not the IWC.

Lonely Resistance

In any case of fishing rights, either salmon or whale, the process to recover what I defined as the indigenous rights was not easy at all. Over 150 years' history of assimilation, and 50 years of denying my Ainu identity, made it difficult for me to know what it really meant to be an Ainu, and what the Ainu substantive rights should really look like. I had little support when I first began my activism, and I did not know whom to ask.

I developed my thoughts around rights claim while visiting other Ainu elders and experts who knew the local history, knowledge and practices. Physical evidence, or 'written' documents, that could prove the history of Ainu whaling practice was extremely difficult to locate. Few studies had been conducted to show the relationship between whales and the Ainu culture. This was further complicated by the fact that such studies were based on the systemic analyses of places in Hokkaido and Ainu's folk stories, many of which were lost in the assimilation process. All the information that I collected was fragmented, missing or even manipulated by the Japanese people. I had to fight against the Japanese systems for his goal to be achieved, but I did not know what to target or how to do it. The rights claim to salmon fishing and whaling was particularly difficult, as these were connected to the economic and political interests of the Japanese government in a very complex way. I was re-weaving the lost Ainu memories with his life experience as a fisherman in the modern Japanese context.

I consisted of trial and error for twenty years. I tried every method that seemed an effective way to change the policy. I learnt from fishermen and contractors and copied their way of getting close to the politicians. I approached potential politicians and paid to lobby them. I do not know how much money I wasted in 20 years. I looked for anyone who could support him, including fishermen friends and various researchers. Whenever I found a relationship with supporters that were inconsistent or unsuccessful, I turned away from them. Many came and left me over the twenty years.

Development Plan for the Industrial Waste Management Facility

In 2005, a critical event pushed my activism into the limelight. Mombetsu City Government (MCG) decided to stop accepting industrial waste at the public waste landfill site as they estimated the site would be full within a few years. This decision created economic problems for the food manufacturers' association and the farmers, including animal husbandry and dairy husbandry unions, who now had to take their waste to an industrial waste management plant outside the city and pay a disposal fee.

---

the government claims that whaling is the part of Japanese culture, in order to maintain the political and economic interests of the government, business and public corporations (MSN, 2012).

These groups put pressure on the MCG to build an industrial waste management plant in Mombetsu City. MCG responded to this request and proposed the construction of a 41-hectare industrial waste plant on a mountain in the Toyooka District of Mombetsu, citing that this would also help revitalise economic activity. The chosen site was also the source of Mobetsu River, where I had been hosting kamuy chep nomi. I was concerned about the planned construction. I saw the potential environmental damage to the river, the forest and the marine ecosystems as an extension of over 100 years of colonisation. This could erode the Ainu's life foundation and our potential access rights to the natural resources.

But my activism became more difficult. The Hokkaido Government granted permission to MCG for the plant's construction in 2007. MCG organised public hearing meetings for the local residents. I attended, but the proposed plan seemed irreversible. I was able to say what I was concerned about and gained the necessary information. In reality, I had no rights to change the plan. The plan was predetermined, prioritising the interests, mostly economic interests, of the majority. The developer justified the plant in terms of local economic benefits and claimed that strict environmental safeguards would be in place.

Eventually, the Fishermen's and Dairy Husbandry Unions decided to support the construction plan and signed a pollution prevention agreement with the developer, and only a few groups of local residents and I remained the opposition. Many AAH-MC members also left me, as the Mombetsu fishermen union, to which most AAH-MC members belonged to as part of their fishing businesses, supported the proposal. I became very isolated.

Encountering Global Frameworks

In this process, my local friend told me about the UN Declaration of the Rights of Indigenous People (UNDRIP) (United Nations, 2007) and the Convention on Biological Diversity (CBD) (United Nations, 1992a). These opened up my eyes. I felt that these justify my indigenous rights claim.[9] At the public hearings held under environmental impact assessment regulations, I asserted the necessity of receiving prior consensus from the local indigenous community for such developments, drawing on international indigenous rights protection laws.

In 2008, I went to the indigenous peoples' event at G8 Toyako Summit held in Hokkaido. There, I met a staff of Sapporo-based NGO (Sapporo NGO staff A), the organiser of the event.[10] Sapporo NGO staff A got interested in my rights claim and

[9] The Article 29 of the UNDRIP ensures the following three points: (i) their right to the conservation and protection of the environment and the productive capacity of their lands or territories and resources; (ii) no storage or disposal of hazardous materials shall take place in the lands or territories of indigenous people without their free, prior and informed consent; and (iii) programmes for monitoring, maintaining and restoring the health of indigenous people, as developed and implemented by the people affected by such materials, are duly implemented (United Nations, 2007)

[10] In these workshops, both Ainu and non-Ainu participants identified the key Ainu issues and explored a possible path to develop Hokkaido, in which Ainu and non-Ainu people could live together. The workshops resulted in forming a pressure group of Ainu and non-Ainu citizens, called *Chi Kara Nisatt,* to influence the Advisory Committee on Ainu Policy and Hokkaido Toyako G8

invited me to his workshops on ESD in Sapporo in the same year. Since then, I got supporters through him and my individual activism developed into the collective one.

1.1 A Journey in Two Parts

The book reports my practice and research journey both ***within*** and ***beyond*** the theory of socially-critical approach to ESD. Compared with just providing individuals with knowledge and skills for living sustainably, a critical approach to ESD aims to create 'a world where everyone has the opportunity to benefit from education and learn the values, behaviour and lifestyles required for a sustainable future and for positive social transformation' (UNESCO, 2005, p. 6). This aspiration has significant transformational potential, not just in its scope and goals but also because of its wide societal focus. This wide focus involves all people, young and old, and people in all sectors related to sustainable development, including people in formal, non-formal and informal education, and continues a lifelong process (UNESCO, 2005, 2012).

The meaning of 'everyone' in this definition challenged my practice and research journey. While this approach was implemented to ESD during the work as a community educator for a marginalised, indigenous Ainu people's community in northern Japan (the first part of the journey—ESD *within* socially-critical approach), it became apparent to me that the socially-critical orientation of ESD was limited. Its principles and pedagogical practices were unable to empower all members ('everyone') in the community to achieve sustainable development. An analysis of the reasons for this led to the second part of my practice and research journey. This necessitated me going *beyond* the current theories and methodologies to support socially-critical ESD and exploring the possibilities of integrating a decoloniality perspective, not just a socially-critical one, in the approach. Viewing and studying this approach from the perspective of decoloniality required me replacing socially-critical lenses with a more empathetic openness to the experiences of colonised and marginalised participants.

However, like ESD, my first practice and research journey began with my theoretical interests in critical environmental education (EE) or education *for* the environment (Fien, 1993; Huckle, 1993; Huckle & Sterling, 1996; Robottom & Hart, 1993).

Summit in 2008. *Chi Kara Nisatta* (discussions for tomorrow in Ainu language) conducted a rally walk called, *Pirika Kéutom Apkashi* (Walk with Heart). Ainu and non-Ainu youth walked 400km from Wakkanai to Ebetsu, in commemoration of Ainu who had been displaced from Sakhalin to this area in the territorial dispute between Japan and Russia in the 1980s (Sapporo NGO staff A, 2010).

1.2 Theoretical Context

Critical EE has provided the theoretical foundation of ESD. Critical EE is based upon a socially-critical orientation and political action goals (Stevenson, 2007), which challenge the education's reproductive functions in perpetuating unsustainable social and economic development (Fien, 2004). Critical EE is based on the critical theories of Jürgen Harbamas, particularly his theory of communicative action (Huckle, 1993, 1996b), and the critical pedagogies of Paulo Freire and, therefore, seeks to advance learning for social critique and empowerment of the oppressed (Fien, 1995; Huckle, 1993, 1996a).

Global policy discourses have accepted critical approaches in the policies on EE, Education for Sustainability (EfS) and ESD since the 1970s without critically examining what the word 'socially-critical' really means.[11] However, there have long been 'rhetoric-reality gaps' (Fien, 1995, p. 78). These policies do not mean that critical EE is universally accepted (Jickling, 1992, 1999, 2006) or that critical EE is easy to implement (Lucas, 1991; Stevenson, 1987, 2007; Walker, 1997). The recent United Nations Decade of Education for Sustainable Development (UNDESD, 2005–2014), which promoted ESD by the United Nations Educational, Scientific and Cultural Organisation (UNESCO) members' state governments, was no exception.

At the end of the UNDESD conference in Nagoya, 2015, participants evaluated the UNDESD as 'successful' in two ways (Heila Lotz-Sisitka, 2015; The Government of Japan, 2015; UNGA, 2015a). Firstly, the UNDESD was seen as successful at infusing the concept of *sustainable development* into education. The Nagoya conference showcased some of these efforts, including regional strategies, initiatives, projects and networks.[12] Secondly, the UNDESD infused *education* into sustainable development. The UNDESD impacted on the wider global community's ability to achieve

[11] The discussions and outcome documents from international and intergovernmental conferences contributed to the development of EE, EfS and ESD. Education conferences included Belgrade Charter (UNESCO, 1975), International Conference on Environmental Education in Tbilisi (UNESCO, 1978), UNESCO-UNEP International Congress on Environmental Education and Training in Moscow (UNESCO, 1997) and International Conference: Environment and Society: Education and Public Awareness for Sustainability in Thessaloniki (UNESCO, 1997). Programs include such as UNESCO-UNEP International Environmental Education Programme (IEEP: 1975–1987) and the UNDESD (2005–2014). Broader global community for sustainable development, including CSD, has also responded the claim of the global education community on the significance education in achieving sustainable development. The importance of education has been clearly remarked in the reports and outcome documents from the conferences, such as *Our Common Future* (WCED, 1987), *World Conservation Strategy: Living Resource Conservation for Sustainable Development* (IUCN, UNEP, WWF, FAO, & UNESCO, 1980), Chapter 36 of Agenda 21 (United Nations, 1992b), and Future We Want (UNGA, 2012). In forty years, the interrelationship of the unsustainable problems between/amongst the fields, generations and species became widely understood (WCED, 1987); the views, scope and methods of educators in EE became widened and broadened. The debates on EE produced a new concept of Education for Sustainability (EfS) in the 1980s and provided the foundation to grow Education for Sustainable Development (ESD) after Earth Summit in 1990.

[12] These included the UNESCO Associated School Project (ASP), the Higher Education for Sustainable Development (HESD), the Promotion of Sustainability in Postgraduate Education and Research

sustainable development, particularly through the process of the UN Commission on Sustainable Development (UNCSD) specifically at the UN World Conference on Sustainable Development (Rio+ 20) in 2012.[13] Similarly, *the Future We Want,* a document prepared by Rio+ 20 for the 66th Session of the UN General Assembly, called for the further promotion of ESD beyond the UNDESD (UNGA, 2012, p. 41). Now, ESD is incorporated into the framework for Sustainable Development Goals (SDGs) and Target 4.7 supports the promotion of ESD (UNGA, 2015b). Furthermore, UNESCO developed the key strategies towards 2030 through *The Global Action Programme (GAP) on ESD* (UNESCO, 2013) and the Incheon Declaration by the World Education Forum confirmed UNESCO's commitment to promoting the SDGs through ESD (UNESCO, 2015).

Experiences from the UNDESD led to the question of who 'everyone' was. The efforts made during the UNDESD remained largely within formal education by schools and higher education institutes. At the Nagoya conference, the efforts in formal education were evaluated by the same formal education and schooling experts. The UNDESD generally overlooked the informal education experiences in the everyday life of a local community. The educational dimensions of community development were silent in the UNDESD. As a result, overlooking community development during the UNDESD devalued the concept of 'everyone' in ESD.

These top-down statements, however, are not enough. They reflect the views and interests of the governments and majority members of a society or community, and do not respond well to the needs and interests of the minority or marginalised people (Gboku & Lekoko, 2007). Marginalised people, like Hatakeyama, experience their problems comprehensively and totally, while top-down policies can only see the problems of marginalised people partially and abstractedly, often overlooking the totality of the problems (Kitoh, 2009). This mismatch in understanding, and the way of dealing with problems of the local community, particularly of marginalised people, is often silenced by those in power.

Sustainable development can only be achieved when its associated values and lifestyles are internalised and contextualised in real life. As Tilbury and Fien (2002) argue:

> Yes, governments and international agencies can hold conferences, issue reports and create structures that encourage individuals, communities and companies to change, and these are important in setting broad goals and catalysing action. However, we can only effectively change the things we have most time to work on and, for most of us, this is ourselves and our local communities. (p. 6)

Network (ProSPER.Net) in Asia, the Regional Centre for Expertise (RCE) movement and the European Network on Higher Education for Sustainable Development (COPERNICUS Alliance, 2015). For example, ASP successfully increased the number of ASP schools to 9,556 in 180 countries (ASPnet, 2015). The United Nations University (UNU) has catalysed 136 Regional Centres for Expertise (RCE) to support ESD through partnerships between the higher education institutes and the local community (UNU IAS, 2014).

[13] Reports from the three Rio Conventions, including the United Nations Framework Convention on Climate Change (UNFCCC), the Convention on Biological Diversity (CBD) and the United Nations Convention to Combat Desertification (UNCCD) emphasised the importance of education in achieving goals of these conventions (Sarabhai et al., 2012).

Change from below through community education and development echoes the goals of ESD and its theoretical grounding in critical EE. Change from below is the heart of community development (Ife, 2016), particularly when marginalised people are the key participants. Experiences of community development could contribute to a bottom-up approach to ESD and enrich ESD policies and practices.

The endogenous development theory of Japanese sociologist, Kazuko Tsurumi (b. 1918–d. 2006), explains the process of change from below:

> [The] ultimate goal of endogenous development is to seek the process, in which no one is excluded, and no one is killed. Bringing the marginalised, those who are disadvantaged and those who are discriminated to the centre and treat them as Sui-ten (Sui 萃 means meeting and ten 点 means point in Japanese). By moving Sui-ten, the member of the society will be shuffled, and the society will be transformed. (Tsurumi, 1999, p. 344)

The goal of endogenous development is 'no-one's exclusion'. No-one's exclusion demands a decentralisation of the system and the creation of small Mandala-like networks at the local level.[14] A society could be transformed by decentralising and repositioning its members, thereby changing its power balance. Thus, the genuine change from below will involve some aspects of an informal unlearning and re-learning process of different members of society if we are to achieve holistic structural changes. Both majority and marginalised people may experience discomfort, pain and resistance. Their emancipation and empowerment involve their realisation of the injustice caused by the power structure of the society in which they are embedded. The political and economic sensitivities and interests of dominant social groups may come under question, thus rendering the ideas and interests of various marginalised people and groups of 'dangerous knowledge' (Maher, 1986). This is a process of *consientização* (conscientisation) (Freire, 1972).

Critical EE emphasises local experiences and places, and that education only becomes meaningful when people learn and act in a real-life context (Fien, 1993; Maser, 1996; Tilbury & Fien, 2002). So far, however, critical EE research has largely focused on formal education and schooling. There are discussions on how adult environmental education differs from education *in/about* and *through* the environment; however, the role of critical EE in adult environmental education remains unclear (Clover, 2002; Clover & Hill, 2013; Clover et al., 2013).

To make critical EE-based practices meaningful to our everyday life context, Inoue and Imamura (2012) advise:

---

[14] Tsurumi owed the idea of Mandala-like society and Sui-Ten on the works of Kumagusu Minakata (1867–1941), a Japanese ecologist, natural historian and folklorist. Minakata attempted to merge two philosophies, the causality principles of Western natural science and Buddhism Karma theory, resulted in the development of his Mandala theory and the idea of Sui-ten (Tsurumi, 1998). Tsurumi was trying to posit a non-Western and non-violent model based on the history, traditions and ecological circumstances of a society at the grassroots level based on Minakata's work. Tsurumi explains that the 'Minakata-Mandala' is 'a sketch for the interaction and inter-comparison of the way of all living flora, fauna and human on everywhere on the Earth' (Tsurumi, 1998, p. 349), and describes *Sui-ten* as meeting point where things are caused by the necessity and contingency and all the relationships, such as cause and effects, necessity and accident, meet each, influence each other and are converged beyond time and distance (Tsurumi, 1998).

> The concepts of 'sustainability' and 'sustainable society' can embody its real meaning, only when environmental education steps in the area of efforts that are often regarded as radical, without being restrained with the 'common sense' and 'routine of a dominant society'. This is the very point where the value of environmental education is challenged. (Inoue & Imamura, 2012, p. 18)

Thus, the first part of my journey in this book investigated the value of critical EE as it stepped into an area of dangerous knowledge to the common sense and the radical challenge to a dominant society.

1.3 The Search for Socially-Critical ESD in a Community Development Context

Guided by the critical EE theories and practices learnt during the late 1990s, the meanings and effectiveness of critical EE in the people's everyday life outside of formal education (i.e. in community development) for the last twenty years were studied. My work from 2003 to 2015 for the Japan Council on Education for Sustainable Development (ESD-J),[15] a non-governmental organisation (NGO), guided the conduct of this study. These ESD-J experiences facilitated research into the meanings, roles and value of critical EE in community development in a real context at a time when theories, policies and practices for ESD were being developed during the UNDESD.

---

[15] Founded on 21 June 2003, the Japan Council on Education for Sustainable Development (ESD-J) is a networking organisation dedicated to promoting education for a sustainable society, given impetus by the UN Decade of Education for Sustainable Development (DESD). ESD-J was established by a civil group of NGOs and individuals of Environmental Education Working Group of the Japan Forum for Johannesburg (JFJ), who advocated the UNDESD with the Government of Japan at the WSSD. ESD-J members included those who are with the background of the environment, development, human rights, peace, gender and youth education. ESD-J has created the consortium for the multistakeholders inviting citizens, governments, local authorities, companies and educational institutions to promote ESD. The organisation's name changed in 2015 from the Japan Council on Education for Sustainable Development, following the conclusion of the UNDESD. See ESD-J (2016). A community-based approach was also the key organisational principle of ESD-J. ESD-J has emphasised: (i) the importance of a community-based approach in ESD, (ii) the significant role that NGOs could play and (iii) the importance of informal learning in the community development process. See ESD-J (2016).

Mainly, two types of works were engaged at ESD-J: (i) networking with NGOs in Asia[16] and policy advocacy with the national government and international communities for sustainable development and ESD and (ii) promoting ESD to community development NGOs. The NGOs that participated in the ESD-J projects were from Asia and had extensive expertise in working with rural and local community development, post-war peacebuilding, reproductive health, etc. Such projects at ESD-J facilitated opportunities to work across multiple social sectors, scales (global, national and local), communities, as well as the policy, theory and practice nexus, and to experience the tensions between and across all of them.

The discussions and projects with community development NGOs on the theme of ESD provided insights about the potential of dynamic learning processes, through which sustainable development could be embedded in community development. This could be identified as 'informal ESD in a community development context'. This insight became an underlying pillar of my policy advocacy. It also highlighted that there were confusion and contestation over ESD at the local community level.

These were particularly noticeable in the initial stages of my ESD-J work. While most practitioners agreed that community empowerment was the foundation of any actions to achieve sustainable development, few saw linkages between community empowerment and ESD as it was being conceptualised internationally. For them, ESD was something to do with formal education. Sustainable development was something to do with environmental protection and conservation (ESD-J, 2009, 2010, 2011b). They found little relevance for it in their work.

Nevertheless, the local community continues to be a key focus in efforts for sustainable development. Governments and experts can provide legal frameworks, economic incentives and technologies, which may facilitate and mobilise local communities. Indeed, global policies have recognised the importance of the local community in development. For example, strategies were developed to implement Agenda 21 (United Nations, 1992b)[17] at the local community level after the Rio

[16] Three projects at ESD-J that I coordinated gave me the insights of informal ESD in the community development context. The one is Asia Good ESD Practice Project (AGEPP: 2006–2008). AGEPP aimed to network the Asian community development NGOs on the theme of ESD. Six NGOs from six Asian countries were selected through the open application process and participated in this project with ESD-J. During the project, the participants explored the meaning of ESD in the community development context and reported 34 practices based on their own understanding of ESD in English and key Asian national languages (ESD-J, 2016). The other is ESD X Biodiversity Project (2008–2010). Nine NGOs reported their activities from the perspectives of biological diversity conservation and community empowerment. Workshops and meetings were also cordinated to share the understanding of ESD and biological diversity among the project perticipants. The third one was NGO Networking Project from 2009 to 2011. Japanese NGOs that worked for rural and community development in the other Asian countries, education, agriculture and foreign affair ministries, Japan International Cooperation Agency (JICA) and United Nations University (UNU) had discussions to identify ESD and the necessary policy to support Japanese civil efforts for ESD and sustainable development in Asia (ESD-J, 2009, 2010, 2011a, 2011b).

[17] Agenda 21 recognises the importance of the commitment by local communities in the efforts to achieve sustainable development. It points out in Chapter 28 on *Agenda 21* as: '…Local authorities construct, operate and maintain economic, social and environmental infrastructure, oversee planning processes, establish local environmental policies and regulations, and assist in implementing

Earth Summit in 1992. Later, the local community was one of the key priorities in the UNDESD (UNESCO, 2005). *Accelerating Local Level Actions* is still identified within five key strategies in the *Global Action Plan (GAP) on ESD* (UNESCO, 2013) and *ESD for 2030* (UNESCO, 2019). Yet, informal ESD in a community context could not be found within the national and international institutional policy frameworks. The education ministries understood informal ESD in a community development context as 'capacity building' and therefore found very little relevance for it (ESD-J, 2013). Non-education ministries, such as those for the environment, industries, and rural and community development, did not see the relevance of ESD either, despite the clear statement of ESD promotion through formal, non-formal and informal education and learning throughout the UNESCO ESD frameworks since 2005. ESD has been often seen as solely about formal education and, hence, the responsibility of education ministries.

Indeed, the nature, scope and purpose of the processes observed in discussions and projects with community development NGOs in Asia had many of the characteristics of critical EE. The actual practices of educators in local communities reflected a broader meaning, similar to the concept of praxis (Freire, 1972). While previous experience provided insights into informal ESD in a community development context, these lacked theoretical rigour; they were too empirical to challenge the dominant understanding and perceptions of ESD.

The problem of a policy-theory-practice gap and of a global-national-local gap around informal ESD in a community development context became explicit when I met Hatakeyama and started the projects with the Mopet Sanctuary Network (MSN) in Hokkaido, Japan, 2009. The MSN seeks sustainable community development through a focus on the indigenous Ainu rights claim by Hatakeyama. Theoretically guided by critical EE, I incorporated the insights on ESD into the practice at the MSN. My engagement with MSN began in the situation where it was difficult to find the relevant literature and theorising for the application of critical approaches in the community development context.

1.4 Two Questions: ESD and Community Development

The gaps and problems in ESD encountered in the work seemed to ultimately stem from the gap between two fields: ESD and community development. The silence in ESD over community development has possibly arisen from the lack of linkage and interaction across these disciplinary fields. Now, the ESD for 2030 addresses, *ESD can promote critical and contextualized understanding of the SDGs by raising questions on the inter-linkages and tensions among different SDGs* (UNESCO, 2019). This statement admits the possibility of ESD to become a valuable tool in building

---

national and subnational environmental policies. As the level of governance closest to the people, they play a vital role in educating, mobilizing and responding to the public to promote sustainable development … (United Nations, 1992b)'.

capacity for sustainable community development and, likewise, the potential of sustainable community development approaches to enrich the theory and practice of ESD.

In this book, I investigate this gap and explore the way in which both fields can contribute to each other, by conducting two critical ethnographies of MSN. For me doing so, I focus on my interactions, as a community educator, with the key participants of MSN, Ainu people in a local community, in particular, the Ainu elder fisherman, as we sought to identify the meaning, role and value of critical ESD.

Thus, the aim of the book is:

> To develop a praxis framework to integrate ESD and community development to be mutually supportive, ultimately strengthening the practices in both ESD and community development field.

This aim seeks to find out how critical ESD can contribute to (or be integrated within) community development, and vice versa, and how a community development practice can enrich critical ESD discussions. It is grounded in three assumptions about informal ESD in a community development context.

The first assumption is that the sustainable community development and empowerment process could be understood as informal ESD in a community development context. The second assumption is that informal ESD in a community development context from the marginalised people's perspective can carry key characteristics of praxis and have significant implications on the theory and practice of critical ESD, such as the meaning of ESD to a local community and the role of the educator.

The third assumption is that imbalances in 'power' in both ESD and community development practice can deflect practitioners and researchers into directions that overlook the diverse learning and knowledge of local communities and silence the voices of those who convey these.

As a result, the following three sub-questions were developed to explore informal ESD in a community development context:

1. How useful is critical EE in understanding ESD in a community development context? Answers to this question might provide an understanding of the relevance and effectiveness of critical EE to ESD in a community development context.
2. What are the key elements of ESD that can facilitate the empowerment of marginalised community member in efforts to achieve sustainable community development? Answers to this question might contribute to the development of a praxis framework for ESD in a community development context.
3. How might this praxis framework be validated and how might it add new insights to current critical EE? Answers to this question would lend validity to a praxis framework for ESD in a community development context.

The investigation of these questions (and sub-questions) was primarily informed by critical theory acknowledging that there is no value-free and neutrality in research. It is value-laden and concerns dominant social systems that have created perpetuating social and economic injustice, as well as environmental problems in a society and within institutional frameworks aimed at supporting sustainable development and ESD. To ensure consistency, the socially-critical approach to the practice of ESD that was investigated in this study was guided by a socially-critical orientation to research (Malone, 1999; Robottom & Hart, 1993). Such was the case in my practice and research journey, at least.

In the course of my practice, issues of decoloniality (Ndlovu-Gatsuheni, 2013, 2015) arose and increasingly influenced the second part of my journey. Decoloniality recognises the limitations of critical theory and aims to go *beyond* it to generate knowledge of the marginalised people through their own epistemologies. Integrating these ideas into the research helped to enrich the research by ensuring the perspectives of the Ainu people in MSN were taken seriously.

Informed by the critical and decoloniality theories that guided my practice, this book employs critical ethnography method. Unlike interpretive ethnography which brackets out any a priori assumptions, critical ethnography emphasises both 'understanding and critique in research' (Fien & Hillcoat, 1996, p. 35) and uses the phenomenological approaches of interpretive enquiry guided by theoretical frameworks such as critical theory and decoloniality (Cohen et al., 2011; Masemann, 1982; May, 1997; Quantz, 1992). Critical ethnographic research produces a thick description of the meaning, but creates socially-critical, reflexive and emancipatory empowerment processes between the lived experiences and a priori theory for both the researcher and participants.

1.5 Significance of This Book

This book is significant in five ways, which, together, contribute to further enriching the theory and practice of socially-critical approaches to EE and ESD. These five ways are: (i) challenging the rhetoric-reality gap; (ii) listening to unheard voices; (iii) enriching the practice of critical ethnography; (iv) contributing to the 'others'; and (v) giving a direction for my own praxis.

i. **Challenging the rhetoric-reality gap**

Despite the critical and socially transformative bases of ESD theories, policies and practices in ESD have prioritised formal education, generally on scientific and technological themes, while overlooking informal education in a community development context. As a result, much current EE and ESD have not responded to (un-) sustainability issues in real life (Huckle & Wals, 2015). This book questions the power structures in the fields of EE and ESD that have caused the exclusion and silencing of community development experiences, diverse knowledge systems and everyday learning experiences in a local community. Such investigation is important particularly now. As stated in *ESD for 2030*, ESD is expected to be a catalyst for SDGs which can provide the holistic and inclusive understanding beyond the differences and tensions among goals and targets of SDGs. This book brings the issue of power to light within the process of knowledge production using current critical EE and ESD. Thus, this study explores the value of critical approaches to EE and ESD and seeks ways to update these approaches by responding to community life experiences through informal education.

ii. **Listening to unheard voices**

Secondly, this book draws its significance from its concerns for the unheard voices in the field. Despite its broad scope, nature and perspective, critical EE predominantly looks at formal education and only a part of non-formal and informal education that can be captured within the lens of formal education. This book attempts to hear the unheard voices that can identify the diverse knowledge and learnings in a local community, particularly from the marginalised people. Identifying these from the perspectives of informal ESD in a community development context helps to enrich the current theoretical and political discourses of EE and ESD. Theory and practice can complement each other's shortcomings, and that will bring a new dimension to critical EE and ESD in achieving sustainable development.

iii. **Enriching the practice of critical ethnography**

Thirdly, the use of the critical ethnography method with the help of decoloniality in this study presents an example of ESD research that can create a process where the researcher and participants can mutually emancipate, empower and produce knowledge together. This book allows the practice and voices of a local community to engage in a dialogue with theory-based discussions of ESD. Integrating decoloniality into a critical ethnography makes the unheard voices and the experiences of the local community to be heard, by finding 'communicable words' with participants. This is 'the journey to connect our inquiry and learning with *their* inquiry and learning, and have a conversation about where we saw things differently' (Wadsworth & Patton, 2010, p. 61).

iv. **Contributing to the 'others'**

Fourthly and lastly, I wish this book may help not only myself but stakeholders who are concerned with empowerment as a goal in community development. In this book, a search was carried out to determine an effective approach for local community empowerment, especially for marginalised people to solve the local community problem towards sustainable development. Hopefully, it can guide both practitioners and community members to know where they stand, what they are doing, how they work together, and what to do next in improving their lives in situations where there is no clear role for facilitators and participants, unlike in formal education and schooling.

1.6 Limitation

Writing this book provided me the opportunity to stop and critically reflect on my ESD practices. In the process of developing a praxis framework, conversations between practice and theory were engaged, providing the key for future practice. Although this is not action research, it is a part of a series of action research cycles being conducted through this researcher's life. Like the research by Julie Davis (2003), this book has contributed to the development of the researcher's own 'living theory'. Thus, this book articulates current concerns and living theory, which may remain and/or be challenged again in future practice. Nevertheless, it is guiding the direction to follow in the field. Thus, this book is 'a work-in-progress' (Davis, 2003, p. ii): the more the research proceeds, the more questions may arise and the more that is learnt about practice. The more practices experienced, the more research into the researcher's own living theory of ESD in a community development context will continue.

1.7 Outline of This Book

Chapter 2 reviews literature from the field of Ainu studies, EE and ESD and national (Japanese) and international policy documents on the indigenous peoples, ESD and sustainable development. This chapter investigates the gap in the field of ESD, which was empirically observed through my work. It explores the relevance of critical EE theory to ESD in a community development context and any issue of power that facilitates the development of theory, policy and practice in formal and science-based ESD. Chapters 3, 4, 5 and 6 are divided into two parts. Part I contains Chaps. 3 and 4. It portrays the application of critical EE approaches to ESD in a community development context and attempts to understand socially-critical ESD *within* the understanding of critical theory. Chapter 3 reviews the ESD practice of Mopet Sanctuary Network (MSN) and the interaction among the key stakeholders inside/outside Mombetsu community, including Ainu members, and myself and evaluates the effectiveness and relevance of ESD activities that were taken place from 2010 to 2012. It investigates the learning and empowerment process of those stakeholders of MSN, informed by critical theory. Chapter 4 critically reflects the ESD intervention within socially-critical approach and investigated how socially-critical approach to ESD was effective to the majority of the MSN stakeholders but disempowered a few Ainu members, particularly focusing on Ainu elder fisherman's behaviour. Part II includes Chaps. 4 and 5. It reports the revised ESD practice beyond socially-critical approach. Chapter 4 provides and discusses the methodological and epistemological limitation of critical theory, which provides the theoretical ground of socially-critical ESD. Chapter 5 analyses the issue of Ainu elder fisherman's disempowerment, based on the theoretical and methodological understanding beyond critical EE, that is, decoloniality. Chapter 6 is the conclusion of this book, which re-engages back the key findings from Chapter 7 with the theoretical discussions. Finally, this chapter presents a praxis framework for ESD from the below. This chapter also presents limitations and recommendations for further ESD practice and research in a community development context.

References

ASPnet, U. (2015). *UNESCO Associated Schools Project Network (ASPnet)*. http://www.unesco-school.jp/eng/

COPERNICUS Alliance. (2015). *The COPERNICUS Alliance, the European network on higher education for sustainable development*. http://www.copernicus-alliance.org/

Clover, D. (2002, March). Environmental Adult Education. *Adult Learning, 13*, 2–6.

Clover, D., & Hill, R. (2013). Adult learning, education and the environment. *New Direction for Adult and Continuing Education, 138*(Summer), 49–59.

Clover, D., Jayme, B. D. O., Hall, B. L., & Follen, S. (2013). *The nature of transformation environmental adult education*. Sense Publishers.

Cohen, M., Manion, L., & Morrison, K. (2011). *Research methods in education* (7th ed.). Routledge.

Davis, J. (2003). *Innovation through action research in environmental education: From project to Praxis*. Griffith University, Nathan, Australia.

ESD-J. (2009). *平成 20 年度 NGO 間の連携等に関する推進検討業務* [Report on project for promoting networking and cooperation among NGOs: 2008–2009]. Ministry of the Environment, Japan.

ESD-J. (2010). *平成 21 年度 NGO 間の連携等に関する推進検討業務* [Report on project for promoting networking and cooperation among NGOs: 2009–2010]. Ministry of the Environment, Japan.

ESD-J. (2011a). *アジアの持続可能な地域づくりのための国際環境協力政策へ!* [Towards international environmental cooperation for sustainable community development in Asia]. ESD-J.

ESD-J. (2011b). *平成22 年度NGO 間の連携等に関する推進業務報告書* [Report on project for promoting networking and cooperation among NGOs: 2010–2011]. Ministry of the Environment, Japan.

ESD-J. (2013). 国連持続可能な開発のための教育の 10 年および UNDESD 以降のアジアの市民社会によるさらなる ESD 推進にむけて (ESD promotion by civil society organisations in Asia towards the rest of and post UNDESD). ESD-J.

ESD-J. (2016). *About ESD-J*. http://esd-j.org/english/about-esd-j/organization

Fien, J. (Ed.). (1993). *Environmental education: A pathway to sustainability*. Deakin University Press.

Fien, J. (1995). *Education for the environment: Critical curriculum theorising and environmental education*. Deakin University.

Fien, J. (2004). *Education for sustainability: Educational policy and practice for sustainable development*. Encyclopaedia of Life Support Systems (EOLSS). http://www.eolss.net/sample-chapters/c11/e6-61-05-01.pdf

Fien, J., & Hillcoat, J. (1996). The critical tradition in research in geographical and environmental education. In M. William (Ed.), *Understanding geographical and environmental education: The role of research* (pp. 16–40). Cassell Education.

Freire, P. (1972). *Pedagogy of the oppressed*. Penguin Books.

Gboku, M., & Lekoko, N. (2007). *Developing programmes for adult learners in Africa*. UNESCO Institute for Lifelong Learning.

Greenpeace Japan. (2017). *捕鯨問題への取り組みについて* [Our efforts on whaling issues]. http://www.greenpeace.org/japan/Global/japan/code/whale/index.html

Hokkaido Prefectural Library. (1731). *津軽一統史巻十之中* [History of Tsugaru Vol. 10.2]. Tsugaru Han.

Huckle, J. (1993). Environmental education and sustainability: A view from critical theory. In J. Fien (Ed.), *Environmental education: A pathway to sustainability*. Deakin University Press.
Huckle, J. (1996a). Realizing sustainability in changing times. In J. Huckle & S. Sterling (Eds.), *Education for sustainability*. Earthscan.
Huckle, J. (1996b). Teacher education. In J. Huckle & S. Sterling (Eds.), *Education for sustainability*. Earthscan.
Huckle, J., & Sterling, S. (Eds.). (1996). *Education for sustainability*. Earthscan.
Huckle, J., & Wals, A. (2015). The UN decade of education for sustainable development: Business as usual in the end. *Environmental Education Research, 21*(3), 491–505.
Ife, J. (2016). *Community development in an uncertain world: Vision, analysis and practice*. Cambridge University Press.
Inoue, Y., & Imamura, M. (Eds.). (2012). *環境教育学: 社会的公正と存在の豊かさを求めて* [Environmental education studies: Searching for social jusice and well-bings]. Houritsu Bunka Sha.
Institute of Cetacean Research. (2017). *Welcome to the Institute of Cetacean Research*. http://www.icrwhale.org/eng-index.html
International Whaling Commission. (n.d.). *Commercial whaling*. https://iwc.int/commercial
Ito, S. (2006). *アイヌ語地名II: 紋別* [Names of places in Aiu language: Mombetsu]. Hokkaido Syuppan Kikaku Centre.
IUCN. (1980). *World conservation strategy: Living resource conservation for sustainable development*. IUCN.
Japan Whaling Association. (2017). *About organisation*. http://www.whaling.jp/english/intro.html
Jickling, B. (1992). Why I don't want my children to be educated for sustainable development. *Journal of Environmental Education, 23*(4), 5–8.
Jickling, B. (1999). Starting points: Questions of quality in environmental education. *Canadian Journal of Environmental Education, 4*(Summer), 104–124.
Jickling, B. (2006). The decade of education for sustainable development: A useful platform? Or an annoying distraction? A Canadian perspective. *Australian Journal of Environmental Education, 22*(1), 99–104.
Kitoh, S. (2009). 環境破壊をめぐる言説の現場から [Critical review on the discourse sites over the environmental problems]. In T. Iida, K. Ito, T. Inoue, T. Kawamoto, S. Kumano, M. Shinohara, T. Simizu, F. Sueki, N. Nakaoka, M. Nakahata, K. Noe, & J. Murata (Eds.), *岩波講座8 生命/環境の哲学* [Iwanami lectures 8: Philosophy of life/environment] (pp. 151–170). Iwanami Shoten.
Kyodo Senpaku Co., Ltd. (n.d.). 会社概要 [About us]. http://www.kyodo-senpaku.co.jp/corporate.html
Lotz-Sisitka, H. (2015). *UNESCO world conference on education for sustainable development conference report by the general rapporteur* (ED/TLC/ESD/2015/RP/1). UNESCO.
Lucas, A. (1991). Environmental education: What is it, for whom, for what purpose, and how? In S. Keiny & U. Zollar (Eds.), *Conceptual issues in environmental education* (pp. 25–48). Peter Lang.
Maher, M. (1986). Environmental education: What are we fighting for? *Geographical Education, 5*(2), 21–25.
Malone, K. (1999). Environmental education researchers as environmental activists. *Environmental Education Research, 5*(2), 163–177.
Masemann, V. L. (1982). Critical ethnography in the study of comparative education. *Comparative Education Review, 26*(1), 1–15.
Maser, C. (1996). *Resolving environmental conflict: Towards sustainable community development*. Lucie Press.
May, S. (1997). Critical ethnography. In H. Hornberger & D. Corson (Eds.), *Encyclopedia of language and education, Volume 8: Research methods in language and education* (pp. 197–206). Kluwer Academic Publishers.
MSN. (2012, February 18). *Mopet Sanctuary Network Okhotsk Mombetsu ESD seminar report*. Mopet Sanctuary Network.

Ndlovu-Gatsuheni, S. (2013). Why Decoloniality in the 21st Century? *The Thinker, 48*, 10–15.

Ndlovu-Gatsuheni, S. (2015). The decolonial Mandela: Embodiment of peace, justice and humanism. *Journal of Developing Societies, 31*(3), 305–332.

Quantz, R. A. (1992). On critical ethnography (with some postmodern considerations). In M. LeCompte, W. L. Millory, & J. Preissle (Eds.), *The handbook of qualitative research in education* (pp. 447–506). Academic Press.

Robottom, I., & Hart, P. (1993). *Research in environmental education: Engaging the debate*. Deakin University.

Sarabhai, K., Ravindranath, S., Schwarz, R., & Vyas, P. (2012). ESD and the Rio conventions. *Journal of Education for Sustainable Development, 6*(2), 181–190.

Shiraiwa, T. (2011). *魚附林の地球環境学ー親潮・オホーツク海を育むアムール川* [Global environmental studies for fish-breeding forest: Amur River that nurtures Oyashio Current/Okhotsk Sea]. Showado Publisher.

Stevenson, R. (1987). Schooling and environmental education: Contradictions in purpose and practice. In I. Robottom (Ed.), *Environmental education: Practice and possibility*. ECT339 Environmental Education, Deakin University.

Stevenson, R. (2007). Schooling and environmental education: Contradictions in purpose and practice. *Environmental Education Research, 13*(2), 139–157.

The Government of Japan. (1949). 漁業法 [Fisheries Law]. The Government of Japan.

The Government of Japan. (2015). *持続可能な開発のための教育(ESD)に関する UNESCO 世界会議の概要報告* [Overview of UNESCO World Conference on Education for Sustainable Development (ESD)]. Ministry of Education, Culture, Sports, Science and Technology.

Tilbury, D., & Fien, J. (2002). The global challenge of sustainability. In D. Tilbury, R. Stevenson, J. Fien, & D. Schreuder (Eds.), *Education and sustainability: Responding to the global challenge*. IUCN.

Tsurumi, K. (1998). *コレクション鶴見和子曼荼羅V: 南方熊楠のコスモロジ* [Collection Tsurumi-Kazuko Mandala V: Essays on Minakata Kumagusu]. Fujiwara Shoten.

Tsurumi, K. (1999). *コレクション鶴見和子曼荼羅 IX: 環の巻* [Collection Kazuko Tsurumi Mandala IX: Circulation]. Fujiwara Shoten.

UNESCO. (1975, October 13–22). *The Belgrade Charter: A framework for environmental education*. Paper presented at the UNESCO-UNEP International Workshop on Environmental Education, Belgrade.

UNESCO. (1978). *Final report: International Conference on Environmental Education in Tbilisi, 1997*. Paper presented at the Intergovernmental Conference on Environmental Education, Tbilisi, Georgia, USSR.

UNESCO. (1997, December 8–12). *The declaration of Thessaloniki*. Paper presented at the International Conference: Environment and Society: Education and Public Awareness for Sustainability, Thessaloniki.

UNESCO. (2005). *UN decade of education for sustainable development: International implementation scheme (IIS)*. UNESCO Education Section.

UNESCO. (2012). *Shaping the education of tomorrow: 2012 report on the UN decade of education for sustainable development*. UNESCO.

UNESCO. (2013). *Proposal for a global action programme on education for sustainable development as follow-up to the United Nations Decade of Education for Sustainable Development (DESD) after 2014*. UNESCO.

UNESCO. (2015, May 19–22). *Incheon declaration education 2030: Towards inclusive and equitable quality education and lifelong learning for all*. Paper presented at the World Education Forum, Incheon, Republic of Korea.

UNESCO. (2019). *Framework for the implementation of education for sustainable development (ESD) beyond 2019* (40 C/23), UNESCO. https://unesdoc.unesco.org/ark:/48223/pf0000370215.locale=en

UNGA. (2012). *Future We Want*. Paper presented at the United Nations Conference on Sustainable Development (A/RES/66/288), Rio de Janeiro, Brazil.

UNGA. (2015a). *Review of the implementation of the United Nations decade of education for sustainable development, 2005–2014*. (A/70/228). United Nations.

UNGA. (2015b). *Transforming our world: The 2030 agenda for sustainable development* (A/RES/70/1). United Nations.

United Nations. (1992a). *The convention of biological diversity*.

United Nations. (1992b, June 2–14). *Agenda 21*. Paper presented at the UN Conference on Environment and Development, Rio de Janeiro, Brazil.

United Nations. (2007). *United Nations declaration on the rights of indigenous peoples (UNDRIP)*. United Nations.

UNU IAS. (2014). *Ten years of regional centres of expertise on education for sustainable development*. http://www.rce-network.org/portal/sites/default/files/public_resource/01_UNU_10yearsBook_web.pdf

Wadsworth, Y., & Patton, M. Q. (2010). *Building in research and evaluation: Human inquiry for living systems*. Allen & Unwin.

Walker, K. (1997). Challenging critical theory in environmental education. *Environmental Education Research, 3*(2), 155–162.

WCED. (1987). *Our common future*. Oxford University Press.

Chapter 2
Unpacking of History, Policies and Theory from the Margin

2.1 History of Hokkaido from a Colonial Perspective

2.1.1 Ainu Mosir

In Ainu language, the land where people live is called *Ainu mosir* ('Ainu' means '(good) human/people' and 'mosir' means land). Before their land became the current Hokkaido of the Japanese territory, their land did not have any specific name with territorial boundary, but just called as Ainu mosir. Now, however, the land of Hokkaido is rarely viewed as a colonised area in Japan. This is because, in addition to the *Wajin*, even the Ainu people often believe 'nothing happened' in the history of Hokkaido.

Due to long-lasting assimilation policies and discrimination (Kaiho, 2008), colonisation has been concealed in educational, social and political systems in Japan, despite the indigenous recognition of the Ainu people in 2008.

The major areas of Hokkaido were inhabited by the indigenous Ainu people before the modernisation of Japan in the late the nineteenth century (Fig. 2.1). These areas encompassed the current Japan-Russian border, including Hokkaido, the Chishima (Kuril or Kurile) Islands, Sakhalin and a part of Kamchatka Peninsula. Before colonisation, these areas were called Ainu *Mosir* by Ainu people or *Ezo-chi* by Wajin Japanese, which stands for 'foreigners' land' in Japanese; they did not see Ainu Mosir as part of Japan.

The Ainu people sustained their lives and society in Hokkaido before the Wajin settlement, having their own social system and cultural traditions, including their own language. They engaged in the fishing, hunting, extensive agriculture and trading

F. Noguchi, *Rethinking Education for Sustainable Development in a Local Community Context*, Education for Sustainability 6,
https://doi.org/10.1007/978-981-16-9464-6_2

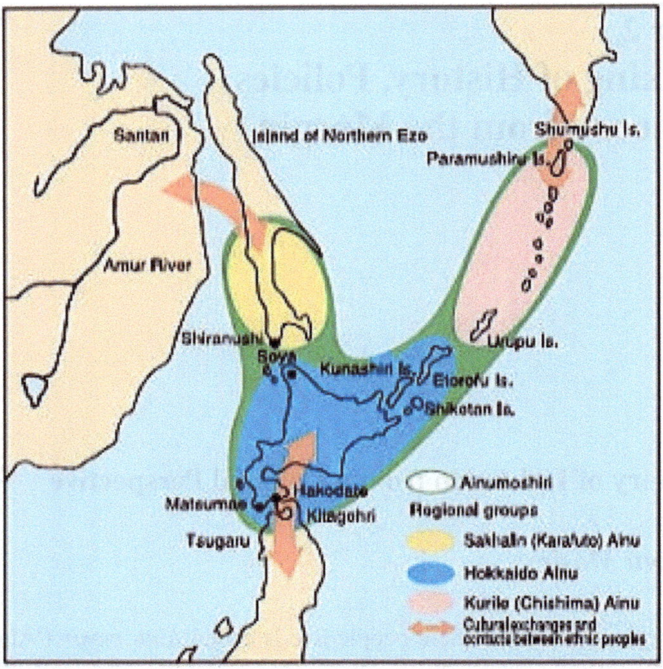

(AAH, 2017a)

Fig. 2.1 Map of Ainu Mosir (traditional Ainu Land). *Source* (AAH, 2017a)

in the greater areas including Japan, Eastern Russia and Northern China.[1] Their knowledge to sustain such life should constitute the core of the indigenous rights.

Wajin Japanese people began colonising Ainu Mosir and assimilating Ainu people in the 1850s, while the Wajin Japanese were under colonial pressure from the Western countries who eagerly expanded their territories all over the world around that time. The United States, England, France, Holland and Russia pressured the Tokugawa Shogunate (feudal government) to open their country. In the negotiation process for the Japan-Russia Treaty of Amity and Commerce in 1855, Japan took a stealthy approach to the negotiations on the northern national border with Russia. The Wajin Japanese claimed their territorial rights to Ezo-chi by depicting the Ainu people as Japanese and under Japanese dominion, and Ezo-chi as *terra nullius*, or belonging

[1] The *Edo* Shogunate had their missionary, Matsumae-*han* (clan) in *Ezo-chi*, which set four trading districts in 1670 s and gained the economic profits by depriving the trading rights from the Ainu people (Uemura, 1990). There are extensive evidences to show the economic exploitation by the Japanese people, numerous revolts by the Ainu against feudal rule and discrimination against Ainu by the Japanese during the Edo era (Uemura, 2008). However, the power of the Ainu people is much superior to the Japanese in Ezochi, so that the impact of the Japanese was still far for the Japanese to get the ruling power from the Ainu people (Uemura, 1990, p. 79). Ainu *Mosir* was still regarded as the Ainu's land before the colonisation in 1880s, as this is seen in the way how the Japanese called the Ainu land as *Ezo-chi*, in contrast to the Japanese land as *Wajin-chi* (Uemura, 2008).

to no one. The Wajin regarded the Ainu people as 'non-human' and with no capacity to govern their land, hence, granting them no territorial rights to their land (Uemura, 2008). This treaty confirmed the Kuril (Chishima) Islands as Japanese territory, while the governance of Sakhalin was shared between Japan and Russia (Uemura, 2008).

The Meiji government, founded in 1868 by the fall of the Tokugawa Shogunate, enthusiastically embraced modernisation to become the first Westernised country in Asia. The Meiji government inherited the diplomatic policies of the Tokugawa Shogunate on Ezo-chi and strategically modernised this area. To justify their land claim against Russia, the Meiji government renamed Ezo-chi to 'Hokkaido' and established the Hokkaido Development and Colonial Agency (北海道開拓使: *Hokkaido kaitakushi*) for the promotion of modernisation and development policies in Hokkaido.[2]

The rapid modernisation of Hokkaido dispossessed the Ainu people of everything, including their culture, language and access rights to the natural resources (Siddle, 2003, p. 451). During the negotiation with Russia, the Japanese government forced the Ainu people to choose whether to live in the Japanese or Russian parts of Ainu *Mosir.* At the same time in 1872, the Meiji government nationalised the Ainu land and formally had control over the Ainu people's resources (Siddle, 2003, p. 452).

2.1.2 Assimilation Policies and Formal Education

The government enacted 'the Hokkaido Ex-Aborigines Protection Act (北海道旧土人保護法: *Hokkaido kyudojin hogohou*)' in 1899 and legitimated the assimilation of the Ainu people through economic and social activities, educational systems and research. The original Japanese words for ex-aboriginal are旧土人 (kyu-dojin; former 'uncivilised' people), which showed the government's discriminative attitudes towards the Ainu people. The Ainu people were differentiated from the Wajin and referred to as the 'secondary-class, uncivilised and barbarian citizens' in the policies (Uemura, 2008, p. 54). Under the Act, assimilation of Ainu people pervaded every corner of life in Hokkaido (Momose, 1994; Uemura, 1990, 2008; Yoshida, 2011).

The Japanese government banned Ainu people from using the Ainu language and Ainu names, and from conducting their ritual activities and traditional life practices, including wearing their customary clothes, ornaments and tattoos. The government encouraged the settlers from all over Japan,[3] which displaced the Ainu from their

---

[2] According to Uemura (1990, p. 249), Hokkaido development policy drew much of the model of the Western colonial frontier in the United States. Kiyotaka Kuroda, the first Minister to the Hokkaido Development Agency, and 76 advisors from the United States developed the master plan for Hokkaido development. The chief advisor was Horace Capron, who was the Second Secretary to the Ministry of Agriculture in the United States.

[3] These mainly included people from the poor villages in Tohoku region (northern Honshu) settled in Hokkaido. Convicts were also taken to Hokkaido and engaged in labouring on infrastructure construction, such as roads, bridges and railways (Abashiri Prison Museum, 2017).

ancestral land to less fertile areas. To protect the growing commercial and industrial activities, the government stripped Ainu people of their access rights to natural resources (such as salmon, deer, bear and whale, which had cultural significance as both a staple food and a spiritual symbol) (Iwasaki, 2011; Nomoto & Iwasaki-Goodman, 2000). The 1899 Act enabled the government to enhance commercial agricultural and industrial activities of the Japanese settlers, which in turn contributed to the economic growth of the nation.

Formal education accelerated the assimilation process, which forced Ainu children to become Wajin Japanese. The Meiji government developed the Ex-Aboriginal Children Education Regulation (旧土人児童教育規定: *kyudojin jidou kyoiku kitei*) in 1901 and established 33 Ainu schools for the Ainu children in Hokkaido (Ogawa, 1991, pp. 259–260). This separated the Ainu children from the Wajin and provided a simplified and easier teaching approach compared to the regular primary schools (Ogawa, 1993, p. 58). The teaching content was not sufficient for Ainu children to proceed to the secondary level even if they could finish the primary education (Ogawa, 1993, p. 58). By 1940, Ainu schools were abolished and Ainu children were accepted into the Wajin schools. By then, the government saw that the assimilation education policy had effectively destroyed Ainu language and customs, and successfully entrenched the Japanese language among the Ainu children (Ogawa, 1993, p. 58). The discrimination against the Ainu people became more severe and more explicit at these mixed schools than in the Ainu schools. The school became the place of persecution by the Wajin, which resulted in a large number of Ainu children dropping out of primary school. Ainu discrimination within schools continued until only recently (Nozaki, 2010).

The 1899 Act legitimatised the superiority of the Japanese race, and the inferiority of the Ainu people, which was instilled into both the Ainu people and the Japanese settlers over the generations (Gayman, 2011; Siddle, 2003). Even after the 2008 official recognition of Ainu as the indigenous people, discrimination and superior-inferior views still continued at 'personal and structural levels' (Gayman, 2011, p. 18), at school, in the workplace and in marriages (Gayman, 2011; Hokkaido Prefectural Government, 2006; Siddle, 2003).

Interracial marriages between the Ainu and, mostly, Wajin increased the assimilation process. Siddle (2003) points out the possibility of biological assimilation, following a group of Japanese bureaucrats who encouraged intermarriage, believing that mingling Ainu blood with that of Wajin should bring progress for the Ainu (p. 452). Although there is hardly any research conducted on biological assimilation, mixing Wajin blood with Ainu did not eliminate the discrimination towards Ainu in reality. 'However mixed you are, a tiny single drop of Ainu blood makes you Ainu' (Gonai, 1972, p. 201). The issue of blood still continues even now as current arguments, mostly by the Wajin,[4] seek to recognise Ainu people by their percentage of Ainu blood.

[4] For example, Yasuyuki Kaneko, the former Sapporo City Council member, stated on the social media (Kaneko, 2014, translated by the researcher): *The Ainu people do not exist anymore. At most there are the Japanese who have the Ainu descendants. It is irrational that the Ainu people can*

Aside from losing their culture, Ainu people continue to experience interrelated socio-economic problems, such as low income, unemployment, low school and higher education enrolments, alcoholism and domestic violence throughout the generations (Center for Ainu & Indigenous Studies, 2010, 2014, 2015; Y. Nakamura, 2008; Voice of Ainu Buraku and Zainichi Korean Women, 2016). These problems have pushed Ainu people to migrate from their homelands into 'the anonymity of the working-class ghettos in Japan's large cities' (N. Nakamura, 2015). Here, they are identified as a *dogai* Ainu, a person who left their original homeland of Hokkaido and now live elsewhere in Japan and overseas.

2.1.3 Indigenous Ainu Rights Claim for Whom?

Despite historically having people with multi-cultural backgrounds,[5] the 'myth' that Japan is an ethnically homogenous country has been sustained in every aspect of life in Japan for a long time (Siddle, 2003). Indeed, this was recently observed in a statement made by high-profile politicians.[6] In the Ainu people's fight against the dominant notion of an inferior and 'dying race' (Siddle, 2003, p. 454), they hoped to ensure their participation in political life, access to the wealth and resources of Japanese society, and to re-create their cultural identity in a way that makes them feel at home. Their hope led a movement in the 1920–1930s to establish local Ainu organisations to improve the social status of the Ainu people (Ogawa, 1993, p. 42).

The movement led to the establishment of the Ainu Association of Hokkaido (AAH) in 1931, which was the first organisation for Ainu people at the Hokkaido municipal level. The AAH was closed once during World War II (WWII) and re-established by the Ainu people in 1946. Since then, AAH has networked and supported Ainu people in Hokkaido, and conducted public advocacy for the Ainu people to the general public (AAH, 2017b). AAH drafted the New Ainu Law and proposed it to the government in 1984 as part of their claim for rights recovery.

The 1899 Ex-Aboriginal Act continued until 1997 when the Japanese government officially recognised the Ainu people as an 'ethnic minority' group of Japan through

enjoy their privileges. It is unaccountable to taxpayers. His tweet has triggered the hate speeches towards the Ainu people by the conservatives until now.

[5] The main cultural communities include Ainu people, Ryukyuan in Okinawa Prefecture, Chinese and Korean people. The Ainu people and the Ryukyuan people (琉球民族 Ryūkyū minzoku) are the indigenous people in Japan. They live on the Ryukyu Islands, the Southernmost Islands between Kyushu and Taiwan. Despite their claim on the recognition of the indigenous status and their self-determination rights to the Japanese government and the repeated UN recommendations, the Japanese government does not recognise them as indigenous people, asserting that the Ainu people are the only indigenous people and so far (Aragaki, 2016).

[6] For example, this statement was made by the former Prime Minister, Yasuhiro Nakasone, in 1896, and by the former Education Minister, Bunmei Ibuki, in 2007 (*The Japan Times*, 2007).

the enactment of the Ainu Cultural Promotion Act (CPA) (The House of Representatives Japan, 1997).[7] In the same year, the Hokkaido Former Ex-Aborigines Protection Act was repealed.

In 2008, the Ainu rights recovery movement led the parliamentary resolution for 'indigenous' recognition (The House of Representatives Japan, 2009). The indigenous recognition was also pushed forward by two international events, namely the adoption of the UN Declaration on Rights of Indigenous People (UNDRIP) in 2007 by the UN General Assembly that the Japanese government voted in favour of (United Nations, 2007) and the 34th G8 Summit held in Hokkaido in 2008 (MoFA, 2008). These international events motivated the government to recognise the indigenous status of Ainu people.

Despite all the outcomes that the indigenous rights movement has brought till now, the indigenous Ainu rights recovery is still tokenistic. This tokenism can be seen in the way the CPA, which was founded on the recognition of Ainu people as the ethnic minority of Japan, still continues to support the 'indigenous' policies, even after the 2008 'indigenous' recognition. Indigenous recognition has a clear awareness of 'the pressure to integrate a group of people into the larger society of the national states of which they are a part' (Viergever, 1999, p. 335), but ethnic minority recognition does not. That is, indigenous recognition implies the identification of a colonial power of one group over the other. On the other hand, ethnic minority recognition is vaguer in its identification of this pressure.

The distinction between indigenous recognition and ethnic minority recognition is important. In the case of Ainu people, indigenous recognition includes acknowledging the colonisation of Hokkaido. This comprehends that the Japanese politically forced Ainu people, who were not originally Japanese people, to become Japanese. In contrast, ethnic minority recognition is acknowledging that Ainu people who are Japanese, as a minority group of Japan. The government continues to use the phrase 'ethnic minority' in policies, instead of a more appropriate expression such as 'indigenous people'. The colonial recognition becomes vague in this meaning.

The tokenism of the indigenous Ainu recognition comes from the lack of Ainu's leadership in their rights recovery movement. This is not new. Non-Ainu (mostly Wajin Japanese) scholars and policymakers are dominant in the Ainu rights movement from an early stage. Few Ainu leaders led the early rights recovery movement in the 1920–1930s (Ogawa, 1993, p. 42). In addition, few Ainu leaders of the 1990s took the initiative to lead what would ultimately become the 2008 indigenous recognition.[8] Even AAH could not have been established without a Wajin named Masaaki

---

[7] CPA, in full, the Act for the Promotion of Ainu Culture, and the Dissemination of Knowledge and Education concerning Ainu Traditions, アイヌ文化の振興並びにアイヌの伝統等に関する知識の普及啓発に関する法律 *Ainu bunka no shinko narabi ni Ainu no dento nado ni kansuru chishiki no fukyu oyobi keihatsu ni kansuru horitsu*, Law No. 52.

[8] These leaders include Giichi Nomura (1914–2008) who made the statement to claim the Ainu indigenous rights recovery at the UN General Assembly in 1992 (Uemura, 2008, p. 82), Shigeru Kayano (1926–2006) who became the first National Diet member and claimed the indigenous recognition of the Ainu people at the Diet in 1994 (Uemura, 2008, p. 80) and Ryukichi Ogawa

Kita, who united the local Ainu leaders of the Ainu movement in 1930 (Ogawa, 1993, p. 65).

In 1997, the CPA was formed by Wajin scholars and policymakers, without reflecting the views of a proposed 'New Ainu Law' formed by the Ainu people in 1984. It reflected the narrow and one-sided definition of the Ainu culture, rights and people, by the Wajin scholars and policymakers. As a result, the CPA further 'de-politicised' (Siddle, 2003, p. 454) the Ainu people, who were further discouraged to take leadership in and engage with the rights movement.

After the CPA, the Ainu rights movement was initiated by non-Ainu (mostly Wajin) groups of scholars, policymakers and activists. They can be classified into two groups. The first asserts the validity (or criticism) of the current Ainu rights legislation based on what the current Japanese Constitution permits, and the CPA. The second group points out the limitations of the current law and seeks a solution that goes beyond the current Japanese law, particularly on the international framework for the rights of indigenous people, such as the UNDRIP. For the purpose of this discussion, the first group will be called 'Group A' and the second 'Group B'.

In these two, Group A has a strong influence in maintaining the validity of the CPA. The CPA process established two ad hoc committees and one permanent committee. This includes 'the Advisory Council for Utari Policy' in 1996[9]; 'the Advisory Council for Future Ainu Policy' in 2008; and 'the Council for Ainu Policy Promotion' in 2009 (Chief Cabinet Secretary of Japan, 2016). These committees are organised in a way that is more favourable to the rights claim within the current Japanese law. This is in terms of the Ainu/Wajin representative ratio within the member groups and the way to select Ainu members. The Advisory Council for the *Utari* Policy has no Ainu member (The Advisory Council for Utari Policy, 1996); the Advisory Council for Future Ainu policy has only one Ainu out of eight experts in 2009 (Chief Cabinet Secretary of Japan, 2016); and the Council for Ainu Policy Promotion has five Ainu members out of 14 in 2017 (Council for Ainu Policy Promotion, 2017). The non-Ainu members are influential in selecting who the Ainu members will be in these committees.

N. Nakamura (2014b) justifies the rationale for Group A:

> In Japan, numbers of **ethnic minority groups** are **few** and we do not have the education to support them. Particularly in Ainu case, their lifestyles are much more assimilated to the Wajin than the indigenous people in the other countries. There are some people, who see the Ainu policies as a privilege, contend that the Ainu people do not exist, as **they neither speak their language nor continue their traditional lifestyle**. Hence, it is hardly accepted by the Wajin people the fact that they are living together with other ethnic minority groups... To avoid unnecessary and unconstructive criticism, it is better to propose alternative options. In any case, **rather than criticising the current policies regardless, it is realistic to find the way to recover the indigenous rights step by step**, considering the special situation of the current Ainu people. (N. Nakamura, 2014b, p. 73). *Underlined and emphasis by the researcher.

(1935–) who has committed to the return of the Ainu communal properties and Ainu remains (Yoshida, 2011, p. 41).

[9] Utari is usually glossed as people, family and compatriot in Ainu. This term is also used to refer the Ainu people.

The text above includes four key problems that Group A and Group B argue about in the current understanding of Ainu policies. These are about understanding (i) the indigenous status; (ii) the population; (iii) the culture; and (iv) the indigenous rights. These four problems motivated Hatakeyama to commit to his indigenous fishing rights claim, which is described in the next section.

i. **Indigenous status**

The Ainu people are recognised as an ethnic minority group, not as an indigenous people, in the current policies written since 2008. Koji Sato, an authority on Japanese constitution, based at Kyoto University, and the *Wajin* chair of the Advisory Council for Future Ainu Policy, gives a detailed interpretation on the meaning of 'ethnic minority' of Japan:

> Recognition of 'the Ainu people' as indigenous means that there are ethnic minority groups who are clearly different from the majority, and who call themselves as 'we are the Ainu people' among us, Japanese people. Both groups of people are those who should create and support the normative world of Japanese constitution as the Japanese citizens. (Sato, 2013, p. 39)

Examining the word, indigenous, in an uncritical manner, ignores the connotations associated with colonisation. The scholars of Group B have criticised that such an understanding ignores the responsibilities associated with 'colonisation' and 'assimilation', which the term 'indigenous' implies (Science Council of Japan, 2011). A non-critical understanding of the term, indigenous, has resulted in their attitude of taking assimilation for granted.

ii. **Ainu population**

It is difficult to ascertain the exact number of Ainu people. Government data appears to underestimate the actual numbers. Currently, policies and projects are based on the Ainu population as determined by: (i) a demographic survey of the Ainu people in Hokkaido conducted every seven years by the Hokkaido Prefectural government and (ii) the number of *dogai* Ainu, or those outside of Hokkaido, obtained in 2011 by the Council for Ainu Policy Promotion. The latest 2013 survey shows 16,786 Ainu individuals in Hokkaido (Center for Ainu & Indigenous Studies, 2015) and the 2011 *dogai* Ainu survey counted 210 (Ainu Policy Promotion Council, 2011). Simply adding the two figures accounts for approximately 17,000 Ainu people in Japan.

The method employed for these demographic surveys, however, is flawed. To determine the population number of the Ainu people in Hokkaido, the Hokkaido Prefectural government collated data from returned questionnaire forms provided by the members of the local AAH chapter. These forms were distributed to the local AAH members and their personal relationships (Okinawa Times, 2017). The data did not include AAH members who did not respond and non-AAH members whom the local AAH chapter president did not know. Mostly, the data did not include those Ainu people who did not want to make their identity public. N. Nakamura (2014a, p. 209) argues that AAH members are 'less than half' of the total Ainu population in

Hokkaido (p. 209). Regarding the demographic survey of *dogai* Ainu, once again, a similar method was used as the Hokkaido Ainu survey. The Council for Ainu Policy Promotion collected the data by asking the local AAH chapter presidents if they knew any Ainu people who lived outside of Hokkaido and calculations were based on the number of responses (S. Hatakeyama, personal communication, February 19, 2013). Once again, the data did not include any Ainu people who did not relate to the local AAH presidents or the Ainu people who live overseas. Chikappu (1998, p. 20), an Ainu elder, estimates that there are 50,000–200,000 Ainu people distributed throughout the world (p. 20). Ultimately, there is no reliable data for the Ainu population, but the government has used data that does not provide a solid foundation to develop an understanding of the current Ainu situation and their rights issues. Underestimation of the Ainu population has disadvantaged the rights claim of the Ainu people.

iii. **Ainu culture**

A narrow understanding of the Ainu identity and population is incorporated into cultural promotion policies and projects, which further constrict and dilute the Ainu culture in relation to music, dance and handicraft (Maruyama, 2013, p. 205). The government believe that cultural events and learning activities could raise the understanding of the non-Ainu people. In addition, it could also help the Ainu people learn about their culture, provide employment opportunities and help them regain their indigenous identity and develop pride in recovering their indigenous Ainu rights. In reality, the Ainu culture is defined by the Wajin and is likely based on the experiences of the Wajin, who may not be familiar with other cultures. The Ainu people have to fit into the Ainu culture as defined by the Wajin-driven policy framework, to be Ainu people.

Unfortunately, those who benefit from such cultural products are the non-Ainu people, rather than the Ainu people (Gayman, 2011, p. 21). An example of this is the CPA project, such as the *Iwor* (traditional hunting territory) Restoration Centre development project. This benefited the Wajin Japanese tourists, and visitors to the centre, where they were able to learn the Ainu culture from the Ainu people. The Ainu rights recovery policies provide minimal cultural promotion and dissemination of information about the Ainu to the Wajin Japanese (Levin, 2001, p. 467). Current policies and projects do not encourage the Ainu people to learn and research the real situation of their indigenous identity, culture and rights.

iv. **Ainu rights recovery**

The issues discussed above (i–iii) have created the current situation where Ainu people are forced to fit into a standard set by the Wajin Japanese, to live as Ainu people. The policies and projects have not recognised the critical need to protect the human rights of the Ainu people, including their rights to land and natural resources, as well as an economic base. The assimilation has been implicit in continuing the policies for indigenous rights recovery, but in so doing, has forced the Ainu people to fit in with a standard the *Wajin* decides.

The underlying cause of a narrow, one-sided and paternalistic understanding of the Ainu identity, population and culture is due to the Ainu people's lack of self-determination or collective rights (Gayman, 2011; Levin, 2001; Maruyama, 2013; N. Nakamura, 2014b, 2015; Siddle, 2003). These rights allow the indigenous people to make decisions about policies for themselves, based on their own definition of identity, culture and their rights as 'people' (Australian Human Rights Commission, 2017; Muswellbrook Shire Council Community Services Team, 2017; United Nations Association in Canada, 2013; United Nations Human Rights Office of the High Commissioner, 1966).

Regarding the claim for self-determination and collective rights, the scholars of Group A raised two reasons why the Ainu people should not have self-determination and collective rights. Firstly, they are concerned that there is a lack of solidarity within the Ainu people. 'They do not have their official organisation for the collective decision-making' (N. Nakamura, 2014a, 2014b, p. 69). 'The internalised oppression, disempowerment, and physical distance' (Gayman, 2011, p. 24) have resulted in a lack of solidarity among the Ainu people. These outcomes are the result of assimilation and colonisation by the Japanese. This explanation sounds like an excuse to Group B, however, whose criticisms include that the government 'defers the decision' (Maruyama, 2013, p. 206), which is 'irresponsible evasiveness' (Gayman, 2011, p. 20). In fact, current policies have put the Ainu people in a negative spiral; lacking these rights has disempowered the Ainu people and it hinders them from uniting and recognising the barriers that they face (Gayman, 2011, p. 24). Furthermore, Group B was afraid of the backlash by the majority Wajin Japanese for the 'special treatment' of the Ainu people (Gayman, 2011, p. 20). Hence, they asked the Ainu people to compromise with the current situation and do the best they could within the current laws' framework. This law was developed soon after WWII when the belief in the ethnic homogeneity was much more dominant than it is now.

The rationale behind the second explanation is found in Article 14 of the Japanese constitution that ensures equal individual rights under the law (Gayman, 2011; Maruyama, 2013; N. Nakamura, 2014a; Siddle, 2003). In fact, Tsunemoto, who has been the key member of the governmental committees, says:

> The rights of indigenous people benefit only to the individuals who belong to a particular group of people, so that the recognition of the rights of a particular group of people may conflict with this article. (Tsunemoto, 2011, p. 50)

The government sees that all Japanese are equal under the law and that Ainu people are regarded merely as Japanese citizens (N. Nakamura, 2014a, p. 209). The government believes that any special treatment of Ainu people may result in negative feelings among the non-Ainu people in Japan. Therefore, the government asserts that individual rights provide basic protection of human rights, which covers the protection of the Ainu rights as a Japanese person. Hence, collective rights are not needed.

Ainu people are missing in the Ainu rights recovery movement

The CPA process overarches these four problems and has undoubtedly left the Ainu people in a colonial situation. It does not reflect their real voices (Gayman, 2011, p. 21). A critical problem in the Ainu rights recovery is that the Ainu people are too disempowered to take bold action to advocate their substantial rights recovery (Gayman, 2011, p. 21), or to claim political power or special status as the indigenous people of Japan (Levin, 2001; Maruyama, 2013; N. Nakamura, 2014a; Siddle, 2003; Yoshida, 2011). In any discussions, events and texts, no matter the assertions made by Group A or B, the activist Ainu people were not well numbered at the frontline. This did not mean that they did not have thoughts or opinions about the entire situation, or that the Ainu population is very small. In fact, the discrimination and assimilation over 150 years have created feelings of humiliation and inferiority in the Ainu people, especially those of the older generation (Gayman, 2011, p. 24). The ongoing colonial pressure through the Ainu rights protection policies discourage the Ainu people from *conscientising* and speaking out about their indigenous roots, their unreasonable situation and their potential rights.

Arguments between the two Wajin groups put these few Ainu activists at the frontline in a ‘twisted’, messy situation, without having much control over the outcome. They were swayed and divided by the Wajin arguments. Some Ainu people, who try to fit in with the identity, culture and rights as defined by the CPA, and its policies, work as government policy members. Others who disagree with CPA definitions join in with the other Wajin group and aim to go beyond the domestic legal protection based on international law. The Wajin controls the indigenous rights arguments, which has divided the Ainu people, and made them turn against each other. The remaining individuals, Ainu people, who do not appear in either camp, are unknown, but there are many who would rather stay away from the arguments, remaining silent and confused.

2.2 Policy and Theory of ESD from the Local Community Perspective

2.2.1 Development of ESD

ESD is both an emerging field and a concept that integrates all aspects of learning (Hopkins, 2012). Officially, the following sentence has been used to define ESD in many policy papers: ESD ‘envisions a world where every person has the chance to benefit from educational opportunities and to learn the lifestyles, behaviours and values necessary to create a sustainable future’ (UNESCO, 2005, p. 6).

As with the concept of sustainable development itself, ESD is not fixed, but rather an evolving concept (Tilbury & Fien, 2002). UNESCO (2009) also acknowledges that slightly different interpretations have been made by the international stakeholders for ESD, but share the following descriptions of ESD:

- A transformative and reflective process that seeks to integrate values and perceptions of sustainability not only into education systems but also into people's everyday personal and work lives;
- A means of empowering people with knowledge, skills and commitments that equip people to address the challenges of global society in local everyday contexts both now and in the future;
- A holistic approach to achieve economic and social justice and respect all life;
- A means to improve the quality of basic education: ESD aims to reorient existing educational programmes and to raise awareness (UNESCO, 2009, p. 26).

ESD relates to the major UN-supported education initiatives such as Education for All (EFA) and UN Literacy Decade (UNLD); however, it goes beyond what is commonly understood as 'education', which often narrowly refers to formal education and schooling activities (UNESCO, 2009). Broadly, ESD has two aims. Firstly, ESD aims to reform the current education. This includes transforming the school system, learning contents and teaching approaches. Secondly, ESD aims to transform the society through education. ESD articulates actions and projects for achieving sustainable development in everyday life context at a local community, covering concepts of peace, human rights and economic viability (UNESCO, 2009). The two aims of ESD indicate that it is holistic and inclusive in its efforts to achieve sustainable community development across a wide array of educational approaches including formal, non-formal and informal education.

ESD is an affinitive educational concept with EE and EfS. EE, EfS and ESD are often used interchangeably, by those who emphasise the importance of education that aims to go beyond individual behaviour change and seeks to empower people for systemic change (Tilbury & Cooke, 2005). On the other hand, there have been strong contestations and disagreements over the wording and definitions. The choice of terminology can depend on how the culture of academia and socio-ecologically engaged scholarship, or geo-epistemologies, might interact with each other and challenge the implementation, enactment and evaluation of ESD in the academic, political and economic power structure (Payne, 2016, p. 70).

In Australia, for example, the acronym ESD has been widely understood to refer to Ecologically Sustainable Development (Australian Government, 1992). This meaning came into use before the term Education for Sustainable Development (and its acronym ESD) became popular worldwide after the Rio Summit in 1992. Instead, in Australia, Education for Sustainability (EfS) is commonly favoured. Payne (2016) asserts that such 'mashing' (p. 71) holds together the different histories, purposes, interests, commitments and tensions but results in the word usage of 'critical' uncritically in EE, ESD and ESD. And now, the same 'mashing' seems to apply to the area of Global Citizenship Education (GCED) (see 2.1.3), using 'critical' uncritically.

2.2.2 *Critical EE: Conceptual Foundation of ESD*

Beyond the arguments on the similarities or differences, EE, EfS and ESD share at least one point in common. The theoretical and political discourses on each tend to be founded in the theorising of 'critical environmental education *for* the environment'. Critical EE is developed in the late 1970/1980s by Robottom (1987) and Lucas (1991) and theoretically synthesised in the 1990s by Fien (1993, 1995) and Huckle and Sterling (1996). As the proposition *for* in ESD suggests, EfS and ESD conceptually draw mostly upon critical EE, which gives the socially-critical orientation to ESD.

2.2.2.1 In/About, Through and for

Lucas (1991) described the ideological orientations of environmental education and categorised environmental education into three types: education *in/about*, *through* and *for*, the environment. Among the three, education *for* the environment is contrasted with education *in/about* and *through* the environment. Each of these reflects a set of values and beliefs that may guide educational decisions and explain their consequences (Fien, 1995).

Key features of education *in/about* and *through* the environment are summarised below, according to the description of Fien (1995)

> Education *in/about* the environment emphasises the knowledge about natural systems and processes and the ecological and political factors that influence decisions about how people use the environment.
>
> Education *through* the environment takes a learner-centred approach to add reality, relevance and practical experience to learning. It provides students with an appreciation of the environment through direct contact with it, which may develop skills for data gathering, photography, interviewing and using scientific instruments as well as social skills such as cooperation and group responsibility.

Table 2.1 briefly summarises the differences between *about*, *through* and *for* in EE, which this research does not touch upon in detail.

In contrast to critical EE, education *in/about* and *through* the environment understands 'environment' as the physical environment and the ecological system. Education *in/about* takes a weak or naïve approach to environmental and social issues, and maintains the dominant liberal/progressive and neoclassic education rather than challenge to the current socio-economic systems and education (Sterling, 1996). Critical EE has 'socially-critical and political action goals' (Stevenson, 1987, 2007, p. 140). It views the environment as inextricably linked with social, economic and cultural systems. It is based upon the integration of the New Environmental Paradigm and socially-critical orientation in education which challenges the perpetuation of unsustainable economic development and the reproductive functions of education (Fien, 1995). Hence, it is 'radical' (Sterling, 1996, p. 19).

Fien (1995) identifies five key principles of education *for* the environment. He argues that it emphasises:

Table 2.1 Key characteristics of education *about*, *through* and *for* the environment

Types	Ownership	Methodology	Ideology	Mode	Approach	Content	Levels
About	Teacher	Positivism	Vocational/neo-classical and/progressive	Uncritical	Knowledge based	Environment	Technical
Through	Teacher	Positivism/interpretivism	Liberal/progressive	Romantic and positively reactionary	Skills developement	Environment and social aspect	Technical
For	Teacher and Learner	Critical theory	Liberal/progressive and Socially critical	Counter hegemonic	Social participation	Environment and human life	Political

Source Fien (1995, pp. 14–23)

1. the development of critical environmental consciousness based upon:
    - a holistic view of the environment as a totality of the interdependent relationship between natural and social systems,
    - a historical perspective on current and future environmental issues, and the study of the causes and effects of environmental problems, and alternative solutions to them;
2. the development of critical thinking and problem-solving skills through a variety of practical and interdisciplinary learning experiences which focus on real-world problems and involve the study of a wide range of sources and types of information;
3. the development of environmental ethic based on sensitivity and concern for environmental quality;
4. the development of the understandings, values and skills of political literacy which promote participation in a variety of forms of social action to help improve and maintain environmental quality; and,
5. teaching strategies that are consistent with its goals. These strategies have been called 'critical praxis'. (p. 55)

It should be noted that 'critical praxis' is one of the key principles of critical EE. Praxis is an approach to critical pedagogy that was developed by Freire (1972). It is the integration of theory and practice or reflection and action upon the world to transform it. It aims to raise the consciousness of learners to the ideological interests served by the present construction of their environment and to empower them to engage in reflective action (praxis) and to transform it (Freire, 1972). Praxis occurs through critical reflection on the situation of those who are trapped in the oppressive structure by gaining the language to describe it through *conscientisation* (conscientização) (Souto-Manning, 2010).

2.2.2.2 Theorising of Critical EE

Theorising of critical EE draws mostly on critical pedagogy and critical theory, which determines two contrasting roles of EE: *subject* and *agent* for social change (Sterling, 1996). Firstly, environmental education must contribute to educational reform by breaking away from the reproducing, unsustainable paradigm (a *subject*). Secondly, environmental education has to play a role in changing values and attitudes by problem-solving, developing action skills, raising awareness about the environment and development-related problems (an *agent*). The former helped educators to critically reflect on education, which has functioned as a tool for a reproducing, unsustainable society and alienating, un-official knowledge. The latter brings 'hope' to educators who see education as playing a role in social transformation.

Reforming education through environmental education (a subject)

Critical pedagogy expresses concern that schooling has functioned as a tool for the reproduction of an unsustainable society. Five points of evidence have been offered in support of this.

The first involves questions about the legitimacy of a particular form of knowledge in education, as official knowledge. Authorities in power, such as the government, prioritise and legitimate Western scientific knowledge as official knowledge in its educational policies, believing its contribution to the industrial growth and existing power structures (Apple, 1993, 2000; Carspecken & Apple, 1992; Freire, 1972).

The second involves the institutionalisation of official knowledge. That is, such knowledge has been legitimatised and promoted as official knowledge in formal education, including in schools, universities, vocational schools and government-supported community programmes (Apple, 1993, 2000; Freire, 1972; Illich, 1973).

The third is the one-sided and unidirectional way official knowledge is transferred. Freire (1972) calls this 'banking education' through which official knowledge is poured into 'the students' brains like money banks' (Souto-Manning, 2010, p. 11). Banking education has made official knowledge into 'common sense' through which people can fit into society. It also plays a role as a 'funnel' (Illich, 1973, p. 71), channelling people into academic and vocational education streams, with the former held up as more worthy than the latter (Connell, 1993; Illich, 1973; O'Hern & Nozaki, 2014).

The fourth is the supremacy of official knowledge creating hierarchical relationships between academically-educated people and the non-academic. In creating and legitimising subordinated relationships, schooling excludes other forms of knowledge. This includes the knowledge of not just the non-academic, but also the knowledge of non-Western, indigenous and local communities, which is thus held to be substantively and functionally inferior (Connell, 1993; O'Hern & Nozaki, 2014, p. 24).

The fifth is the unsustainable nature of the world that results from all the environmental problems, injustice and inequality, political alimentation, conflict, etc. This unsustainable world has established a social system where education as a tool for reproduction can be sustained.

Transforming society through environmental education (an agent)

While criticising schooling for reproducing an unsustainable society, critical educators still find hope in education. As Carspecken and Apple (1992) argue, 'Schools can be and are arenas in which alternative and oppositional cultural practices evolve' (p. 509). Similarly, critical environmental educators placed their hope in environmental education to play a role for educational reform as well as social transformation. Education can challenge the dominant beliefs, values and practices that sustain a society.

In support of this point, Tilbury and Fien (2002) assert:

> … education for sustainability would embrace alternative epistemologies, and would value diverse ways of knowing, identify with the people and communities it purports to serve

> and respect community-based approaches to social change. This new outlook would extend the focus of education (and environmental education) from schools into the community. Education would no longer be interpreted solely as an academic subject for schools but as a participatory process which would involve all areas of civil society, including businesses and public services. (p. 10)

These words indicate a key point in making a move away from education as a tool for reproducing an unsustainable society and towards social transformation instead. These words advocate that 'education' in ESD should go beyond the traditional understanding that limits it within a formal setting, and should take a community-based approach, bringing formal and non-formal entities and community development (informal education) together.

To make education an *agent* for social change, environmental educators have drawn on critical theories from the 1980 to 1990s. Critical theory aims for consensus, based on an open and public argument, essential for more sustainable forms of development. Huckle (1993, 1996b) integrates critical theory in the learning and teaching methods for the critical EE and EfS in a school education context.

Huckle (1993) summarises discursive communicative action theory in four points:

- Universal moral consensus is inherent in the nature and use of human language;
- All human communication can be an ideal speech situation in which all participants have equal power to defend their contributions as meaningful, true, justified and sincere;
- Claims to truth and justification to public scrutiny are revealed; and
- A rational consensus is made, based on an open argument, which undermines the false consensus (Huckle, 1993, p. 61).

Discursive communicative action theory has been integrated and practised as a critical approach to EE and EfS. This has occurred mostly in formal education settings, in the form of workshops, peer learning, multi-stakeholder participation and through the facilitation role of teachers.

Fien (1992, 1995) draws on structuration theory by Anthony Giddens to explain the process of integration of critical EE into a school education context. Structuration theory seeks to explain the reflexive and dialectic relationship between the social structure and the individuals as agents within the social structure (Giddens, 2012). It describes that social change is possible as the individuals can determine the social structure, and vice versa, the social structure can determine the resources and rules for the individual. Both can limit as well as enable each other to change. There is a tension between the agent and the social structure, which accompanies the resistance and conflict. Fien (1995) argues that critical EE is possible based on the struggles of teachers who played a role as an intellectual transformative being, struggling in integrating the rhetoric and reality of our lives and works and challenging both the educational systems and the social structure (p. 98).

2.2.2.3 Policy Supports for Critical EE

The attributes of critical EE outlined in previous sections emphasise a transformational intent. One highlight of the theorising of critical EE is its strong interaction with international policies. Critical EE has influenced international organisations, particularly UNESCO, who has also responded to the critical EE discourses. UNESCO and its member government states have incorporated the key concepts of critical EE into their policies. These policy commitments have facilitated the conceptual growth of their sustainability-related approaches to education through more research and implementation of practices.

The policy commitments have drawn political and economic interests that affect what the sustainability-related educations could be named and how it should be interpreted and implemented. EfS became popular at the same time as sustainability and sustainable development concepts became widely accepted. For example, during the 1997 Thessaloniki Conference and until the 2002 World Summit on Sustainable Development (WSSD), UNESCO preferred to use the phrase, Education for Sustainability (EfS) (UNESCO, 1997). Then, Hopkins (2012) chose to use ESD, rather than EfS, during the drafting process of Chapter 36.

Hopkins (2012) explains the reason of the name change from EE/EfS to ESD is that the broad scope and settings of EE and EfS tended to be ignored and narrowed to one of adjectival education during implementation. It remained as an elective outside the core curricula or as an after-school activity, despite the strong statements from international documents such as Tbilisi Declaration. To avoid repeating the problem, ESD was chosen and expected to simply overcome the problem of EE.

Despite the name changes, the history shows that critical EE has been consistently taken up in international policy documents, even if only as rhetoric. Lucas (1991) states that the international community on EE, and later for EfS and ESD, has moved towards a critical, or *for*, view of EE. This includes the Belgrade Charter (UNESCO-UNEP 1975), which contains a statement of the goal of environmental education based on *for*.

The history of education and sustainable development has experienced five waves where educational concepts become broadened and widened, as Table 2.2 shows. The first wave was the time around the 1960s to the late 1970s, which includes Stockholm Conference in 1972. The educational debates around the issues of the environment established the field of EE. This conference designated the UNESCO as a responsible UN organisation that should lead educational debates in relation to the environment, development and sustainable development. Although the main focus of EE around this time was school education, the policy documents show some of the key elements of critical EE. The Belgrade Charter in 1975 emphasised not only gaining skills, knowledge and attitude but also action through participation to solve the environmental issues, based on the broad understanding of the interrelatedness of culture, environment, economy and society (UNESCO, 1975).

The second wave is the time around the late 1970s–1980s, which includes the Tbilisi Conference in 1978. The interrelationship of the unsustainable problems between/among the fields, generations and species became widely understood in the

Table 2.2 Interaction between sustainable development and EE, EfS and ESD policies

	Emerging educational concepts	Key sustainable development events	Key essence in relation to education	Key educational documents	Key essence	Key discussions of critical EE
1st Wave late 1970s	EE	**1972** **UN Conference on the Human Environment (Stockholm, Sweden)** **Stockholm Declaration, No. 19**	- EE is essential to enhance the knowledge to understand and to protect the environment - Role of UNESCO to promote EE			
				1975 **Belgrade Charter**	- Recognition of inter-linkage between society, economy, culture, peace and environment - Framed five EE objectives to change **awareness, knowledge, attitude, skills, evaluation ability, and participation**	
2nd wave late 1970s late 80s	EfS			**1978** **Inter-governmental Conference on Environmental Education (Tbilisi, USSR)** **Tbilisi Declaration**	- Re-emphasised Belgrade Charter EE framework in the global political context	
		1980 **IUCN, UNEP, WWF: "World Conservation Strategy"**	- Inter-relationship between environment and development			1980s, 1990s - Critical approach to EE, *"for"* - Set the aim of EE for social transformation - Conceptualising EfS

(continued)

Table 2.2 (continued)

	Emerging educational concepts	Key sustainable development events	Key essence in relation to education	Key educational documents	Key essence	Key discussions of critical EE
		1987 **Bruntland Report: "Our Common Future"**	- Conceptualising of sustainable development			
3rd wave late 80s early 2000s	ESD	**1992** **UN Conference on Environment and Development: UNCED Agenda 21**	Agenda 21, Chapter 36 , - Role of education for SD - Start attempt to merge EE and Development education into ESD concept - Formal and nonformal education in all disciplines - Reaffirm the Belgrade charter framework			1990s, 2000s - Conceptualising ESD - Merging EE/EfS and EFA streams together - Arguments and tensions about the differences between EE, EfS and ESD - Arguments and resistance from EFA on merging into ESD
				1997 **The Declaration of Thessaloniki**	- Conceptualising of Education for sustainability - EE can be referred as education for environment and sustainability	
		2000 **UN Millennium Summit Millennium Development Goals (MDGs) by 2015 EFA Goals Target 2.A**	- Ensured that the children's full access to primary education			

(continued)

Table 2.2 (continued)

	Emerging educational concepts	Key sustainable development events	Key essence in relation to education	Key educational documents	Key essence	Key discussions of critical EE
		2002 World Summit on Sustainable Development: WSSD	- Resolved to start the UN Decade of Education for Sustainable Development (UNDESD) and adopted at the 57th session of the United Nations General Assembly in December			
				2005 (–2014) International Implementation Scheme (IIS) on UNDESD	- DESD aimed to build "a world where everyone has the opportunity to benefit from education and learn the values, behaviour and lifestyles required for a sustainable future and for positive **social transformation**"	
4th wave early 2000s		**2012 Rio+20 Future We Want (Article 231)**	- ESD should be promoted beyond the UNDESD			

(continued)

Table 2.2 (continued)

	Emerging educational concepts	Key sustainable development events	Key essence in relation to education	Key educational documents	Key essence	Key discussions of critical EE
				2014 **Shaping the Future We Want: UN Decade of Education for Sustainable Development (2005–2014) Final Report** **Roadmap for Implementing the Global Action Plan on Education for Sustainable Development** **Muscat Agreement**	- UNDESD succeeded in infusing ESD into both education and sustainable development concept - Presents five key strategies for the ESD promotion after 2014 - Understands that ESD is holistic and transformational education and aims **transforming society** - Included ESD as target for EFA and proposal for SDGs	
5th wave? Post 2014	GCED	**2015** **Sustainable Development Goals (SDGs): 2030 Agenda for Sustainable Development Target 4.7**	- Ensures the knowledge and skill for sustainable development through ESD and Global Citizenship Education (GCE)	**2015** **Incheon Declaration: Education 2030**	- Develops skills and attitudes to make informed decisions and respond to global challenges through ESD and GCE	

Source IUCN (1980), UNESCO (1975, 1978, 1997, 2005, 2014a, 2014b, 2014c, 2015, 2017), UNGA (2000, 2002, 2012, 2015); United Nations (1972, 1992), and WCED (1987).

1980s (WCED, 1987), and such recognition resulted in the birth of the sustainable development concept. Responding to the sustainable development debates, critical educators aimed to go beyond school- and science-based EE, and developed a new concept of EfS in the 1980s. The main focus of EfS was still school education, but the life-long non-formal and informal education became identified in the EE/EfS debates.

The third wave is the time around 1990–2000, which follows the 1992 UNCED and the formation of the UNCSD. Chapter 36 of Agenda 21 from UNCSD clearly states the role and meaning of education in achieving sustainable development (United Nations, 1992). This meets the critical educators' assertion of education for the environment covering environment, society, economy and culture. Chapter 36 emphasised a practical approach by emphasising EE and EfS at the local community level. In parallel to EfS, the follow-up process of Chapter 36 generated the concept of ESD.

The fourth wave is the time that the policy commitments became intensified to establish the UNDESD, which called for the commitments of member state governments. The word social transformation, which was long-argued in the critical EE/EfS, was firstly used in the UNDESD documents. While EE and EfS play the central role of the debates, ESD became an umbrella concept to embrace all sustainability-related educational initiatives. This included the Millennium Development Goals (MDGs), UN Literacy Decade and Education for All, which all recognised the UN Declaration of Human Rights in 1948 (UNESCO, 2005, p. 25), and included peace, human rights and gender education.

'Criticism of the concept of sustainable development itself is an integral part of ESD' (Hopkins, 2012, p. 27), and ESD does not intend to teach about the concept of sustainable development. Now, the criticism towards ESD has been leading the fifth wave, a new educational concept for the post-UNDESD; Global Citizenship Education (GCED) is said to complement the education that ESD does not include, such as human rights and peace education (UNESCO, 2017). The UNESCO acknowledged, however, that ESD embraced these forms of education even at the beginning of the UNDESD (UNESCO, 2005). It could be argued that the difference between ESD and GCED is subtle or even nil. There could be political interests behind the emergence of this new concept, which are not investigated in this book.

2.2.3 Recurring Rhetoric-Reality Gap

Strong policy commitments to EE, EfS and ESD have created power pressures that draw the political and economic interests to interpret and implement in a particular way. As a result, conservative interpretations of EE/EfS (*in/about* and *through*) have dominated. This is the 'rhetoric-reality gap' (Fien, 1995; Huckle, 1996b) between the theory of critical EE and its practice. The objectives of critical EE have tended to be 'diluted' and 'deleted' in practice in many parts of the world throughout the history of EE, EfS and ESD (Fien, 2004; Greenall, 1981a; Tilbury & Fien, 2002). The UNDESD was no exception.

Is policy support empowering?

In 2014, the UNESCO and the Government of Japan co-organised the end of the UNDESD conference in Nagoya, Japan. This conference celebrated the achievements of the last decade and presented the further commitment of UNESCO for ESD promotion beyond 2014. The UNDESD successfully infused sustainable development concepts into the educational strategies of member states and conducted initiatives, projects and networks globally.[10] It is also said to have impacted on the wider global community particularly through the UNCSD.[11] These successes showed that the concepts and methods of ESD were actively promoted during the UNDESD. The dialogue of policy, research and practice contributed to the advancement of ESD. However, there are critiques that the UNDESD was a failure. As Huckle and Wals (2015) noted:

> Our central argument is that the Decade represents 'business' as usual in the end' since the majority of those who determined its rationale and develop educational projects and programmes under its umbrella failed through inadequate guidance, misplaced idealism or the censoring of more critical ideas and content, to face up to current global realities. (Huckle & Wals, 2015, p. 492)

One of the main causes of the failure seems to be the imbalance in the policies during the UNDESD. All the efforts were made mostly for formal education and schooling rather than for informal education. The review of the UNDESD showed how significant the evaluation of formal education and schooling efforts of the member governments were, while how little information on informal education and community development was included (UNESCO, 2009, 2012, 2014c). Indeed, UNESCO (2014c) states, 'Non-formal and informal ESD is increasing' (p. 9); however, they understand narrowly the informal ESD as public-awareness through campaigns and media (UNESCO, 2014c, p. 132). This understanding did not include informal learning and empowerment processes through social participation and actions for sustainable development, which should relate to critical EE principles for social change.

This lack of informal ESD brings many of the claimed successes into question. Indeed, as early as 1991, Lucas had argued that there was 'little reliable evidence of success in meeting the goals of education *for* the environment' and that many claims

---

[10] These included the UNESCO Associated School Project (ASP), Higher Education for Sustainable Development (HESD), Promotion of Sustainability in Postgraduate Education and Research Network (ProSPER.Net) in Asia, Regional Centre for Expertise (RCE) and the European Network on Higher Education for Sustainable Development (COPERNICUS Alliance, 2015). ASP successfully increased the number of ASP schools to 9,556 in 180 countries (ASPnet, 2015). RCE United Nations University (UNU) has conducted Regional Centre for Expertise (RCE) (UNU IAS, 2014) to support ESD conducted based on the strong partnership between the higher education institutes and the local community. 136 local areas were acknowledged as RCE in the world (UNU IAS, 2015).

[11] The three Rio Conventions, including the United Nations Framework Convention on Climate Change (UNFCCC), the Convention on Biological Diversity (CBD) and the United Nations Convention to Combat Desertification (UNCCD), have gradually infused the importance of education in achieving goals of these conventions (Sarabhai et al., 2012).

of successes were either 'self-praise' descriptions of courses by their producers or 'pious hopes' 'that the goals of programs were being achieved' (p. 36). It could be argued that the celebrations of the UNDESD at Nagoya were similar 'self-praise' or 'pious hopes'. The reports on the decade mostly represented the stakeholders of formal education evaluating their own formal education efforts. That is, the idea of ESD for 'everyone' in the eyes of the UNDESD was not a part of the Nagoya discourse.

2.2.4 Articulating the Silencing of Educational Modes and Characteristics

Very often when people hear the word 'education', they think of learning in formal education organisations such as kindergartens, schools and universities, or learning activities such as music lessons, craft-making and gardening classes hosted by private and community learning organisations. However, education also happens outside schools. There are mainly three forms of education, which are applicable to ESD:

- Formal education is carried out in the school, college and university system, and is provided by state, regional, municipal and local educational authorities, and by individual schools and teachers.
- Non-formal education occurs outside the formal school system, but through other organised learning settings, e.g. youth groups, women's associations, zoo and park programmes, extension systems, community and church organisations, adult literacy classes, and other settings to provide information and encourage practices.
- Informal education reaches audiences outside organised groups. It is provided by news media, traditional and entertainment media, community mobilisation efforts and other channels of communication (Fien et al., 2001, p. 388).

ESD has inherited the broad approaches of integrating formal, non-formal and informal education, rather than the single approach offered through only formal education. However, ESD has still largely remained an adjectival education, or optional add-on, and formal education has mainly dominated ESD during the UNDESD (Hopkins, 2012, p. 28). Contrary to this, what is not commonly regarded as 'education' was overlooked, including the works of practitioner and researchers who tackled the issues of poverty, exclusion and economic issues in everyday life contexts (Hopkins, 2012, p. 28). These are mostly covered and tackled in the disciplinary field of community development.

The categorisation of educational modes and characteristic types of La Belle (1982) helps us clearly to identify the gaps of the UNDESD (Fig. 2.2, see next page). From the perspective of educational mode, the UNDESD focused on formal education efforts and any efforts that could be understood from formal education (schooling). From the perspective of educational characteristics, the UNDESD looked at the works and stakeholders that could be understood with the methods and

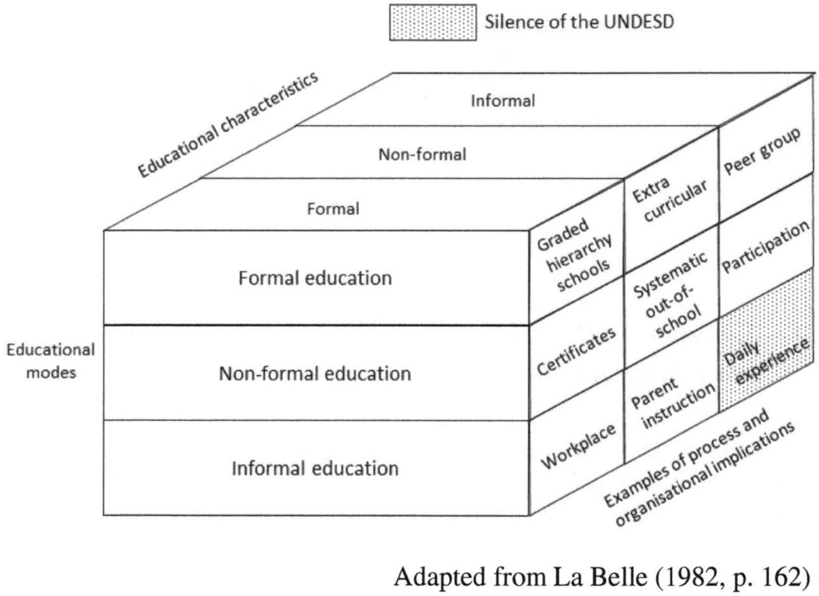

Fig. 2.2 Silence of the UNDESD in educational modes and characteristics. *Source* La Belle (1982, p. 162)

approaches of formal educational characteristics, or schooling. These included structured learning and training activities by government, NGOs and business/industries. An area the UNDESD overlooked was informal education, in particular, where the informal education mode and informal education characteristics overlap; informal education through daily experiences.

Out of three educational approaches, formal education and schooling dominated discussions in educational research and policies for EE, EfS and ESD, by the UNDESD. By focusing on formal education and schooling, the UNDESD overlooked the area where informal learning characteristics and informal education modes cross; informal education through 'daily experience'. This diminishes the fact that the most education happens informally outside of what people normally see as 'education' (Illich, 1973, p. 20).

Informal education through everyday life experiences accounts for only one of nine cubes of Fig. 2.2, but it qualitatively comprises vast parts of human life. Illich (1973) says that most learning is commonly believed to be the result of teaching at formal education and schooling is in 'illusion' (p. 20). In fact, the time we spend in formal education and schoolings is only a part of our lives, considering how little time people are likely to be in formal or non-formal learning situations across one's lifetime. Most learning happens casually outside school, throughout our lives, in an unstructured and intangible way (Illich, 1973, p. 20). There may not be qualified teachers, official curriculum, learning purpose, objectives and textbooks, but we still

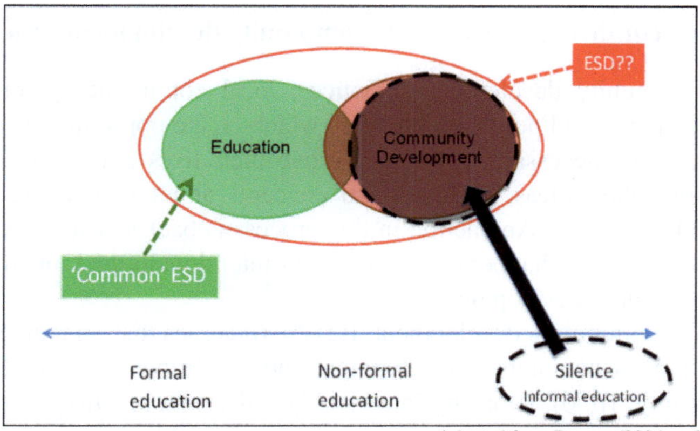

Adapted from Rogers (2004, p. 262)

Fig. 2.3 Silence of informal ESD in a community development context. *Source* Rogers (2004, p. 262)

learn. We think, learn and decide to act through our everyday lives, joys, struggles and acts of resistance.

Community development is the area that covers mostly informal education through everyday life experience. The part that is overlooked by the dominant ESD policies and research includes informal education that happens in a community development context. Figure 2.3 shows the overlooked part in the UNDESD. This part can be named as ESD in a community development context, which comprises informal learning processes embedded in community development efforts for sustainability.

2.2.5 *Community Development as a Praxis*

Community development concerns people's everyday reality of life in their local communities and is the initial context for sustainable development (Ife, 2016; Ledwith, 2005). It is 'an ongoing and complex process of dialogue, exchange, consciousness-raising, education and action aimed at helping the people concerned to construct their own version of community' (Ife, 2016, p. 117). A few community development writers have focused on the overlap between community development and education. Warburton (2013) sees this process as 'an educational process in the broadest sense, where participants learn by doing' (Warburton, 2013, p. 28). They see that praxis, which constitutes the ultimate goal of critical EE, is also the integral part of community development (Ife, 2016; Warburton, 2013).

The following five elements of community development as praxis identify the significant implications of adopting a socially-critical approach to ESD in a local community development context.

i. **Empowerment through sustainable community development practice**

Through community development practices, local community people reflect their social, economic and political structures which create opportunities and challenges, and take the necessary steps to improve their lives and their communities. They enrich their ideas, thoughts and concepts about sustainable development in a real-life context. Any action in this process is backed with new learning and re-learning. Learning happens informally, un-intentionally and un-structurally throughout community development process.

In the field of community development, Ife (2016) argues that, 'genuine empowerment is the aim of community development and can bring effective changes in a local community' (p. 6). Learning inextricably links with practice; learning and practice empower community people and result in sustainable community development. Sustainable community development coincides with a process of community empowerment. Learning in a real-life context at a local community level can bring a real change (Tillbury & Fien, 2002). Governmental agreements or new institutional structures and programmes alone do not bring real change effectively. Learning helps community people to take an action to change their situation, and they also learn through doing a practice.

Conscientisation is at the heart of genuine community empowerment. It involves the local community people's articulation of real-life experiences, sufferings and aspirations and analysis of the relationship between their problems and the broader social, economic and political structures causing their oppression by the people themselves (Ife, 2016). Through conscientisation, community people become able to control their own lives and the conditions under which they live (Tilbury & Fien, 2002). This is the point that attributes community development as praxis.

ii. **Change from below**

'Change from below' is the heart of community development (Ife, 2016, pp. 138–139). This 'from below' idea challenges the hierarchical relationship between local community people and experts that is commonly accepted in many community works. The experts, who have 'degrees or diplomas or who are members of a recognised profession' (Chambers 1993 and 2005 in Ife, 2016, p. 139), often play a key role in applying universal knowledge onto a complex reality of a local community. Community development challenges the power relationship between these parties, attempting to regain the autonomy or self-determination of a local community in relation to government and international organisations, or marginalised people in relation to the majority, with regard to their future. At the same time, it humbles the expert who works simply as 'a resource that may be used by the local community people' (Ife, 2016, p. 122).

Particularly, in this book, 'from below' perspective concerns people in 'a form of acute and persistent disadvantage rooted in underlying social inequalities' (UNESCO, 2010, p. 135). Social, economic, cultural and/or political factors inextricably cause the marginalisation of a particular group of people in a local community.

Marginalised people are often the hardest hit by the challenges created by development proposals with short-term goals and often have the least resilience in major conflicts and crises. Their difficult situation is exacerbated in this process as their accumulated educational, health and livelihood problems pose major obstacles for them in responding to problems appropriately and taking initiatives to preserve or improve their situation. Community development aims to make the marginalised people visible, hear their voices and bring them to the centre of any sustainable development efforts for the local community. This point echoes with the central concept of endogenous development by Tsurumi and Kawada (1986).

iii. **Mutual learning between community people and experts**

The process of 'from below' becomes the learning approach for both the experts and the local community. This process challenges the fixed image of the roles and knowledge that both parties normally have. Community people often see that experts in authority who can provide all (or even some) of the answers (Ife, 2016), such as problem identification, establishing the approach to the solution of problem and designing and making a decision on a project. They often devalue their experiences and knowledge about their own community and do not even think that they have a right to participate in their local community development process. Experts also often do not expect that they can learn from the local community people.

Together they can re-think their position, attitudes to each other, and the knowledge they already have while in search of new knowledge for the local community. Experts have to be willing to listen and learn from the local community. Community people need to know that they have knowledge which is locally contextualised and often difficult to convey or be understood based on the dominant universal 'expert' knowledge. This process requires new learning and unlearning from both sides about what they have possessed from their previous experiences, which leads to mutual liberation (Warburton, 2013, p. 28).

iv. **Lifelong learning**

Formal education and schooling have been major target areas of ESD policies, practices and research. However, formal education engages with a part of everyday life and targets specifically children and youth. Learning contents are determined based on governmental policies and the interests of teachers. The vast majority of people in everyday life contexts at a local community level have little or almost nothing to do with shaping the contents of formal education and schooling. The issues that local community people find very important may not be identified or prioritised as learning contents for formal education and schooling.

Sustainable development relates to all humans and involves all aspects of our lives, and learning must, therefore, be part of a lifelong process (UNESCO, 2005, p. 6). Formal education and schooling are not enough to achieve sustainable development. Fien (1995) argues that whether education can function for reproduction of unsustainable society or social change depends on 'how they (educators) work together with efforts for social change in and beyond the school' (p. 90). The field of community development holds the clue for social change beyond the school.

Community development often tackles the locally identified issues in the everyday lives and involves people beyond those whom formal education and schooling activities could involve. Education also happens informally and un-structurally in a community development process, which dominant ESD discourses do not often see from their limited perspective of 'education'. Understanding and analysing community development processes from the perspectives of ESD can therefore have a significant implication as praxis.

v. **Structural approach**

Community development challenges the structural basis of individualised community problems and seeks alternatives to the commonly accepted assumptions of the existing social, economic and political system (Ife, 2016). This approach is more than a community-based approach, which has 'an individualised and professional orientation' (Ife, 2016, p. 127). A community-based approach is an important aspect of community development. It has been emphasised by many international and government policies, NGOs and research, as well as integrated into programmes and initiatives for sustainable development, including EE, EfS and ESD. However, a community-based approach by itself is not enough and can at times even be problematic in trying to solve problems fundamentally.

The community-based approach does not necessarily challenge the social, economic and cultural systems that have been producing these problems. It focuses on the most obvious issues but may not see them holistically, in relation to other problems and the systems that create the problems. The professional orientation permits a hierarchy between experts, as a central player, and the community, as subordinates, by only including the experts' knowledge. Professional orientation also makes it economically unviable for the local community to receive continuous community service. Such an orientation of a community-based approach does 'not empower communities or consumers, because knowledge and wisdom tend to be confined to the professional and not shared with others' (Ife, 2016, p. 127).

Community development attempts to bridge different contexts (global-local), knowledge paradigms (modern-traditional/indigenous), theory and practice, localities (urban-rural), peoples (majority and marginalised people) and times (past-present-future). In such efforts, it aims to identify colonial pressures and oppression between/among these and facilitate the participation of diverse stakeholders to a community practice and the mutual learning among them (Ife, 2016). Community participation and mutual learning contribute in empowering the local community members for achieving sustainable development. Such challenges of community development to the systems based on participation and empowerment share the key features of praxis.

Therefore, these above five elements indicate that community development is itself a bottom-up mutual learning process for all the stakeholders in everyday life settings. The experience of community development could enrich the theory and practice of critical EE's application to ESD in a local community context.

2.2.6 Causes of Silencing

Critical educators in EE, EfS and ESD have seen the problem of the rhetoric-reality in critical EE as inescapable because of critical EE's strong linkage with policies. Politics seeks to accommodate all views and therefore, makes it impossible to present one's favoured view of sustainable development or philosophy of education (Fien, 2004, p. 4; Greenall, 1981a; Tilbury & Fien, 2002). Policies for ESD were planned and implemented in a politically acceptable manner that did not offend anyone during the UNDESD (Hopkins, 2012, p. 24). The earlier discussions identified that the policies for the UNDESD manifested the rhetoric-reality gap as a form of silencing of ESD in a community development context. As a result, critical components that were declared in the UNDESD policies were 'diluted and deleted' again. So, given the fact that the rhetoric-reality gap of critical EE comes from the unchangeable nature of politics, it is possible to conclude that the silencing of ESD in a community development context was an unavoidable result.

An important question to address is whether critical EE should stay where it is or move beyond the rhetoric-reality. Critical EE practitioners, who have struggled and attempted to break this cycle, suggest that we undertake a situational analysis or 'read the context' of ESD programmes (Fien, 2000; Tilbury & Fien, 2002). Understanding the silencing of ESD in a community development context involves asking questions such as: (i) What is the nature, cause and impact of the silencing of ESD in a community development context? and (ii) How has the theory of critical EE responded to this?

Two factors seemed to have caused this silencing of the praxis-based learning experiences of community development. The first one includes the dominant beliefs in education and community development among many stakeholders. Following Greenall (1981b), Fien (2004) has traced that the dominant influences of mainstream beliefs and practices have turned socially-critical and transformative objectives into acceptable forms of education *in/about* and *through* in the history of EE, EfS and ESD. Fien's words also imply the mainstream beliefs and practices in ESD and what can be named as a 'common understanding' of ESD. The nature of critical ESD that figured in the rhetoric of the UNDESD is outlined below.

The second factor is the political and economic pressures inside/outside of the UNDESD that formed the 'common understandings' of ESD. This came through policies and initiatives of power authorities such as UNESCO and member governments. Thus, it was deemed legitimate and prevailed among the wider stakeholders.

In this power relationship, UNESCO has authority to decide the policies of the UNDESD at the international level, but at the same time, they are also under the pressure of the governments of member states. The success of the UNDESD was evaluated, at least in part, by how many member states accepted and implemented ESD.

Given that education ministries were generally the contact point for the UNDESD,[12] UNESCO had to focus on educational areas that these ministries could understand and work in—and these were in almost every case, formal education and schooling (ESD-J, 2013).

Given these internal and external pressures, it is not surprising that the UNDESD was dominated in practice by forms of ESD that were considered politically 'safe'. In other words, non-transformative practices focused on formal education to the detriment of transformative education in the informal settings of community development. The 'common understanding' of ESD, alluded to above, required elucidation to justify this claim. Such evidence may be seen in the epistemology of ESD that emerged during the UNDESD, particularly how key elements of ESD came to be understood. These were: (i) the meaning of sustainable development (end goal); (ii) the process of ESD (education); and (iii) the content that ESD promotes (knowledge).

i. **Sustainable development (end goal)**

Sustainable development has been interpreted in many ways, with many criticisms. As a result, the meaning of sustainable development has become 'multifaceted and fluid' (Hoppener, 2016, p. 102), 'ambiguous' (Yvon, 2009, p. 24), 'ambivalent' (Mitcham, 1995, p. 311), 'contradicted' (Lélé, 1991, p. 608) and 'oxymoronic' (Radclift, 2006, p. 66). Such ambiguity reflects the everyday (rather than scientific) nature of sustainable development and helps make the concept acceptable to most people. As a result, sustainable development can be accepted as 'necessary' and 'noble' even though the exact intended meaning tends to be interpreted to various stakeholders' advantage. This is similar to the way in which the word 'peace' is understood, as noted by Galtung (1969, p. 167). A non-scrutinising approach acts to conceal issues of power and justice. Thus, the political interests and economic influence of dominant stakeholders in ESD mean that all terms, especially sustainable development (and education), must be 'value-laden'.

Various writers have described the many interpretations of sustainable development as being along a continuum with polar opposites, such as 'technological' or 'ecological' (Orr, 2011, p. 94) or 'strong' or 'weak' (Huckle, 1996a, p. 9). The technological or weak approach is directed at maintaining current approaches to economic growth, but minimises the negative environmental impact through new technologies and legal frameworks. This is a top-down approach and is driven by experts, science and technological advancement. The technological approach has contributed to the rise of the environmental science and management field, which Huckle (1996a, p. 9) describes as strongly linked to the spread of modernity and economic development. This is also known as 'ecological modernization' (Dryzek, 1997, p. 169) and was referred to in the recent discussion on the 'green economy' (Bina, 2013; Brand, 2012) after Rio+20 in 2012. This leaves the current model of

[12] 'Commented by Dr Yoko Mochizuki, the former Programme Specialist UNESCO ESD Section, Paris, at the ESD-J International Open Forum: Further ESD promotion by Civil Society Organisations in Asia towards the end of the UNDESD and beyond', on 30 November 2013, Tokyo, organised by the Japan Council on the UN Decade of Education for Sustainable Development (ESD-J).

economic growth and its basis in neo-liberalism and globalisation unchallenged. In particular, Rostow's (1960) 'stages of economic growth' model provides a framework for all the nations to aim for to achieve industrialisation, commercialisation and a centralisation of social and political systems through the progress of science, technology and supporting legal systems (Baker, 2006; Mitcham, 1995).

On the other hand, the ecological or strong approach to sustainable development aims for a structural transformation of the current systems. This could occur by integrating the social, economic, environmental and political dimensions of development to optimise a more balanced matrix of sustainability outcomes. This requires expert, technology-based, scientific knowledge to be complemented by local and indigenous knowledge. This approach requires societal collaboration driven by the shared efforts of both experts and ordinary citizens. Such a democratisation of science also reflects moves towards a democratisation of society and power.

A number of global initiatives were launched with the objective of integrating ecological approaches with the technological efforts for sustainable development. This included the creation of new forms of governance and collaborative projects involving multiple stakeholders.[13] These tend to be rhetorical, however, as conceptual fluidity renders these policies and practices prone to political and economic priorities. Global politics on sustainable development emphasises the technological or weak approach by seeking to minimise the negative environmental impacts until appropriate new technology is discovered (WCED, 1987). Hence, knowledge of the technological approach tends to be recognised and valued, whereas the ecological approach is generally unrecognised and not fully appreciated in policy discourses.

ii. **Education (process)**

Socio-economic and political pressures have enhanced the formal education and schooling concept (Apple, 1993; Freire, 1972; Illich, 1973; Shor, 1986). This is the same for ESD. The dominant technological approach to sustainable development has impacted the way education is conceived and highlighted the role of educational experts.

Formal education and schooling detach people from everyday life experiences (Illich, 1973, p. 19). They act as a funnel to channel people, particularly youth and children, into educational programmes developed and packaged by governmental authorities (Illich, 1973, p. 71). This is the prevailing form of education, which Freire (1972) refers to as the 'banking concept'. In these educational approaches, knowledge transfer is one-way, from the teacher (depositor) to the students (depositories) (Freire, 1972, p. 53). The students are treated as empty containers to be filled with the knowledge by the teacher, educational institutes and other authorities who can decide what knowledge is and how it should be transmitted. This way of knowledge transfer makes students dependent on teachers and educational institutes as experts, and at the same time, renders them incapable of organising their lives around their own experiences and resources within their own communities (Illich, 1973, p. 12).

[13] For example, Earth System Governance Project (http://www.earthsystemgovernance.org/) and Future Earth Project (http://www.futureearth.org/).

The UNDESD highlighted formal education and schooling by focusing on the education experts, including formal education organisations such as schools and higher education institutes. They also looked at a selection of non-formal education organisations, including community learning centres and public sectors who incorporate a schooling approach to their activities. These included business industries and governments that all provided structured learning opportunities targeting the vast local community. On the other hand, the UNDESD did not provide an opportunity for community organisations to participate in ESD debates. In addition, community organisations hardly found any relevance in the common understanding of ESD. The policies ignored the point made by critical educators that formal education cannot make a major contribution to the sustainability transition unless major educational reforms are enacted (Fien, 2004).

iii. **Knowledge (content)**

The technological orientation of sustainable development, and a strong emphasis on formal education and schooling concepts, also influenced which 'knowledge' should be priorities for ESD. Critical educators have pointed out that particular knowledge is legitimised and transmitted through formal education institutes and schooling concepts. Apple (1993, 2000) refers to this as 'official knowledge'.

The legitimised or 'official knowledge' is the result of complex power relations (Apple, 1995). Indeed, this was the case for knowledge enhanced and transferred under the UNDESD. In addition, official knowledge in ESD refers to environmental management knowledge and all the knowledge that basic education can provide, particularly in the developing countries. Critical educators have noted that prevailing economic and political pressures tend to make education facilities choose content that minimises the factors that contribute towards unsustainable problems, but do not challenge the fundamental basis of these social systems (Berberet, 1989; Fien, 1995, 2004).

The government and authorities' definition of ESD tends to be accepted as a standardised norm by practitioners, when promoted by the official institutes. ESD policies overlooked the unmeasurable experiences outside of school. This included everyday life experience and other local and indigenous knowledge (Illich, 1973, p. 71). Emphases on scientific knowledge, environmental and basic education have made ESD overlook the diverse knowledge that exists outside of the official knowledge, particularly within the indigenous and local knowledge, and opportunities for their integration.

The official knowledge creates a hierarchy between teacher and students, where the teachers determine both the content and the learning process. As Illich (1973) argues, schooling allows the learners' imaginations to be formed by curricular instruction and conditioned to institutional learning of every sort. Content determined by someone else can deprive the opportunity for *conscientisation.* Such education also excludes knowledge held by the socially subordinate groups (Connell, 1993, p. 39). This is also the same to EE, EfS and ESD.

Gough (1997, 2014) has argued about this marginalisation in EE, EfS and ESD over the years. The 'official knowledge' in this field has silenced the voices of women, indigenous, gay and disabled people, as well as those defined by race, class and body size. They are not being given the opportunity to participate in EE, EfS and ESD and have their voices heard.

Exclusion in ESD has two problems. Firstly, excluding these people also excludes their knowledge, because they are the knowers and the agents of the knowledge (Gough, 2014; Gough & Whitehouse, 2003). This is despite the fact that their knowledge may carry useful insights for sustainable development that have not been adequately pursued (Gough & Whitehouse, 2003). Teachers could take something from the local community groups and their vast knowledge systems, and work with it so it still fits with their intention and/or the mainstream education goals. Instead, the second problem of exclusion in ESD is that the local and indigenous knowledge presented in classroom activities does not relate to the reality of local community. Rather, they tend to reflect views of 'romanticism and/or wish for an idealistic return to a lost Eden which was never an Eden at all' (Le Roux, 1997, p. 17).

2.2.7 Is the Current Critical EE Theoretically Enough?

A critical question in addressing the rhetoric-reality gap in ESD is whether critical EE is sufficiently potent and efficacious to respond to the broader scope and settings of ESD. UNESCO has recognised local community and informal education as key focus areas for promotion of ESD during and post-UNDESD (UNESCO, 2014c) as detailed in the *GAP* (UNESCO, 2014b). There are a number of projects that took community-based approaches; however, formal education dominated the implementation of ESD.[14] Few projects to date included informal education processes in the community development efforts.[15] Of the research that is available, most studies of EE and ESD are *in/about* or *through* sustainable community development, which can be categorised as any of the following three types of research detailed below.

The first type of research includes case-practice reports for community development, which describes sustainable development efforts. These only provide minimal analysis of how and why they are educational, however, and how they relate to the socially-critical and transformative objectives of EE, EfS and ESD. The second type of research is the literature, which examines the learning processes involved in formal education (i.e. schools) within community projects (see Andrzejewski et al.,

[14] For CSD, Agenda 21 was localised in 6000 local authorities as Local Agenda 21 (United Nations, 2012, p. 6). Community-based ESD projects included 'Regional Centres of Expertise on ESD (RCE)' by the United Nations University (UNU), 'COE Programme for ESD' and 'Innovation Programme for ESD' by Asia/Pacific Cultural Centre for UNESCO (ACCU), and 'Asia Good ESD Practice Project (AGEPP)' and 'Asia NGO Network on ESD (ANNE)' by the Japan Council on the UN Decade of Education for Sustainable Development (ESD-J).

[15] Formal education organisations such as universities and government-supported non-formal education organisations played central roles in UNU-IAS and ACCU projects. ESD-J showcased the community development efforts by NGOs from informal ESD perspectives, which are discussed in Chapter 4.

2009; Oikawa, 2009; Shaw & Oikawa, 2013; Smith et al., 2012). In these efforts, community leaders, experts and indigenous/traditional knowledge holders participate in the learning activities of formal education. School-community partnerships may enrich the content of education and the curricula. These forms of education may also have some impact on the wider community; however, the impact is often indirect and many community members are left uninvolved. The third type of research is on environmental adult education, for example, Clover (2002), Clover and Hill (2013), and Clover et al. (2013), which provides many examples of appropriate pedagogies that address the power and marginalisation issues that exist within a local community. These pedagogies still carry a schooling focus, however, and the community education is still viewed within a very structured framework in terms of its curricula, facilities and teacher qualifications. These programmes do not teach the dynamic *process* of learning that occurs in community development.

Research in these three categories is critically important to EE, EfS and ESD. These have broadened the concept, process and content of socially-critical and transformative education and, however, are more focused on formal education or schooling, in comparison with community development. These research areas provide little guidance on appropriate pedagogical practice, especially in relation to knowledge creation and learning processes through community development.

Educators such as Jickling and Walker have criticised critical approaches to EE and ESD. Jickling (1991) contends, 'environmental education is not problem solving and the students in education *for* the environment are simply participating as intelligent individuals in the constant re-examination and re-casting of society' (p. 155). Walker (1997) points out its inefficiency: 'While the theory is an effective mechanism to critique practice, it does not provide the strategies to solve educational problems. If environmental education is to become important in school education, a more adequate theory is required (p. 155)'. These statements relate to ESD in a formal setting rather than within a community development context.

These critiques overlook an important aspect of theorising education *for* ESD. That is the critical educators' understanding of the limitation of achieving social change through only formal education. Critical EE could be socially transformative only if education works closely with other struggles in/beyond school education (Fien, 1995; Whitty, 1985). From this view, these critiques do not look at EE, EfS and ESD that occur outside of formal education and schooling. They still look at critical EE from the dominant perspective of formal education or within a schooling context. Little attention is paid to informal education in a community development context, which could have significant value for praxis.

The current critical EE is not sufficient to counter these critiques or the power pressures around EE, EfS and ESD policies because of its strong focus on formal education and schooling. These words pose an assumption that the critical EE also may be trapped in the modern education thinking, which sees education as a funnel.

Wals (2007) elaborates on critical EE in the social learning process, which may in part share the same issues as informal education in a community development context. His work is not explicit about the problems of power and tension among the stakeholder groups, however, particularly between the dominant majority and the marginalised within a local community. Thus, it is still unclear what critical EE in a social learning process really means to community development as detailed below.

Theorising about ESD in a community development context has yet to adequately recognise the learning, capacity-building pathways and potential outcomes of its own practices particularly with regard to empowerment for social change. This is needed for two reasons. Firstly, it can update the current critical EE by providing a realistic approach to its social transformation goal. Secondly, it can provide a firm theoretical grip that critical EE can hold on in their communication with community development practitioners. It may help the practitioners to become explicitly conscious about community empowerment as the foundation of their works and its relevance to ESD. Eventually, theorising of ESD in a community development context can contribute to bridging the disciplinary gap between ESD and community development.

2.3 Summary of Chapter 2

Colonial perspectives clearly showed that the Ainu issues were the hidden central factor in achieving sustainable development in Hokkaido. Ongoing assimilation of the Ainu people has been creating an unfair and unjust situation to them throughout their lives in Hokkaido. Despite the official indigenous rights recovery movement since the 1930s, and the 2008 official indigenous recognition, the policies for the 'indigenous rights protection' still have a significant way to go. The Wajin stakeholders dominated the indigenous rights recovery efforts in Japan, who were further classified into Group A and Group B. These two groups argue within themselves, while excluding the proactive participation or the leadership of Ainu people in their own rights recovery claim.

ESD is the concept that grew based on the conceptual and policy development on sustainable development since 1970s. Critical EE has provided the conceptual framework to the EE, EfS and ESD policies, in particular UNESCO. Strong policy commitments, however, caused a rhetoric-reality gap in the implementation of policies, which critical EE practitioners repeatedly pointed to over the years (Fien, 1995, 2004; Tilbury & Fien, 2002). The real meaning of a critical approach has tended to be 'diluted and deleted' (Greenall, 1981a) when these are implemented through the policies, including the UNDESD. Policies on ESD have tended to focus mostly on formal education and schooling, while overlooking informal education through everyday life experiences, due to the economic and political power pressures. The silencing of the community development experiences resulted in ESD's not responding to the problems within the local community. ESD within a community development context has important implications as praxis to critical EE.

Reviewing ESD discourses from the local community perspectives informs that the effectiveness and applicability of critical EE to ESD in a community development context is unknown.

Despite lacking the efficient and relevant theoretical framework, however, the socially-critical and transformative approach was essential to ESD in Hokkaido.

These should involve an unlearning for both Ainu and Wajin people about the history of Hokkaido from the colonial perspectives and the conscientisation of the Ainu people about their indigenous roots, their unreasonable situation and their potential rights. This focus of ESD was obtained from the discussion of this chapter about the ongoing assimilation that has created a complex situation of the Ainu rights recovery movement in Japan. The Ainu people have been de-politicised that they do not wish to proactively commit to improving their situation or do not even realise what they could have as their indigenous rights. In this very situation, Hatakeyama, a Mombetsu-based Ainu elder, was distinctive in the current Ainu rights recovery movement in Japan, and the indigenous rights claim seems to contain the critical elements for Hokkaido ESD.

In the following chapters, this research conducts an empirical study that examines the relevance and effectiveness of current critical EE within a community development context. If not relevant and effective, it explores how critical EE can be updated through developing a praxis framework for it.

References

AAH. (2017a). *Map of Ainu Moshir (traditional Ainu settlement areas).* https://www.ainu-assn.or.jp/english/begin.html

AAH. (2017b). *Outline of the organisation.* https://www.ainu-assn.or.jp/english/outline.html

Abashiri Prison Museum. (2017). *Land Hokkaido where a prisoner opened it.* http://www.kangoku.jp/world/data3.htm

Ainu Policy Promotion Council. (2011). *「北海道外アイヌの生活実態調査」作業部会報告書* [Ainu outside Hokkaido living conditions survey Working group report]. Chief Cabinet Secretary of Japan.

Andrzejewski, J., Baltodano, M., & Symcox, L. (Eds.). (2009). *Social justice, peace, and environmental education: Transformative standards.* Routledge.

Apple, M. (1993). The politics of official knowledge: Does a national curriculum make sense? *Discourse: Studies in the Cultural Politics of Education, 14*(1), 1–16.

Apple, M. (1995). *Education and power.* Routledge.

Apple, M. (2000). *Official knowledge: Democratic education in a conservative age.* Routledge.

Aragaki, T. (2016, April, 28). 「先住民族」撤回要求 琉球王国の認識に違い ["Indigenous people": Calling for revise—Incorrect understanding of Ryukyu kingdom], Newspaper. *Ryukyu Shimpo.*

ASPnet, U. (2015). *UNESCO Associated Schools Project Network (ASPnet).* http://www.unesco-school.jp/eng/

Australian Government. (1992). *National strategy for ecologically sustainable development.* Australian Government.

Australian Human Rights Commission. (2017). *Right to self determination.* https://www.humanrights.gov.au/right-self-determination

Baker, S. (2006). *Sustainable development.* Routledge.

Berberet, G. (1989). *Education for sustainable development.* Paper presented at the Globescope Pacific Conference, Los Angeles, USA.

Bina, O. (2013). The green economy and sustainable development: An uneasy balance? *Environmental Planning C: Government and Policy, 31*, 1023–1047.

Brand, U. (2012). Green economy—The next oxymoron? No lessons learned from failures of implementing sustainable development. *GAIA—Ecological Perspectives for Science and Society, 1*, 28–32.

Carspecken, P., & Apple, M. (1992). Critical qualitative research, theory, method, and practice. In M. LeCompte, W. L. Millory, & J. Preissle (Eds.), *Handbook of qualitative research in education*. Academic Press.

Center for Ainu & Indigenous Studies. (2010). *北海道アイヌ民族生活実態調査報告* [Report on the 2008 Hokkaido Ainu living conditions survey]. Center for Ainu & Indigenous Studies, Hokkaido University.

Center for Ainu & Indigenous Studies. (2014). *北海道アイヌ民族生活実態調査報告 その2* [Report on the Hokkaido Ainu living conditions survey Vol. 2]. Center for Ainu & Indigenous Studies, Hokkaido University.

Center for Ainu & Indigenous Studies. (2015). *北海道アイヌ民族生活実態調査報告 その3* [Report on Hokkaido Ainu living conditions survey Vol. 3]. Center for Ainu & Indigenous Studies, Hokkaido University.

Chief Cabinet Secretary of Japan. (2016). *Council for Ainu policy promotion*. http://www.kantei.go.jp/jp/singi/ainu/index_e.html

Chikappu, M. (1998). 1997年秋-アイヌの人権についておもうこと [My reflection on the rights of the Ainu peoples]. In H. Osaka (Eds.), *アジア太平洋の先住民族-権利回復の道* [Indigenous peoples in Asia-Pacific region: The path towards their rights recovery]. Kaiho Shuppan.

Clover, D. (2002). Environmental adult education. *Adult. Learning, 13*(March), 2–6.

Clover, D., & Hill, R. (2013). Adult learning, education and the environment. *New Direction for Adult and Continuing Education, 138*(Summer), 49–59.

Clover, D., Jayme, B. D. O., Hall, B. L., & Follen, S. (2013). *The nature of transformation environmental adult education*. Sense Publishers.

Connell, R. (1993). *Schools and social justice*. Pluto Press; and Temple University Press.

COPERNICUS Alliance. (2015). *The COPERNICUS Alliance, the European network on higher education for sustainable development*. http://www.copernicus-alliance.org/

Council for Ainu Policy Promotion. (2017). *アイヌ政策推進会議 名簿* [List of members for the council for Ainu policy promotion]. Chief Cabinet Secretary of Japan.

Dryzek, J. (1997). *The politics of the earth: Environmental discourses*. Oxford University Press.

ESD-J. (2013). *国連持続可能な開発のための教育の10年およびUNDESD以降のアジアの市民社会によるさらなるESD推進にむけて* [ESD promotion by civil society organisations in Asia towards the rest of and post UNDESD]. ESD-J.

Fien, J. (1992). *Education for the environment: A critical ethnography*. (PhD), University of Queensland, Brisbane, Australia

Fien, J. (Ed.). (1993). *Environmental education: A pathway to sustainability*. Deakin University Press.

Fien, J. (1995). *Education for the environment: Critical curriculum theorising and environmental education*. Deakin University.

Fien, J. (2000). Education for the environment—A critique: A response. *Environmental Education Research, 6*(2), 179–192.

Fien, J. (2004). *Education for sustainability: Educational policy and practice for sustainable development*. Encyclopaedia of Life Support Systems (EOLSS). http://www.eolss.net/sample-chapters/c11/e6-61-05-01.pdf

Fien, J., Scott, W., & Tilbury, D. (2001). Education and conservation: Lessons from an evaluation. *Environmental Education Research, 7*(4), 379–395.

Freire, P. (1972). *Pedagogy of the oppressed*. Penguin Books.

Galtung, J. (1969). Violence, peace and peace research. *Journal of Peace Research, 6*(3), 167–191.

Gayman, J. (2011). Ainu right to education and Ainu practice of 'education': Current situation and imminent issues in light of Indigenous education rights and theory. *Intercultural Education, 22*(1), 15–27.

Giddens, A. (2012). *Consequences of modernity*. Polity Press.

Gonai, M. a. W., M. (1972). *明日に向かって: アイヌの人びとは訴える* [Towards future: An Ainu appeal] Maki Shoten.
Gough, A. (1997). *Education and the environment: Policy, trends and the problems of marginalisation* (Vol. 39). Australian Council for Educational Research.
Gough, A. (2014). *Voices from the margins: Towards anti-oppressive environmental education.* Unpublished.
Gough, A., & Whitehouse, H. (2003). The "nature" of environmental education research from a feminist poststructuralist viewpoint. *Canadian Journal of Environmental Education, 8*(1), 31–43.
Greenall, A. (1981a). Environmental education in Australia: Phenomenon of the seventies (a case study in national curriculum development). *Occasional Paper, 7*.
Greenall, A. (1981b). Environmental education: A case study in national curriculum action. *Environmental Education and Information, 1*(4), 285–294.
Hokkaido Prefectural Government. (2006). *平成18年北海道アイヌ生活実態調査報告書* [Report on the 2006 Hokkaido Ainu living conditions survey]. Hokkaido Prefectural Government.
Hopkins, C. (2012). Reflections on 20+ years of ESD. *Journal of Education for Sustainable Development, 6*(1), 21–35.
Hoppener, M. (2016). 'We think we're helping, but are we really?' Critical reflections on engineering for sustainable development. In G. Nhamo & V. Mjimba (Eds.), *Sustainability, climate change and the green economy* (pp. 84–114). Africa Institute of South Africa.
Huckle, J. (1993). Environmental education and sustainability: A view from critical theory. In J. Fien (Ed.), *Environmental education: A pathway to sustainability*. Deakin University Press.
Huckle, J. (1996a). Realizing sustainability in changing times. In J. Huckle & S. Sterling (Eds.), *Education for sustainability*. Earthscan.
Huckle, J. (1996b). Teacher education. In J. Huckle & S. Sterling (Eds.), *Education for sustainability*. Earthscan.
Huckle, J., & Sterling, S. (Eds.). (1996). *Education for sustainability*. Earthscan.
Huckle, J., & Wals, A. (2015). The UN decade of education for sustainable development: Business as usual in the end. *Environmental Education Research, 21*(3), 491–505.
Ife, J. (2016). *Community development in an uncertain world: Vision, analysis and practice.* Cambridge University Press.
Illich, I. (1973). *Deschooling society*. Penguin Books.
IUCN. (1980). *World conservation strategy: Living resource conservation for sustainable development*. IUCN.
Iwasaki, M. (2011). 先住民族による捕鯨活動 [Whaling by the indigenous peoples]. In H. Matsumoto (Ed.), *国立民族学博物館調査報告書97: 海洋環境保全の人類学* [Senri ethnological reports 97: An anthropology of the Marine environmental conservation] (pp. 97–224). National Museum of Ethnology.
Jickling, B. (1991). Environmental education, problem solving, and some humility please. *Trumpeter, 8*(3 Summer), 153–155.
Kaiho, Y. (2008). 近代のアイヌ民族史 [Modern history of Ainu people]. In *The foundation for research and promotion of Ainu culture* (Ed.), *平成13年度普及啓発セミナー報告* [2001 public awareness raising seminars report]. The Foundation for Research and Promotion of Ainu Culture.
Kaneko, Y. (2014). アイヌ民族なんて、いまはもういないんですよね。せいぜいアイヌ系日本人が良いところですが、利権を行使しまくっているこの不合理。納税者に説明できません。[The Ainu people do not exist anymore. At most there are the Japanese-Ainu people. Unreasonableness is that (the Ainu people) can enjoy their privileges. It is unaccountable to the taxpayers]. https://twitter.com/kaneko_yasuyuki/status/498816070531031041
La Belle, T. (1982). Formal, nonformal, and informal education: A holistic perspective on lifelong learning. *International Review of Education, XXVlll,* 159–175.
Le Roux, K. (1997). Towards sustainable conversation: Developing environmental education processes. *Southern African Journal of Environmental Education, 17*, 47–52.
Ledwith, M. (2005). *Community development: A critical approach.* A BASW/Policy Press.
Lélé, S. (1991). Sustainable development: A critical review. *World Development, 19*(6), 607–621.

Levin, M. (2001). Essential commodities and racial Justice: Using constitutional protection of Japan's Indigenous Ainu people to inform understandings of the United States and Japan. *New York University of International Law and Politics, 33*, 419–526.

Lucas, A. (1991). Environmental education: What is it, for whom, for what purpose, and how? In S. Keiny & U. Zollar (Eds.), *Conceptual issues in environmental education* (pp. 25–48). Peter Lang.

Maruyama, H. (2013). Japan's post-war Ainu policy. Why the Japanese government has not recognised Ainu indigenous rights? *Polar Record, 49*(249), 204–207.

Mitcham, C. (1995). The concept of sustainable development: Its origins and ambivalence. *Technology in Society, 17*(3), 311–326.

MoFA. (2008). *G8 Hokkaido Toyako Summit*. http://www.mofa.go.jp/policy/economy/summit/2008/index.html

Momose, H. (1994). 北海道旧土人保護法の成立と変遷の概要 [Establishment of law to protect aborigine in Hokkaido and overview of its change]. *Sion, 55*, 64–86.

Muswellbrook Shire Council Community Services Team. (2017). *Walking with aboriginal and Torres Strait Islanders and their communities: Practice implications—Self-determination*. http://www.workingwithatsi.info/content/PI_selfdetermination.htm

Nakamura, N. (2014a). Realising Ainu indigenous rights: A commentary on Hiroshi Maruyama's 'Japan's post-war Ainu policy. Why the Japanese government has not recognised Ainu indigenous rights? *Polar Record, 50*(253), 209–224.

Nakamura, N. (2014b). 「アイヌ政策のあり方に関する有識者懇談会」報告書に関する論考の比較検討 [Comparative study of the commentaries on the report of the advisory council for future Ainu Policy]. *Hokkaido Minzokugaku* [Hokkaido Ethnological Studies], *10*, 67–76.

Nakamura, N. (2015). Being Indigenous in a non-Indigenous environment: Identity politics of the Dogai Ainu and new Indigenous policies in Japan. *Environment and Planning A, 47*, 660–675.

Nakamura, Y. (2008). 現代アイヌ民族の貧困 [The current poverty issues of the Ainu people]. *教育福祉研究* [Journal of Education and Social Work], *14*, 15–25.

Nomoto, M., & Iwasaki-Goodman, M. (2000). アイヌ民族と鯨の関わり [Relationship between Ainu people and whale]. In K. Kitamuro (Ed.*), モーリー2(Morie 2)*: Hokkaido Shinbun.

Nozaki, Y. (2010). アイヌ民族の教育不平等 [A study on the educational inequality of the Ainu]. *The Bulletin of Kokugakuin University, Hokkaido Junior College, 27*, 41–53.

O'Hern, D. M., & Nozaki, Y. (2014). *Natural science education, Indigenous knowledge, and sustainable development in rural and urban schools in Kenya: Toward critical postcolonial curriculum policies and practices*. Sense Publishers.

Ogawa, M. (1991). 「アイヌ学校」の設置と「北海道旧土人保護法」・「旧土人児童教育規程」の成立 [A historical study on "Ainu School" (an elementary school in Ainu Community) in Hokkaido(1): The forming process of Ex-Aboriginal Children Educational Regulation]. *The Annual Reports on Educational Science, 55*, 257–325.

Ogawa, M. (1993). 「アイヌ教育制度」の廃止-「旧土人児童教育規定」廃止と1937年「北海道旧土人保護法」改正 [Abolition of Ainu education policy: Abolition of Ex-Aboriginal Children Education Regulation and Revision of Hokkaido Ex-Aborigines Protection Act in 1937]. *The Annual Reports on Educational Science, 61*, 37–79.

Oikawa, Y. (2009). *Mobius for sustainability*. Kesennuma City Government.

Okinawa Times. (2017, August 7). アイヌ支援へ生活状況調査-政府全国規模で [Supporting Ainu; government conducts Ainu living condition nationwide survey]. *Okinawa Times*.

Orr, D. (2011). *Hope is an imperative: The essential David Orr*. Island Press.

Payne, P. G. (2016). The politics of environmental education. Critical inquiry and education for sustainable development. *The Journal of Environmental Education, 47*(2), 69–76.

Radclift, M. R. (2006). Sustainable development (1987–2005)—An oxymoron comes of age. *Horizontes Antropológicos, 12*(January/June), 65–84.

Robottom, I. (1987). *Environmental education: Practice and possibility*. Deakin University Press.

Rogers, A. (2004). *Non-formal education: Flexible schooling or participatory education?* Kluwer Academic Publishers

Rostow, W. (1960). *The stages of economic growth: A non-communist manifesto*. Cambridge University Press.
Sarabhai, K., Ravindranath, S., Schwarz, R., & Vyas, P. (2012). ESD and the Rio conventions. *Journal of Education for Sustainable Development, 6*(2), 181–190.
Sato, K. (2013). *日本国憲法と先住民族であるところのアイヌの人びと* [Japanese Constitution and Ainu persons as Indigenous people]. Hokkaido University Center for Ainu and Indigenous Studies.
Science Council of Japan. (2011). *報告 アイヌ政策のあり方と国民的理解* [Report on the situation of Ainu policies and national understanding].
Shaw, R., & Oikawa, Y. (Eds.). (2013). *Education for sustainable development and disaster risk reduction*. Springer.
Shor, I. (1986). *Cultural wars: School and society in the conservative restoration 1969–1984*. Routledge & Kegan Paul.
Siddle, R. (2003). The limits to citizenship in Japan: Multiculturalism, indigenous rights and the Ainu. *Citizenship Studies, 7*(4), 447–462. https://doi.org/10.1080/1362102032000134976
Smith, J., Wheeler, L., Guevara, J. R., Gough, A., & Fien, J. (2012). *Conversations on school—Community learning partnerships for sustainability (A guidebook)*. RMIT University.
Souto-Manning, M. (2010). *Freire, teaching, and leaning: Culture circles across contexts*. Peter Lang.
Sterling, S. (1996). Education in change. In J. S. Huckle & S. Sterling (Eds.), *Education for sustainability*. Earthscan.
Stevenson, R. (1987). Schooling and environmental education: Contradictions in purpose and practice. In I. Robottom (Ed.), *Environmental education: Practice and possibility*. ECT339 Environmental Education, Deakin University.
Stevenson, R. (2007). Schooling and environmental education: Contradictions in purpose and practice. *Environmental Education Research, 13*(2), 139–157.
The Advisory Council for Utari Policy. (1996). *報告書* [Report]. Ministry of Land, Infrastructure, Transport and Tourism, Japan.
The House of Representatives Japan. (1997). アイヌ文化の振興並びにアイヌの伝統等に関する知識の普及及び啓発に関する法律 [Ainu cultural promotion act: CPA in full, the act for the promotion of Ainu culture, and the dissemination of knowledge and education concerning Ainu traditions]. http://www.shugiin.go.jp/internet/itdb_housei.nsf/html/houritsu/14019970514052.htm
The House of Representatives Japan. (2009). アイヌ民族を先住民族とすることを求める決議案 (第一六九回国会、決議第一号) [Resolution calling upon the government to recognize the Ainu people as indigenous to Japan, 169 National Diet Session, Resolution No. 1]. http://www.shugiin.go.jp/internet/itdb_gian.nsf/html/gian/honbun/ketsugian/g16913001.htm
The Japan Times. (2007, 26 February). Ibuki: Japan 'extremely homogenous'. *The Japan Times*. http://www.japantimes.co.jp/news/2007/02/26/national/ibuki-japan-extremely-homogenous/#.V-ipOfl96Uk
Tilbury, D., & Cooke, K. (2005). *A national review of environmental education and its contribution to sustainability in Australia: Frameworks for sustainability*. Australian Government Department of the Environment and Heritage and Australian Research Institute in Education for Sustainability (ARIES).
Tilbury, D., & Fien, J. (2002). The global challenge of sustainability. In D. Tilbury, R. Stevenson, J. Fien, & D. Schreuder (Eds.), *Education and sustainability—Responding to the global challenge*. IUCN.
Tsunemoto, T. (2011). *アイヌ民族と教育政策~新しいアイヌ政策の流れのなかで~* [The Ainu people and education policy: In the new Ainu policy current]. Sapporo University Research Institute.
Tsurumi, K., & Kawada, T. (1986). *内発的発展論* [Endogenous development theory]. University of Tokyo.

Uemura, H. (1990). *北の海の交易者たち-アイヌ民族の社会経済史* [Traders in Northern sea: Socio-economic history of the Ainu people]. Dobunkan Publisher.

Uemura, H. (2008). *知っていますか?アイヌ民族一問一答* [Do you know the Ainu people?: Q & A]. Kaiho Shuppansha.

UNESCO. (1975, October 13–22). *The belgrade charter: A framework for environmental education.* Paper presented at the UNESCO-UNEP International Workshop on Environmental Education, Belgrade.

UNESCO. (1978). *Final report: International conference on environmental education in Tbilisi, 1997.* Paper presented at the Intergovernmental Conference on Environmental Education, Tbilisi, Georgia, USSR.

UNESCO. (1997, December 8–12). *The declaration of Thessaloniki.* Paper presented at the International Conference: Environment and Society: Education and Public Awareness for Sustainability, Thessaloniki.

UNESCO. (2005). *UN decade of education for sustainable development: International Implementation Scheme (IIS).* UNESCO Education Section.

UNESCO. (2009). *United Nations decade of education for sustainable development (DESD, 2005–2014): Review of contexts and structures for education for sustainable development 2009.* UNESCO.

UNESCO. (2010). *Education for all global monitoring report 2010: Reaching the marginalized.* UNESCO.

UNESCO. (2012). *Shaping the education of tomorrow: 2012 Report on the UN decade of education for sustainable development.* UNESCO.

UNESCO. (2014a). *2014 GEM final statement: The Muscat agreement.* UNESCO.

UNESCO. (2014b). *Roadmap for Implementing the global action programme on education for sustainable development.* UNESCO.

UNESCO. (2014c). *Shaping the future we want: UN decade of education for sustainable development (2005–2014) final report* (UNESCO Ed.). UNESCO.

UNESCO. (2015, May 19–22). *Incheon declaration education 2030: Towards inclusive and equitable quality education and lifelong learning for all.* Paper presented at the World Education Forum, Incheon, Republic of Korea.

UNESCO. (2017). *Global citizenship education.* https://en.unesco.org/gced/approach

UNGA. (2000). *United Nations millennium declaration* (A/RES/55/2).

UNGA. (2002). *57/254 United Nations decade of education for sustainable development.* (A/RES/57/254). United Nations. http://www.un-documents.net/a57r254.htm

UNGA. (2012). *Future we want.* Paper presented at the United Nations Conference on Sustainable Development. A/RES/66/288, Rio de Janeiro, Brazil.

UNGA. (2015). *Transforming our world: The 2030 Agenda for sustainable development* (A/RES/70/1). United Nations.

United Nations. (1972). *Declaration of the United Nations conference on the human environment.* Stockholm, Sweden. http://www.un-documents.net/unchedec.htm.

United Nations. (1992, June 2–14). *Agenda 21.* Paper presented at the UN Conference on Environment and Development, Rio de Janeiro, Brazil.

United Nations. (2007). *United nations Declaration on the Rights of Indigenous Peoples (UNDRIP).* United Nations.

United Nations. (2012). *Sustainable development in the 21st century (SD21): Review of implementation of agenda 21 and the Rio principles.* https://sustainabledevelopment.un.org/content/documents/641Synthesis_report_Web.pdf

United Nations Association in Canada. (2013). *The human rights approach to sustainable development: Environmental rights, public participation and human security.* United Nations Association in Canada.

United Nations Human Rights Office of the High Commissioner. (1966). *International covenant on civil and political rights.* United Nations.

UNU IAS. (2014). *Ten years of regional centres of expertise on education for sustainable development*. http://www.rce-network.org/portal/sites/default/files/public_resource/01_UNU_10yearsBook_web.pdf

UNU IAS. (2015). *RCEs worldwide*. http://www.rce-network.org/portal/rces-worldwide

Viergever, M. (1999). Indigenous knowledge: An interpretation of views from Indigenous Peoples. In L. Semali & J. Kincheloe (Eds.), *What is indigenous knowledge? Voices from the academy*. Taylor & Francis.

Voice of Ainu Buraku and Zainichi Korean Women. (2016). *Situations and challenges of minority women in Japan: For review of seventh and eighth periodic reports of government of Japan on the implementation of the convention on the elimination of all forms of discrimination against women (CEDAW)*.

Walker, K. (1997). Challenging critical theory in environmental education. *Environmental Education Research, 3*(2), 155–162.

Wals, A. (Ed.) (2007). *Social learning: Towards a sustainable world*. Wageningen Academic Publishers.

Warburton. (2013). *Community and sustainable development: Participation in the future*. Earthscan.

WCED. (1987). *Our common future*. Oxford University Press.

Whitty, G. (1985). *Sociology and school knowledge: Curriculum theory, research and politics*.

Yoshida, K. (2011). アイヌ民族の補償問題-民法学からの近時の有識者懇談会報告書の批判的考察 [Compensation issues of the Ainu people: Critical review on the recent report by expert's panel on Ainu countermeasures from civil law perspectives]. *Nomos, 26*, 19–47.

Yvon, P. (2009). Sustainable development: A vague and ambiguous "theory." *Society and Business Review, 4*(3), 231–245.

Part I
ESD *within* Socially-Critical Approach—Light and Shadow

Part I reports the first part of the two critical ethnographies in this research. This part portrays the application of socially-critical approaches to ESD in a community development context and attempts to understand socially-critical ESD *within* the understanding of critical theory. It contains one chapter. This chapter (Chapter 3) depicts the process of integrating socially-critical approaches to ESD efforts by MSN and analyses the effectiveness and challenges of ESD informed by critical theory.

Chapter 3
Socially-Critical ESD: Light and Shadow

Colonisation of Hokkaido resulted in a double-faceted outcome is depicted by light and shadow. 'Light' means that the colonisation modernised the nation through rapid economic growth, which brought prosperity to the majority of Wajin Japanese people and the nation. 'Shadow' means that this prosperity was achieved through loss of the land, resources and society of the Ainu people. Ongoing assimilation and suffering of the Ainu people still exist unrecognised in the everyday life of Hokkaido, while most of the Wajin believe nothing ever happened.

The indigenous rights recovery of the Ainu people, and their empowerment, are the 'hidden' central issues in the search for sustainable development in Hokkaido. These require the consientisation and emancipation of both the Ainu and Wajin Japanese people through unlearning and new learning. Due to the unfathomable degree of assimilation, however, the Ainu people are too disempowered to question their situation and assert their rights for self-determination in regards to identity, culture and needs. This search for a path to sustainable development requires more work to look back at the past, as well as to look forward into the future. It should begin with determining if it is necessary for Ainu people to know who they really are, reveal their concealed history and discuss the future that both Wajin and Ainu people want to achieve.

Following this interplay between 'light' and 'shadow' of the continued colonisation of Hokkaido, the activities of the Mopet Sanctuary Newtork (MSN) became apparent. Contributing to the MSN movement required a learning process that was referred to as ESD. This was guided by the discussions in Chap. 2 that defined ESD as a transformative, empowering, holistic and quality education needed to achieve sustainable development, largely drawing on critical EE.

This story of implementing an ESD process is documented in this chapter, which illustrates the process of how the socially-critical ESD was infused into the MSN activities from 2010 to 2013. Therein, the next step as community educators was to meet Hatakeyama, get to know his struggles for his indigenous rights recovery and commit to developing his efforts into collective and collaborative social actions, and learning through taking a socially-critical ESD approach.

F. Noguchi, *Rethinking Education for Sustainable Development in a Local Community Context*, Education for Sustainability 6,
https://doi.org/10.1007/978-981-16-9464-6_3

3.1 Connecting Dots—From Individual Activism to Collective Action

I met Hatakeyama and his indigenous rights claim in 2009 for the first time at the study tour in Mombetsu that Sapporo NGO staff A and the participants of the ESD workshop in Sapporo in 2008. Sapporo NGO staff A's strong interest in developing ESD based on Hatakeyama's indigenous claim was shown in his email from 2009.

> Until now, there are efforts for environmental education and environmental conservation in Hokkaido, which makes use of Ainu's nature views and their spirit. But I think these are not enough. The perspectives on recovering the social and economic rights of the Ainu people are necessary for such efforts. (Isn't it ESD?) I am really interested in Hatakeyama's efforts because I can see the elements that could link to the recovery of social and economic rights of the Ainu people.
>
> Yet, it is also true that this type of rights claim is often taken as '(ethnic) egoism' generally. I think that it would be better if we could express such rights claim and could positively work on conserving the local natural environment and establishing a self-sufficient economy. We also need the widespread sharing of this strategy within the public arena.
>
> Indigenous Ainu issues tend to be well understood by outsiders rather than locals, outside Hokkaido rather than inner Hokkaido, and overseas rather than inner country. The locally based approach is, in a sense, the most difficult but most important. If we could make such process, it would be a great success to the Ainu people, the majority Wajin Japanese and ESD. (Sapporo NGO staff A, personal communication, October 29, 2009)

As Sapporo NGO staff A argued, the Ainu's knowledge tends to be 'particularised' (Agrawal, 2002, p. 290) as an 'educational' resource based on the environmental educator's needs in mostly the formal and non-formal education settings.[1] As argued in Chap. 2, the current EE and ESD activities in Hokkaido do not go beyond the narrow cultural understanding, such as dance, songs, music and the demonstration of traditional fishing technique. These could benefit the general public, particularly, the majority Wajin Japanese, who might enhance their understanding of the Ainu culture. These could not touch colonial history, however, and could not improve the social and economic situation of the Ainu people, who could not fit within this narrow cultural understanding.

Hatakeyama's indigenous rights claim echoed with my investigation of ESD from the margin. Herewith, I joined his activism and examined his rights claim from a socially-critical ESD perspective. Then, I began my practices with Sapporo NGO staff A, starting with problem identification within Mombetsu community and the search for key strategies based on the study tour experience.

---

[1] For example, Sapporo City council developed the education modules for Ainu education for the schools in Sapporo City. Schools in Sapporo City shows the case practices of the primary and junior high schools in Sapporo which have conducted Ainu lessons about traditional salmon fishing, the traditional life practices around salmon and the Ainu's spiritual connection with salmon (Sapporo City Council, 2017). *Ureshipa* Club of Sapporo University, which develops Ainu youth to be Ainu educators, has also provided the visiting lectures by Ainu youths on the Ainu culture, such as traditional dance and songs at schools in Sapporo (Sapporo University, 2017).

3.1.1 Problem Identification

The study tour included visits to six local learning organisations, which were based on themes such as local history, environmental conservation and Ainu culture. From the study tour, two problems were identified with current local learning activities in relation to Hatakeyama's indigenous rights claim. Firstly, the learning activities overlooked the Ainu people following modernisation (or colonisation). Secondly, these tended to objectify the natural environment, by separating nature and humans, and seeing nature only as an entity to be protected or to be utilised. Underlying the two problems of local learning activities was the dominant modern, Western and scientific educational views, which seek 'scientific and technological solutions to the environmental problems without addressing the root social, political and economic causes' (Tilbury & Fien, 2002, p. 9). Such a view did not facilitate participants reflecting on current lifestyles in Hokkaido, or eliminate the fact that modernisation was achieved through colonisation of the Ainu land and people.

This modern, Western and scientific educational view created two types of gaps in Mombetsu, which could have obstructed Hatakeyama's indigenous rights claim within the Mombetsu community. The first gap was between the Ainu and Wajin people, as well as within the Ainu people. Previously, the local Ainu and Wajin Japanese never had a chance to discuss or work together on local indigenous issues. In addition, the local Ainu people were not united in their rights claim. Few Ainu people like Hatakeyama were active. Some Ainu people did not wish to publicly identify themselves as Ainu people, especially, the older generations. They were afraid of recalling their experiences of discrimination and abuse. Furthermore, younger generations were not even aware of their Ainu blood because they were not told about it by their families.

Interest in the proposed industrial waste management plant development in Mombetsu complicated the situation. The local community and local Ainu community were divided into those in favour, and those against, the development plan. Through the study tour, I observed that there was hesitation from local Wajin and Ainu members in supporting Hatakeyama's indigenous rights claim and AAH. They supported Hatakeyama's claim in their minds, but they did not want to support him publicly because their organisations, such as the Fishermen's Union, Farmers' Union and Mombetsu City Council, had already made an agreement with the developer.

The second gap which could have obstructed Hatakeyama's indigenous rights claim was the knowledge gap. Local learning activities understood local history and issues predominantly from the Wajin Japanese perspective. At the same time, the dominant Wajin Japanese influence dismissed Ainu knowledge and history. This occurred for two reasons.

Firstly, long lasting assimilation policies, particularly formal education, played a key role, as discussed in Chap. 2. The situation remained unchanged until now, even after the 2008 official indigenous recognition. Ainu education is not compulsory, and it really depends on the teachers' interests and efforts (Shinada, 2010). Even though teachers are interested in it, it is still difficult to find space for it in an already busy curriculum and to identify how to teach it effectively. As a teacher in Mombetsu describes, years three and four might be the only space for teachers to integrate Ainu study, however, students at that age are too young to comprehend sensitive colonisation issues and the indigenous rights recovery (MSN, 2010c). Needless to say, teachers outside Hokkaido find little relevance in teaching Ainu issues, which are not considered local issues.

Lack of teaching materials and guidelines also makes it difficult for Mombetsu teachers to conduct Ainu education. A statement about Ainu people in the primary and high school textbooks are 'fragmented, inappropriate and limited' (Shinada, 2010, p. 68).[2] Teachers also find that existing supplementary textbooks are also not enough.[3]

Secondly, the nature of the modern, Western knowledge dismissed the Ainu people's knowledge, which was orally transmitted through tales, legends, experiences and morals for everyday life from generation to generation (Ainu Museum, 2017). Lack of written records makes difficult for anyone to access Ainu knowledge. Assimilation policies of the past and present discouraged Ainu people from keeping their language,[4] or passing their culture on to future generations. Reflecting this, Hatakeyama recalled a critical memory from his childhood:

> In Japan, if the Wajin were to find out that the Ainu were speaking in Ainu, they would have strictly punished them for it. So, my grandmother and her friends totally stopped speaking in Ainu whenever they saw me near. Because of such things, Ainu people cannot understand Ainu language after my generation. (S. Hatakeyama, personal communication, December 22–24, 2015)

Even if the Ainu people had some local knowledge, they also became unsure about it in relation to the evidence-based, modern, Western knowledge. This was assumed from Hatakeyama's words, as he often said that there were no (written) records to prove the local historical sites in Mombetsu (S. Hatakeyama, personal communication, December 13, 2013). All these factors resulted in erasing the existence of the Ainu people, and their knowledge, when juxtaposed against the modern Wajin and their knowledge.

---

[2] In April 2016, the Ministry of Education made a modification on the statement in the junior secondary school text book regarding the ex-Aboriginal policy on the Ainu people in 1899. The original draft stated, 'the government enacted the ex-Aboriginal policy in 1899 and took the lands of Ainu, who mostly engaged in hunting and gathering and forced them to engage in agriculture'. The government changed this statement to 'the government… gave the land to the Ainu people and tried to change their life into the Agriculture-based life'. This modification has been criticised by the media and the AAH, who see it as 'distortion of the history' (Kadota, 2015).

[3] The supplementary text books on the Ainu people, which were published with the aim of compliment with what was missing in the curriculum, was first published in the 1984 (Shinada, 2010, p. 68). The side readings for the Ainu education have been published by the four organisations, including Hokkaido Education Board, Sapporo City Education Board, Hokkaido Teachers' Union and Foundation for the Research and Promotion of Ainu Culture.

[4] UNESCO categorises Ainu language as 'critically endangered' (UNESCO, 2009).

3.1.2 Embodying ESD Concept in a Local Community Context: Mopet Sanctuary Network

Based on these possible 'people' and 'knowledge' gaps in Hatakeyama's indigenous rights claim, two strategies were engaged for ESD in Mombetsu during this initial phase. This included 'multi-stakeholder' and 'participatory' approaches. These were the key approaches that characterised critical EE. It was assumed these could help open up Hatakeyama's rights claim to a broader stakeholder audience in/outside of the local community. This could reveal the complex connections of local Ainu issues to diverse fields, raise their '*tojisha ishiki* (当事者意識)'[5] and, hopefully expand Hatakeyama's solo activism into dynamic and collective social actions.

Initial works, from February till June 2010, involved workshops and meetings in Mombetsu, Sapporo and Tokyo with Ainu and Non-Ainu individuals. This brought together organisational resources from SFSY and ESD-J. The multi-stakeholders had expertise in diverse fields, including human rights, local primary industries, Ainu issues, environmental issues both inside and outside Mombetsu. Many of them had never met or previously worked together.

At all the workshops and meetings, Hatakeyama shared his life story and concerns on indigenous rights, particularly in relation to the Ainu culture and its practices around salmon and whale. A facilitated discussion of the participants was also carried out. These discussions highlighted the complex link between Hatakeyama's concerns with issues from diverse fields, and the limitations of current Japanese and international legal frameworks. These were limited by their ability to respond to his claims and concerns in a holistic manner (MSN, 2010a, 2010b, 2010c).

Discussions held over a six-month period crystallised the 'Mopet Sanctuary Concept' (Fig. 3.1) and established the MSN to bring collective actions and learnings to realise this concept. This concept aimed to achieve sustainable community development based on Hatakeyama's rights claim.

Three principles constituted the Mopet Sanctuary Concept. The first principle was to understand Hatakeyama's claim from a local and historical perspective. His life story showed that his individual experiences were deeply rooted in the history of colonisation. The trauma and emotional scars, which he, his family and people experienced in the past, continued to the present, creating the ongoing economic and social problems of the Ainu people. The second principle was to understand Hatakeyama's claim from the bio-regional perspective. Hatakeyama pointed out the impact of farming, and industrial activities, on the marine ecosystem. As Hatakeyama observed, the sea, forests and rivers were a unified concept, and the traditional Ainu

[5] There is no appropriate English word to translate '*tojisha-ishiki* (当事者意識)'. This word is often used to describe the degree of commitment of a person to a social and economic issue from which he/she is not directly affected. The online-based Digital-*Daijisen* Japanese dictionary (Shogakukan Digital-Daijisen, 2017) explains: 'An understanding that he/she directly related to a particular issue. An awareness to be a part of connected party'. This world could be translated in English as: a person who sees the other's problem as if his/her problem and feels 'responsible' and 'committed' to the solution. There is no single word to describe it in English. Thus, I used the original Japanese word in this book.

Fig. 3.1 Ainu participant explaining the Mopet Sanctuary Concept

people's lives, values and knowledge were interwoven in *Iwor*, a sphere where the Ainu lived and conducted their traditional hunting and gathering. His story indicated the necessity of the bio-regional approach in the solution of the marine environmental problems.

The third principle was to understand Hatakeyama's claim from a practical, everyday life perspective. One participant said:

> Now we have UNDRIP, and the government recognised Ainu as indigenous people. However, these are nothing more than abstract. The Ainu rights recovery movement won't proceed without the movement for claiming the right in the real-life context. Thus, Hatakeyama's indigenous fishing rights claim is meaningful. More people will resonate with him if we keep passing his claim to the public rightly. We have to deliver his claim to those who are around us in a compelling manner. (MSN, 2010a)

While understanding the importance of substantive indigenous rights recovery stemming from an everyday life context, participants were concerned that any legal framework for indigenous rights recovery was too great a stretch to affect indigenous rights substantively. They found that the international legal framework such as UNDRIP and CBD could give more relevant guidance to Hatakeyama's claims than the current Japanese legal framework. They found, however, that these were still too abstract to make sense of in a real-life context.

Finally, participants agreed to establish MSN. This became the space for members to share information related to Hatakeyama's rights claim with each other, the wider community as well as connect stakeholders in/outside of the local community with

Mopet Sanctuary Concept. During the establishment of MSN, the government's construction plan of the final industrial waste management facility became imminent in Mombetsu. Hence, MSN began the activities that were mostly responsible for challenging this local development.

3.1.3 Meaning of ESD and the Role of Educators

As shown in Fig. 3.2. Responding to the social actions made by MSN members, diverse learning activities were organised by 2012. These learning activities were organised in multiple forms, including workshops, seminars, informal meetings and participatory citizenship research activities in/outside of Mombetsu.

It was proposed that all activities should strengthen the linkage between the MSN movement and local schools,[6] as well as with national and global issues on sustainable development.[7] MSN learning activities also included the periodic local environmental and historical studies.[8] The data collected through these studies provided the source of information that supported Hatakeyama's claim at the arbitration process through the Hokkaido Environment Dispute Coordination Commission (HEDCC) (see this chapter). Alongside these events, closed informal meetings were carried out with key members of MSN. The informal meetings became the space for participants to share confronting issues, such as strategies for the arbitration process, and to discuss possible actions to be taken.

---

[6] MSN organised learning activities to link the MSN's Ainu rights movement to schools in Mombetsu and to the global efforts for sustainable development outside Mombetsu. For the school-community linkage, teachers who participated in the MSN workshop organised special classes with Hatakeyama and Close friend A for year six and year eight students at their schools in Mombetsu in 2010 and 2011. In the classes, Hatakeyama shared his life story, and Close friend A taught the colonisation history of Hokkaido and the on-going Ainu issues. The teacher who invited Hatakeyama and Close friend A said that the year three students were still too young to comprehend the complexity of the Ainu issues and the depth of the problems that they have faced historically. He considerd that the ages over year 5–6 seemed appropriate for Ainu study. He also found, however, that it is not easy to conduct Ainu study for these years, as the current primary and secondary school curriculum guidelines do not support these Ainu studies.

[7] These included sustainable fishing and Fukushima Daiichi nuclear disaster debris after the Great East Japan Earthquake in 2011.

[8] A group of MSN has checked the water quality at six fixed points at Mombetsu River every four months since 2010. Interviews of the local community stakeholders of Mombetsu Museum and Okhotsk Sea Ice Museum were conducted. The literature on the local Ainu history was reviewed to confirm the ancestral roots of Hatakeyama, who is a descendent of a Mombets Ainu elder, Kikenimpa, in the oldest record of Mombetsu (Hokkaido Prefectural Library, 1731).

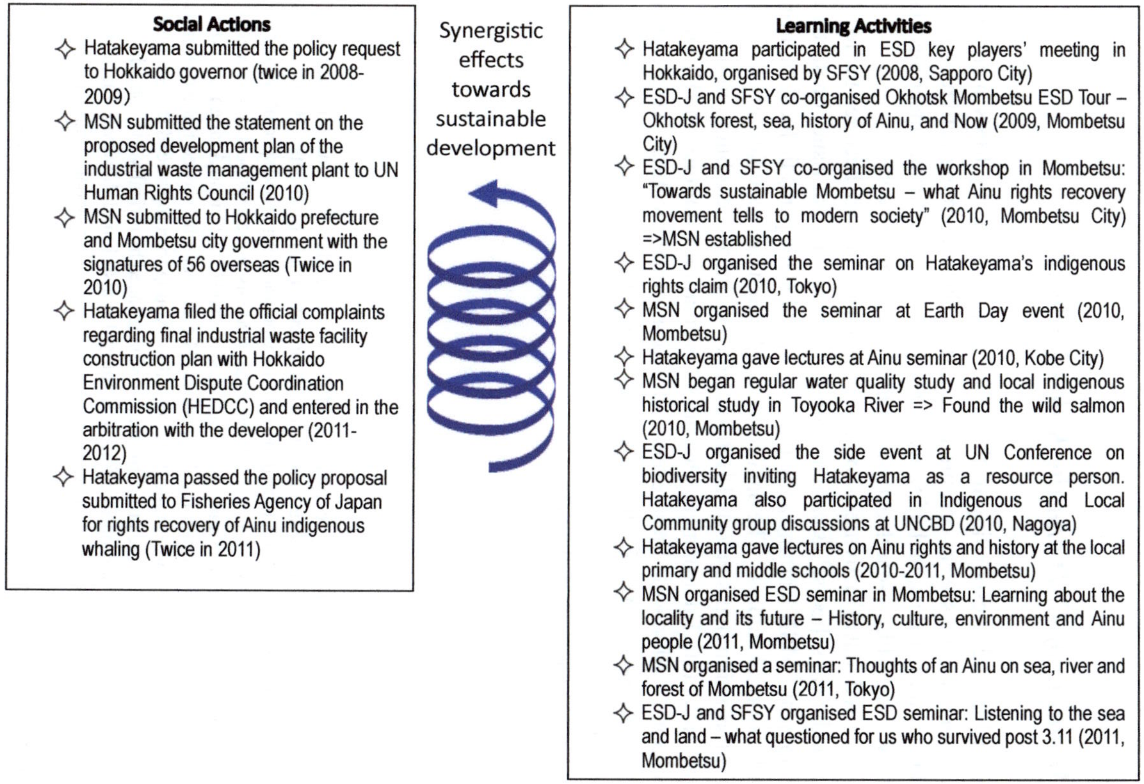

Fig. 3.2 ESD = Social actions X Learning Activities

3.1.4 A Formula for Socially-Critical ESD

Through these activities, a clearer understanding was obtained about socially-critical ESD in a community development context and the role of educators. It was understood that the socially-critical ESD process could be created through coordinating timely and effective learning opportunities that should respond to the social and political actions of a local community. This understanding is described using the formula as ESD = Social actions X Learning Activities (Fig. 3.2).

It was assumed that the learning activities and social actions that the MSN had been conducting could synergistically interact and create a process of socially-critical ESD, as shown in Fig. 3.2. I believed that this idea echoed with the ideas of a socially-critical approach to ESD that should extend beyond formal education by responding to the struggles of a local community (Fien, 1995; Tilbury & Fien, 2002).

Based on this ESD formula, an understanding of the two roles that educators should play in MSN's ESD process was developed.

1. Create learning spaces for local community members to provide detailed, alternative and timely information on the important issues related to the policy advocacy issues and activities;
2. Facilitate participatory processes for the diverse stakeholders to meet, express themselves freely, and learn from one another.

Using this formula, it was postulated that 'learning' could be the key to create the bottom-up process in the MSN, and could prevent further isolation of Hatakeyama and the other Ainu people in Mombetsu. In asserting the indigenous rights against the developer, key members of the MSN appeared to favour the top-down approach to policy change. They conducted public advocacy activities through lobbying, collecting petitions, and making statements through international organisations. Such a top-down approach, which was taken by key MSN members, seemed to naturally and commonly be taken by the rights-based activism in general. Ife (2016) describes, "The conventional approach to human rights has been through the law: legislation, bills or charters of rights, United Nations (UN) conventions and the use of legal mechanisms to work for human rights protection" (p. 79).

This tendency was noticeable in some MSN members who experienced students' social activism in the 1960s to 1970s in Japan.[9] They opted for legislative change as the means to recover their indigenous rights. They believed these could effectively give external pressure to the authorities to change their attitude towards the marginalised groups (MSN, 2010b). With this understanding, some MSN members conducted a number of policy advocacies, such as a written statement to the UN

[9] Some members of the MSN had experienced opposition activism against the treaty of Mutual Cooperation and Security between the United States and Japan, and the opposition movement against the Narita (Tokyo) International Airport Construction in 1960–1970s. Others had commented on the Minamata Disease problems, and were concerned the science was used as a political and economic tool to support development in Japan, which caused Minamata Disease. Underlying their comments in MSN, they commonly had strong criticisms of the governmental structure and the modernisation process that resulted in a destructive pattern of development.

Human Rights Council (2010); a proposal to Hokkaido Prefectural Government, Mombetsu City Council (2010) and the Fisheries Agency of Japan (2011); and the arbitration process through Hokkaido Environmental Dispute Coordination Commission (HEDCC) from 2011 to 2012.[10] Thus, it was considered that a bottom-up process through learning activities in combination with the top-down social actions could empower the local community members effectively. This process of learning and action using both a bottom-up and top-down approach could prevent the isolation of the Ainu people in a local community.

3.2 Critical Reflection on ESD Within Socially-Critical Approach

Reflecting on the MSN experiences from the establishment till 2012, two key questions were investigated to understand informal ESD in the community development context:

1. How effective were the critical approaches to EE, EfS and ESD in community development?
2. What challenges remain regarding empowerment of the local community, particularly socially marginalised Ainu members?

The unstructured interviews and focus group discussions were conducted with key MSN members in February and December, 2012. The next section reports the impact that key members of the MSN, and media reports, considered as 'successes'.

3.2.1 Achievements

There were four successes identified mainly by respondents from MSN who participated in the focus group discussions conducted in 2012, and from the MSN documents from the establishment.

(i) **Recognition of Ainu as the key stakeholder in community development**

In 2012, as a representative of the AAH Mombetsu Chapter, Hatakeyama signed the Industrial Pollution Prevention Agreement with the developer, and the reconciliation process through HEDCC was terminated (Ministry of Internal Affairs & Communications, 2012). The media, the members of MSN regarded this outcome as the first 'success' case (*Hokkaido Shimbun Press*, 2012; *The Asahi Shimbun*, 2012;

---

[10] Participants with expertise in the indigenous rights protection and international human rights issues, organised a petition, which collected 56 signatures from the indigenous people' organisations overseas in 2010. This petition supported these MSN's policy advocacies, such as local and municipal governments, and the UN Human Rights Council in 2010 (UNGA, 2010).

The Mainichi Shimbun, 2012; *The Yomiuri Shimbun*, 2012), although MSN could not stop the construction plan. The agreement recognised the Ainu, as a key stakeholder in the development plan and industrial operation. It secured the rights to allow the Mombetsu Ainu people to inspect the operation at any time based on their free will and to receive regular monitoring reports on the operation of the waste treatment facility.

(ii) **More opportunities for sharing life stories of Hatakeyama**

Through the MSN actions and learning activities of MSN, Hatakeyama had the chance to share his experiences at various occasions, including conferences and seminars at the global, national and local levels. COP10 in 2010 gave Hatakeyama the opportunity to learn more about global indigenous people's rights, develop his own connections with the indigenous people of the world, as well as with the *dogai* Ainu (Ainu people outside Hokkaido), who worked on the same goal of indigenous rights recovery.

Hatakeyama's close friend in Mombetsu (Close friend A), observed that the opportunity to share his life experiences might have eased Hatakeyama's burden that he had carried throughout his life. He went to the primary and secondary schools with Hatakeyama to teach the history of local Ainu people and their issues. He described how he became energetic during his talk.

> Satoshi-san talked happily about Ainu Kamui [God] to the schoolchildren. Moreover, he passionately talked about the Ainu culture and the Ainu fishing rights like a pure, innocent boy. Kids were so fascinated by his talk and just concentrated on it for two hours. His talk seemed to be a cleansing process for Hatakeyama, whose desire for profit and loss of faith in humans had burdened him throughout life. This was like his [Hatakeyama's] emancipation process. (Close friend A, personal communication, December 25, 2015)

Hatakeyama admitted that he had never had the chance to talk about himself before MSN. He even avoided talking about himself in public. It was proposed that sharing his life experience might help him gain back his confidence and self-esteem. During the initial phases of MSN, Hatakeyama often avoided expressing his thoughts and concerns in his own words, even during a closed meeting. Instead, he would ask someone else, often Close friend A, to represent his thoughts and feelings. Whenever he was invited to make a speech, Hatakeyama insisted on going with Close friend A. After a while, he eventually travelled by himself and spoke about his life story of his own words.

(iii) **New information on the local community to fill the knowledge gap**

Data collected from the environment and history survey on Mombetsu Ainu helped fill the knowledge gap, particularly in the arbitration process at HEDCC. The community's public opinion was often based on the information provided, reflecting one-sided views of the developers and local government. Such information provided only a part of the whole picture that tended to be dominated by narrow economic arguments and a bio-physical environmental perspective. The local community members based their opinions on such information from the developers. The political and economic interests of the organisations and industries that the community members belonged to also strongly influenced their decision-making process.

Hatakeyama describes:

> There were Ainu fishermen friends who said that they really agreed with me but their position at the fishermen's union, which supported the construction, made it difficult for them to give me full support. (S. Hatakeyama, personal communication, December 13, 2013)

The change in the attitude and words of the community members caused emotional frictions with those who did not support the proposed plan and information. Scientific and theory-based evidence helped MSN members avoid emotional arguments and justify the Ainu rights during the HEDCC process. Alternative data also helped the MSN attract the interest of a wider range of stakeholders, including the media and researchers.

(iv) **Collective actions and learning for sustainable development**

The meetings and workshops of the MSN motivated diverse participants in/outside Mombetsu to commit to Hatakeyama's rights claim. They developed their sense of '*tojisha ishiki*' (see Sect. 3.1.2) to Hatakeyama's claim and the indigenous issues in Hokkaido through the discussions.

An MSN member commented during a meeting in 2010:

> This is a kind of the movement to re-think where we come from. MSN activism will benefit the wider range of non-Ainu people in/outside of Mombetsu. (MSN, 2010a)

One MSN member felt the weight of Hatakeyama's burden, as a descendant of Wajin colonisers who had taken Ainu Mosir and forced assimilation for their own benefit. Some also saw the Ainu culture as the guiding values that Hokkaido society should emphasise in their search for the post-modern and post-colonial process. Others had shared their concerns about potential environmental damage caused by the local development.

The meetings and workshops produced more collective actions and learning activities by the MSN members through their networks and organisations. The social actions included the policy advocacies to the UN, national and local governments (as shown in Fig. 3.2), and the learning activities in/outside MSN. This included seminars at Earth Day Mombetsu, and local teachers' Ainu education, as well as local historical and environmental citizen' research. The knowledge accumulated through the actions and learnings provided the data that MSN utilised to support Hatakeyama's claims in the arbitration process at HEDCC.

3.2.2 Challenges

While the various outcomes that were considered as success, MSN faced several challenges, which resulted in changing my approach to ESD for MSN later on. Those include mainly empowerment issue of the group members. Ainu people, including Hatakeyama, which were observed at MSN meetings. While MSN activities successfully brought together and empowered mostly Wajin in/outside Mombetsu and some Ainu member who were relatively from a younger generation, those did not bring the same result to few Ainu members in Mombetsu.

In fact, through the activities, I observed that they were diverse, complex and at times contradicted each other within a group and in the relationship with the majority, Wajin Japanese people. The discussions on the proposed industrial management plant showed significant complexity within the Ainu group. The local Ainu people had diverse thoughts on the construction plan and Hatakeyama's rights claim. While Hatakeyama personally heard members of Hatakeyama's AAH-MC support him, few did so publicly (MSN, 2010b).

Other than the Ainu individuals who were under the political and economic pressures from their organisations and industries in Mombetsu, some Ainu individuals did not want to get involved in any action related to the Ainu because of their fear of discrimination. They said:

> Wake not a sleeping baby![11] Don't mention the word of Ainu anymore. I just want to forget about it and live quietly. (MSN, 2010c)

They feared that Hatakeyama's activism would remind them of past discrimination and pain. These were issues that they did not want to recall and would rather forget.

One Ainu MSN member made the following comment that indicates the complex relationship within the Ainu group:

> The Ainu people never come together. They are always busy fighting. Wajin Japanese are more trustworthy than Ainu. (F. Noguchi, 2013)

Colonisation destroyed their community, including their social ties. Current local Ainu people do not have opportunities to unite themselves to share their thoughts and concerns.

Critical EE and critical theory recognise the marginalised people in a society. It identifies their struggles and resistance to the power of the majority. In these theories, however, marginalised people tend to be treated as if they were a homogenous group against the majority. In these theories, the complex relationship within a marginalised group is rarely understood. Likewise in MSN, a socially-critical approach to the activities helped participants understand that there were struggles and resistances of the local Ainu people in relation to the Wajin people. This could not bring participants a clear understanding, however, on what to do with such diversity, complexity and contradiction within a marginalised people when both the marginalised and the majority had to work on the common goal of achieving local sustainable development.

The most symbolic incident of the disempowerment issues was Hatakeyama's 'irrational' behaviour, which is described as 'pendulum-like behaviour' during and after the arbitration process through HEDCC from 2011 to 2012, as detailed in the next section.

---

[11] Japanese idiom. This has the same meaning as 'wake not a sleeping lion' in English.

3.3 Issue of Disempowerment of Ainu Fisherman Elder

3.3.1 Confrontation Between 'Group A' and 'Group B'

Policy advocacies and learning activities[12] by MSN could not effectively stop, or even slow down, the planning of the industrial waste management facility. The Hokkaido Prefectural Government (HPG) which supervises the local city governments at a prefectural level, fully permitted the plan in October, 2011, and construction began. In this situation, MSN came up with the idea of filing a complaint about the potential environmental damage by Hatakeyama's AAH-MC against the developer through the arbitration at the Hokkaido Environment Dispute Coordination Commission (HEDCC), located in Sapporo City, the main city of Hokkaido, 300 km from Mombetsu. The HEDCC arbitration process caused the splitting of the MSN into two groups over the strategies of Hatakeyama's key claim, wherein Hatakeyama lost his leadership.

The fundamental cause of the MSN member's split was that the MSN could not include any of the MSN members as a co-applicant with Hatakeyama or co-agent for him in the application for the HEDCC arbitration, despite that MSN proposed the idea of the arbitration. The arbitration process was strictly closed only to the applicants and the agents. More precisely, the applicants had to be the residents who lived in the area near the proposed construction site. At this point, most MSN members supported Hatakeyama from outside this area. So, they were not eligible to be co-applicants with Hatakeyama. There were a few local residents in MSN, however, they had already been involved in multiple interests in Mombetsu, and this made it difficult for them to be a co-applicant, despite their wish to support Hatakeyama. Other members were part of other local opposition groups and had recently signed the agreement with the developer. Others were fishermen, who were the members of the local fishery cooperative, and they too had already agreed to the development plan. There were also Ainu members who did not want to make public their identity by becoming a co-applicant.

MSN could not choose the agent who would support Hatakeyama, either. MSN ended up inviting a new member (Member A) to be an agent for Hatakeyama. Member A was one of a few law experts in Japan with extensive knowledge in indigenous and environmental rights protection. On March 4, 2011, Hatakeyama submitted the application form that included Member A as the only agent.

Since MSN members could not get involved in any real-time discussions at the arbitration meetings, we had to decide the strategies based on secondary information

---

[12] MSN handed the petitions of over 300 indigenous organisations and individuals in Japan, and from overseas, to Hokkaido Prefectural Government (HPG) and Mombetsu City Government (MCG) (Takenaka, 2010; *Yomiuri Shimbun*, 2010) and made statements at the UN Human Rights Council (UNHRC) (UNGA, 2010). Sapporo NGO staff A and I organised workshops and forums in Mombetsu, Sapporo and Tokyo to attract the attention and raise understanding of indigenous rights, sustainable fishing and environment and development issues.

(mostly provided by Member A). In this process, Hatakeyama struggled with comprehending the unfamiliar legal and scientific terms used at the meetings. However, Member A had enough expertise and knowledge, and he effectively had control of the communication with the MSN and in developing the strategies for the arbitration. This situation, however, created distance, delay and misunderstanding in the communication between Member A and the MSN members and among the MSN members. It made the split between the two groups of MSN members even wider, those who supported, and those who were against, Member A's strategies. Ironically, the MSN's member's confrontation between their split groups followed exactly the same pattern as the confrontation pattern of the Ainu rights recovery movement (as discussed in Chap. 4). That is, the two groups of Wajin Japanese stakeholders who had confronted each other (Group A claiming the indigenous rights claim within the Japanese domestic law and Group B aiming to go beyond the Japanese domestic law and claiming these based on the international legal standard) did so without the Ainu people's active participation.

In MSN, 'Group A' was formed by the members of MSN who supported the strategies of Member A. They wished to take a 'realistic' approach based on what current Japanese legal provisions could provide. Their strategy for the arbitration process was stated in an email to the MSN core members as below;

> I guess that a well-established and active civil movement would be necessary if we seriously want to stop the construction. Without an established civil movement we are now claiming Ainu rights in the waste management construction plan. In this situation, what we could achieve, at most, through the arbitration would be a compromise. What we can do now is to make the Ainu people 'tojisha' [see 5.1.2] as the local stakeholder in community development by signing the agreement rather than asking 'hard requests' at the arbitration to stop the construction. So, we should not intend to stop but to bring them to the surface as 'tojisha' at upfront. (Member A, personal communication, March 5, 2012)

'Group B' was identified by the members who had what was considered 'hard requests' to submit, according to Member A. They intended to use the arbitration to suspend the construction as long as possible, and, eventually, wanted to cancel the construction (MSN, 2011a, 2011c). They asserted that the 'compromise' within the current Japanese legal system was ineffective in realising Hatakeyama's indigenous rights claim, drawing on the UNDRIP and CBD. By so doing, they also intended to open up a new path to the Ainu's indigenous rights recovery by developing a more appropriate legal system in Japan (MSN, 2011b).

The debris issue of the Great East Japan Earthquake (also known as the '3.11' Earthquake) complicated the conflicts within MSN even more. Only a week after the arbitration application submission, a magnitude 9.0 earthquake hit Tohoku (in the Northern region of Japan) on 11 March 2011. In the process of post-disaster rehabilitation, the national government called for the contribution by municipal and local governments to share the debris clean-up, which was estimated at 80 million to 200 million tonnes in the devastated areas (Makinen, 2011).[13] This call from the government grew into a controversy, with the wider residents throughout Japan, concerned about the spread of radiated debris near the tsunami devastated areas around the Fukushima Daiichi nuclear power plant and its potential hazards to health and the environment.

Group B was also concerned about the potential harm caused by the radiated debris if it were to be disposed at the proposed waste management plant in Mombetsu.[14] They thought that the debris issues might attract support from the wider community residents for Hatakeyama. Group B members eventually formed the opinion that Hatakeyama should include the claim that the proposed waste management facility should not accept the radiated debris into his assertion during the arbitration. Group B became more militant in their approach about the earthquake debris as time went by.

3.3.2 *'Irrational' Behaviour*

Hatakeyama was gradually losing his leadership between the two groups. He accepted one group's opinion whenever he went and spoke to them, denied the other group but then repeated the same ideas as he did for the other group. One Group B member, who drove Hatakeyama from Mombetsu to the meeting with Member A and Group A in Sapporo, observed how Hatakeyama changed his words and behaviours before and after the meeting during their travel between Mombetsu and Sapporo. 'Hatakeyama-san changed during the travel back from Sapporo, as if he became a totally different person' (Ex-MSN member, personal communication, February 11, 2013). After the meeting, the ex-MSN member lost his trust in Hatakeyama and completely stopped further communication with Hatakeyama. Hatakeyama's behaviour looked like the 'swinging' of a pendulum between two different opinions: of Group A and B; and also between two locations, Sapporo and Mombetsu.

The time constraints of the arbitration process[15] forced Hatakeyama to make a final decision. In March 2012, Hatakeyama decided to sign the agreement with the developer and followed Group A's strategy. The agreement gave the go-ahead for the developer to finalise the construction for its opening in November. The agreement recognised: (i) the local Ainu as the local key stakeholder; (ii) prevention of the negative impact by the plant operation on their cultural activities; (iii) conservation

---

[13] In a typical year, the entire country generates about 71 million tonnes of household waste and more than 400 million tonnes of industrial waste, according to the Environment Ministry (Makinen, 2011).

[14] Responding to their interests, Sapporo NGO staff A and I organised workshops and meetings for MSN to learn about the radiated debris issues in relation to the impact on the natural environment and human health and the indigenous rights protection (MSN, 2012).

[15] The arbitration process at HEDCC has to be concluded in one year after the submission of the application.

of the local natural environment; and, (iv) the rights of the local Ainu to inspect the plant operation any time upon their request.

3.3.3 Impossible Whaling Dream

In contrast to the praise by the media and the researchers on the outcome that Hatakeyama obtained from the arbitration, Hatakeyama was unsatisfied. The media and the researchers saw the recognition of the Ainu people in the local community development process as the first achievement in the history of the Ainu rights movement in Japan (*Hokkaido Shimbun Press*, 2012; *The Asahi Shimbun*, 2012; *The Mainichi Shimbun*, 2012; *The Yomiuri Shimbun*, 2012). However, Hatakeyama's 'irrational' behaviour continued. Rather than looking into strategies that could optimise what he got from the arbitration, he began to speak a lot about his desire for hunting a minke whale—which is illegal in Japan.

At a focus group discussion in 2013, where the core MSN members reflected on the MSN activities, Hatakeyama was irritated and angry, stating:

> I want to take action [by hunt a whale] in the early summer of this year, when the weather is good... I am ready to be jailed for this. Catching salmon in the river, and hunting whales... I want to catch these based on my decision, on my indigenous rights as a Mombetsu Ainu descendant, not based on the permission of someone else. (F. Noguchi, 2013).

Hatakeyama's words put MSN members into further confusion, particularly those in Group B who were already disgruntled that their opinion was not considered over Group A's:

> "If you hunt a whale now, who would support you?"
>
> "Hunting a whale is illegal. It would make a tremendous impact on your son who is going to take over your fishing license at the Fishermen's Union and your family."
>
> "After hunting the whale, who would process it?"
>
> "You should not cause the local supporters any trouble."
>
> "Yes, the outside experts and the world may say to you that this is your right. However, without getting support from your family and your local community people, your action will be almost like a suicide attack." (F. Noguchi, 2013).

Hatakeyama contended:

> AAH predominantly understands the meaning of indigenous rights only as cultural activities, such as dancing and singing. Our Mombetsu Chapter is the only one claiming indigenous rights connected with our livelihood. We would lose our indigenous spirits if we were to do 'cultural' activities only as they say. Fifteen years ago, I got the permission to catch rays from the Mombetsu City government. My fellow [Wajin] fishermen tore me down by saying that Ainu would get everything. If I sought permission [for whale hunting] from all the Mombetsu residents and fishermen, I am 100% sure that I would never be able to do it. (F. Noguchi, 2013)

MSN members understood well that whaling had been the central indigenous claim of Hatakeyama for over twenty years. Yet, whaling, particularly hunting a minke whale, did not make sense to the MSN members who knew that it is illegal. They could not understand why Hatakeyama clung to the idea of whaling so much. It could be more realistic for them if Hatakeyama just committed to developing the follow-up strategies based on what they had agreed to through the arbitration. Hatakeyama's persistent advocating for whaling puzzled MSN members. Other than political challenges around indigenous whaling rights claims, MSN members found no point in his whaling claim. There had been drastic reductions in economic potential in whaling, particularly the minke whale, in the last thirty years. Whaling was no longer an economically profitable business in the 2010s.

When Hatakeyama began his claim of indigenous whaling rights in 1987, Hatakeyama expected that this would provide income opportunity for the Ainu people to improve their economic situation. Through his work of spearfishing dolphins, he saw the inflated market prices of whale meat compared to the cheap dolphin meat that was consumed as the substitute for whale meat in Japan.[16] Hatakeyama wished to get back whaling rights in the hope it might create jobs and income opportunities for him and his fellow Ainu fishermen.

As Fig. 3.3 depicts, while whale meat is over-supplied in Japan, the demand has drastically dropped.[17] The market supplies whale meat at a low price, not only by catches from scientific research, but also by imported meat, mostly from Iceland (Sakuma, 2012). The golden age when fishermen dreamed of making profits out of the whaling industry had already dissipated. Hatakeyama, of course, knew that whale meat had lost market value in Japan. His 'swing' during the arbitration and his clinging to whaling were totally beyond comprehension for all the MSN members, including myself (where I tried my best to stick with Hatakeyama without agreeing to the assertions of either group).

3.3.4 'Patchy Empowerment': Success or 'Unsuccess'?

The cross-analysis between successes and challenges of MSN's ESD efforts highlighted different degrees of local empowerment. The MSN's ESD efforts resulted in a mosaic; an uneven and unbalanced degree of community empowerment between the larger majority of Wajin, the younger generation of Ainu people, and people in Hatakeyama's generation. Hence, different degrees of local community empowerment were referred to as 'patchy empowerment'.

Patchy empowerment was contrary to the intention of ESD for MSN that aimed to achieve community development with 'no-one's exclusion' (Tsurumi, 1999, p. 344). Among the Ainu members observed as disempowered, Hatakeyama's disempowerment was so critical that it had the potential to eliminate all the successes of the

[16] Greenpeace Japan noted that JPY 650,000,000 (approximately AUD 80,000,000) was gained in 2008 from the trade of the whale meat from scientific research (Greenpeace Japan, 2017).

[17] Sakuma (2012) argues that the annual average amount of the whale meat consumption per capita is only 23.7 g, which is 'virtually the same weight as half of a chocolate bar or a slice of ham' (p. 1).

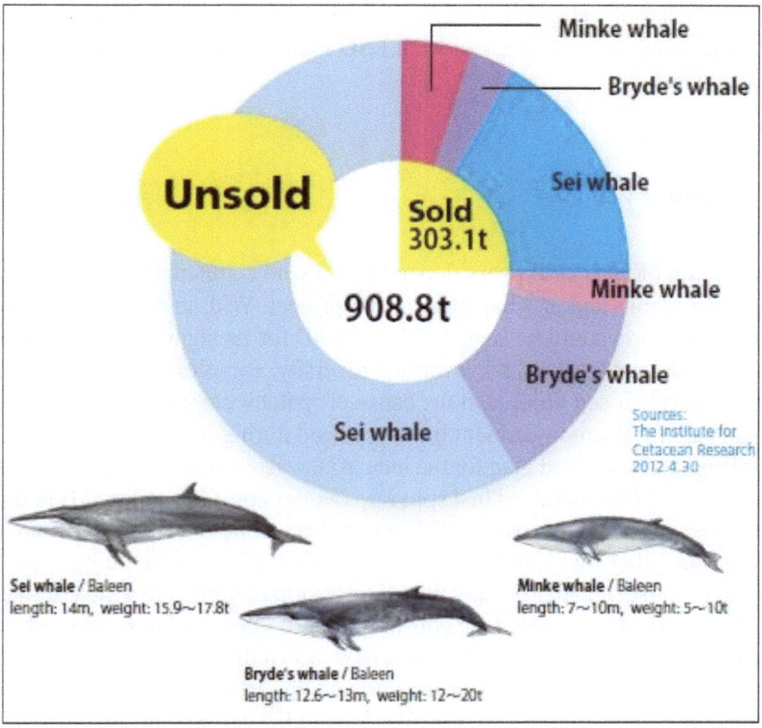

Fig. 3.3 Demand–supply of whale meat in Japan, 2011 (Sakuma, 2012)

MSN. While Hatakeyama's empowerment through the actions and learnings of MSN were of critical importance to ESD, he became the least empowered of all. Patchy empowerment implies a problem in the understanding of a socially-critical approach and in the guiding theories which include critical EE. This sets social actions and empowerment as its own goal of education (Fien, 1995, p. 6).

Audience feedback following my presentation on MSN's ESD practice in 2010 became the very beginning of the investigation into the possible problems in the understanding of ESD. After the presentation, this audience came up to me and commented as follows: 'This is not ESD. How many Ainu people are living in Mombetsu?' It was ultimately assumed that this comment might relate to the struggle in understanding 'patchy empowerment'. Ultimately, it questioned what socially-critical ESD is really *for*.

The assumption was that some degree of utilitarian view might be embedded in critical EE. When the presentation on the MSN was made in 2010, the MSN had only just been established based on the interests of a few individuals and had not yet achieved any large social impact through mobilising the networks of the MSN members. It was assumed that this audience might not have seen the MSN as part of ESD because of this lack of social impact. Based on the same understanding, it was assumed that this audience would see the MSN as part of ESD once they knew of the social impact the MSN's ESD efforts made through collective efforts by 2012. With that in mind, it must be asked what ESD really means to the few Ainu people, like Hatakeyama.

3.4 Summary

The evaluation of ESD could vary depending on who counted it as a success or 'un-success', for whom and at what stage of the project. With this utilitarian view, the MSN's ESD efforts could be seen as 'successful' for its significant social impacts. This view could not explain, however, the diversity, complexity and contradictions within the marginalised group and the cause of 'patchy empowerment'.

Hatakeyama's disempowerment issue emerged during the arbitration process for the governmental proposed plan for the industrial waste management facility. During the process, the MSN members had split into two groups: Group A and B in the arbitration process with the developer. Wajin members of both groups confronted each other, arguing either that Hatakeyama should either: (i) claim his indigenous rights within the premise of Japanese law that did *not* stop or slow down the construction; or, (ii) that he should claim that the construction goes beyond Japanese law based on international legal frameworks, to stop or slow down the construction. Between the two groups, Hatakeyama lost his leadership and his 'irrational' behaviour emerged. This 'patchy' empowerment could be overlooked for the sake of the positive social impact observed on a large scale, on the MSN's ESD.

This eventually led to the disarray of the MSN in the post-arbitration process. Hatakeyama's continued his behaviour (in particular, his avocation for the illegal hunting of minke whales) and went far beyond the tolerance of the MSN members, including myself. The problems of disempowerment of a few Ainu members, including Hatakeyama, could not be improved, and these could not explain the cause of patchy empowerment *within* socially-critical ESD.

The next chapter analyses Hatakeyama's disempowerment from the viewpoint of his idiosyncratic way of understanding and knowing and by letting go of my guiding theory of critical EE. It starts with my reflection, which attempted to explore 'why' socially-critical approaches retain a 'utilitarian' view, yet cannot explain the patchy empowerment that occurs *within* socially-critical ESD.

References

Agrawal, A. (2002). Indigenous knowledge and the politics of classification. *International Social Science Journal, 54*(173), 287–297.

Ainu Museum. (2017). *Ainu history and culture: Oral literature.* http://www.ainu-museum.or.jp/en/study/eng13.html

Fien, J. (1995). *Education for the environment: Critical curriculum theorising and environmental education.* Deakin University.

Greenpeace Japan. (2017). *調査捕鯨船団、早期帰港の本当の理由* [Scientific research whale vessel: the real reason of their early return]. http://www.greenpeace.org/japan/ja/news/blog/staff/blog/33371/

Hokkaido Prefectural Library. (1731). *津軽一統史巻十之中* [History of Tsugaru Vol 10. 2]. Tsugaru Han.

Hokkaido Shimbun Press. (2012, March 10). 儀式で鮭捕獲の川公害防止へ アイヌ協会支部が協定 紋別の産廃業者と [For industrial pollution prevention for the river of the Salmon ceremony: Ainu Association of Hokkaido Mombetsu Chapter signed agreement with the Mombetsu developer]. *Hokkaido Shimbun Press*.

Ife, J. (2016). *Community development in an uncertain world: Vision, analysis and practice*. Cambridge University Press.

Kadota, K. (2015, August 21). 教科書のアイヌ記述、検定で"歴史的歪曲 [The statement of the Ainu people in school text book: "Historical distortion" in the governmental authorisation process]. *The Asahi Shimbun Digital*. http://www.asahi.com/special/kotoba/jinken/SDI201508120064.html

Makinen, J. (2011, April 3). After Japan disaster, disposing of waste creates dilemmas. *Los Angeles Times*. http://articles.latimes.com/2011/apr/03/world/la-fg-japan-trash-20110403

Ministry of Internal Affairs and Communications, Japan. (2012). *Hokkaido heisei 23nen choutei dai 1gou jiken* (Hokkaido 2012 Arbitration No.1 case). http://www.soumu.go.jp/kouchoi/pollutionsystem/pollution/0120016.html

MSN. (2010a, February 21). *Mopet Sanctuary Network meeting report*. Mopet Sanctuary Network.

MSN. (2010b, June 20–21). *Mopet Sanctuary Network meeting report*. Mopet Sanctuary Network.

MSN. (2010c, February 26). *Mopet Sanctuary Network workshop report*. Mopet Sanctuary Network.

MSN. (2011a, February 4). *Mopet Sanctuary Network meeting report*. Mopet Sanctuary Network.

MSN. (2011b, July 11). *Mopet Sanctuary Network meeting report*. Mopet Sanctuary Network.

MSN. (2011c, July 2). *Mopet Sanctuary Network meeting report*. Mopet Sanctuary Network.

MSN. (2012, February 18). *Mopet Sanctuary Network Okhotsk Mombetsu ESD Seminar report*. Mopet Sanctuary Network.

Noguchi, F. (2013, February 11). *Mopet Sanctuary Network focus group record*.

Sakuma, J. (2012). The trend in Whale meat consumption. *IKANet News Special Edition*.

Sapporo City Council. (2017). *アイヌ民族に関する教育* [Education about Ainu people]. http://www.city.sapporo.jp/kyoiku/top/education/ainu/ainu_minzoku.html

Sapporo University. (2017). *ウレシパクラブ* [Ureshipa Club]. http://www.sapporo-u.ac.jp/univ_guide/affiliate/ureshipa.html

Shinada, S. (2010). 「アイヌ」像と北海道の学校教育：教職員用の指導の手引き・指導資料を中心に」 [Image of the Ainu people and school education in Hokkaido: Review of teachers' guide book and teaching materials on Ainu education]. *Graduate Students' Bulletin, Graduate School of International Media, Communication and Tourism Studies, Hokkaido University, 6*, 65–73.

Shogakukan Digital-*Daijisen*. (2017). 当事者意識 [Tojisha-ishiki]. *Digital-Daijisen*. https://dictionary.goo.ne.jp/jn/258546/meaning/m0u/

Takenaka, T. (2010, March 17). 産廃処分場建設問題 アイヌ協会が抗議文: 紋別支部市長と市公害審に [Industrial waste management plant construction, Protest by Ainu Association: Mombetsu Chapter, against the City Governor and Mombetsu Industrial Pollution Council]. *Hokkaido Shimbun Press*.

The Asahi Shimbun. (2012, March 10). 産廃業者と公害防止協定「先住権認めて」 アイヌ協会支部長側 [Industrial pollution prevention agreement 'Recognition of indigenous rights' by Hokkaido Ainu Association Mombetsu Chapter]. *The Asahi Shimbun*.

The Mainichi Shimbun. (2012, March 10). *公害防止協定: アイヌ協会支部藻別川支流の産廃処分場をめぐる業者と 立ち入り調査も* [Industrial pollution prevention agreement: Hokkaido Ainu Association Mombetsu Chapter dispute against the developer over the industrial waste management plant construction at Mombetsu River]. *The Mainichi Shimbun*.

The Yomiuri Shimbun. (2010, March 18). 紋別産廃場問題「意見書未審議は人権無視」アイヌ協会支部市などに抗議文 [Mombetsu industrial waste management issue: "No investigation of proposal is neglect of human rights" Ainu Association Mombetsu protest against the City government]. *Yomiuri Shimbun.*
The Yomiuri Shimbun. (2012, March 10). *産廃処分場をめぐり公害防止協定所 紋別藻別川流域* [Industrial pollution prevention agreement over the industrial waste management plant construction: Mobetsu River region in Mombetsu]. *The Yomiuri Shimbun.*
Tilbury, D., & Fien, J. (2002). The global challenge of sustainability. In D. Tilbury, R. Stevenson, J. Fien, & D. Schreuder (Eds.), *Education and sustainability—Responding to the global challenge.* IUCN.
Tsurumi, K. (1999). *コレクション鶴見和子曼荼羅 IX: 環の巻* [Collection Kazuko Tsurumi Mandala IX: Circulation]. Fujiwara Shoten.
UNESCO. (2009). *UNESCO atlas of the world's languages in danger.* http://www.unesco.org/languages-atlas/
UNGA. (2010). *Written statement submitted by the Shimin Gaikou Centre (Citizens' Diplomatic Centre for the Rights of Indigenous Peoples), a non governmental organization in special consultative status* (A/HRC/15/NGO/24).

Part II
ESD *Beyond* Socially-Critical Approach—Decoloniality

Part II reports on the second part of the two critical ethnographies in this research. This part contains two chapters. The first chapter (Chapter 4) provides and discusses the methodological and epistemological limitation of critical theory, which provides the theoretical ground of socially-critical ESD. The second chapter (Chapter 5) analyses Hatakeyama's Swing based on the theoretical and methodological understanding beyond critical EE, that is, decoloniality.

Chapter 4
Letting Go

This chapter reports my critical reflections on MSN's ESD practice *within* socially-critical approach. In particular, it illustrates the struggle in understanding 'patchy empowerment' and exploring it in the context of the literature within critical EE, ESD and beyond. The reflection process facilitated a more appropriate methodological approach in comparison with the first critical ethnographic study, to get closer to socially-critical ESD in a community development context from the marginalised people's perspectives.

It should be noted that this chapter is not the report of the retrospective analysis on MSN's ESD efforts in the past. 'Patchy empowerment', which emerged in practice, took place simultaneously to this research for this book in 2013. Hence, this chapter presents real-time dilemmas and struggles in the approach taken. The discussions in this chapter assisted in finding a better way of my engagement with the local community, particularly the marginalised people, for the remainder of the research and future practice.

4.1 No-Way Out

The guiding theory (critical EE) used in the MSN resulted in patchy empowerment and the research methodology (critical theory) could not explain the cause of this gap in the community empowerment. There seemed to be no way out beyond the critical situation of the research and practice for MSN. At that time, there were two options.

Option one was to continue the research within the theoretical and methodological understanding of critical EE. With this option, the research would examine the successes of MSN, and analyse the motivations and behaviour changes of the members who initiated a wider range of social actions and learning activities, and the broader impact of these actions to people in Mombetsu and in Japan. It was assumed that the research with option one would still produce 'acceptable' outcomes.

F. Noguchi, *Rethinking Education for Sustainable Development in a Local Community Context*, Education for Sustainability 6,
https://doi.org/10.1007/978-981-16-9464-6_4

However, the struggles of the very few Ainu in the MSN would be ignored in this option, in comparison with the significant 'amount' of social impact, and the 'numbers' of people who were mobilised through the social actions and learning activities of the MSN.

Option two was to go beyond critical EE and critical theory. With this option, a micro-focus analysis would be conducted on a few Ainu members, in particular, Hatakeyama. Concerns over option two included uncertainties about the methodology and timeframe. Hatakeyama's disempowerment was contrary to my intention of ESD and almost derailed this aspect of the project.

The literature was revisited within and beyond critical EE to find a way to break through the critical situation. It was investigated why critical EE appeared 'utilitarian' when it was applied to socially-critical ESD in a community development context. The theories within and beyond critical EE provided a guide to re-engage back with the research questions and option two, by taking on a decoloniality methodology.

4.2 Re-engaging with the Literature

There are two assumptions that indicate the utilitarian aspect of critical EE, which could make critical EE insufficient for socially-critical ESD in a community development context. The first one is the homogenous view of marginalised people in critical theory. This view overlooks the diversity, complexity and contradictions in the power relationships within a marginalised group. Critical theory could create an epistemological oppression in modern knowledge over the knowledge of marginalised people. The other is the schooling concept, which is the built-in formal education settings that most critical EE is based on. Formal schooling in critical EE increases the homogenous view in critical theory so that critical EE overlooks the different degrees of empowerment within a marginalised group and bears the epistemological oppression of those with modern knowledge over the few marginalised people with a different knowledge.

4.2.1 Homogenous View in Critical Theory

The homogenous view in critical theory emerges through classifying whom the marginalised are and identifying what their knowledge is in relation to modern knowledge.

Identifying indigenous knowledge by modern knowledge

Agrawal (2002, 2005) argues that what is generally defined as 'indigenous knowledge', or 'knowledge of the marginalised', is created one-sidedly by those with modern, scientific and Western knowledge. According to Agrawal (2002), those with modern knowledge (particularly scientific knowledge) recognise particular information from indigenous or marginalised people ("*particularisation*"), seek its relevance to science and modern knowledge ("*verification*"), then generalise and apply it to respond to their needs for development and environmental conservation (generalisation) (pp. 290–291). This process is referred to as '*scientisation*' (Agrawal, 2002, p. 291).

Those with modern knowledge are the ones driving *scientisation.* In this process, what they think is necessary as 'knowledge', is separated from the original context while ignoring "multiple, crucial, little-noticed details (Agrawal, 2002, p. 291)". A part of the language, knowledge or experiences of the indigenous and marginalised people is taken (*particularisation*), considered in relation to modern knowledge (*verification*), and integrated to reproduce the modern and scientific knowledge (*generalisation*). A homogenous view characterises the process of scientisation, where marginalised people and their knowledge are simplified and generalised within a complex reality. Following the *scientisation* process, questions remain: 'To what extent is re-defined "indigenous knowledge" by modern knowledge useful to indigenous people and who actually benefits from such knowledge?' (Agrawal, 2002, p. 291).

Epistemological oppression of other knowledges by modern knowledge

The process of scientisation creates an 'oppressive' epistemological power differential between those with modern knowledge and those without, in any form of research including positivism, interpretivism and critical theory. This oppression is caused because of different epistemological approaches between modern knowledge and other knowledges.

Those with modern knowledge have overwhelming control in knowing and understanding what the knowledge means. Drawing on the experiences of environment-development disputes in Japan, in particular, the Minamata disease (Fig. 4.1), Kitoh (2007, 2009) identifies the epistemological power differential between two contrasting views in the research for marginalised people in a local community. The first view is 'policy systemic' and the second is that of 'resisting individuals'.

The policy systemic view characterises the epistemology of the modern knowledge production process. It understands the problems of marginalised people from a general, universal and bird's eye point of view. It seeks its solutions systemically like a policy-maker (Kitoh, 2007, p. 135). The other view is the one of resisting individuals, who are 'forced to crawl on the bottom of the society' (Kitoh, 2007, p. 141) and manage to live taking the burden of the society individually.

There is a power differential between these two views; the policy systemic view oppresses the view of the resisting individuals. The policy systemic view supports those in positions of power—often government officials and researchers, who have a modern knowledge background. This makes resisting individuals abstract and simplifies socially complex and politically sensitive problems so that everyone can easily accept and comprehend them (Kitoh, 2007, p. 135). At the same time, the policy systemic view deflects away from understanding the totality of suffering the

Minamata disease collectively describes the industrial pollution that caused severe health and environmental problems in Japan since the 1950s. It was caused by the release of waste water, contaminated with heavy metals, by the Chisso Corporation (Ui, 1992). Many of the victims were marginalised community members.

In 1956, at a small, poor fishing village in Minamata, Japan, a cat began having seizures and dived into the sea with severe convulsions. Then, other cats and dogs did the same. One day, crows fell from the sky. Local residents were suspicious as to why these animals died in such a strange way. Eventually, they also saw many fish floating in the sea. (NIMD, 2001, p. 2) Then some villagers began suffering from continual convulsions, became unable to walk or talk properly, seemed to lose their mind, and died. One after another had similar problems in the same village, and the same things happened in the surrounding villages (Ui, 1968).

The local public health department called this unknown illness, the 'strange disease' and suspected it was infectious (Ui, 1968). The health department isolated the patients and disinfected their homes. Those affected first were mostly from marginalised and impoverished fishing families. People stopped buying fish from them. They were stigmatised and discriminated against. They became poorer and even more marginalised. Eventually, the problem became more commonly known as 'Minamata disease'.

In 1968, over ten years since the first outbreak of Minamata disease, the government finally admitted its cause. (Some argue victims were already suffering from mercury poisoning since the late 1940s (Soshisha, 2017)) The government, together with Chisso, concealed the interim report in 1959 by the University of Kumamoto. It pointed to the probable cause of Minamata disease as the organic mercury in the waste water caused by the Chisso Corporation. During that time, Chisso kept dumping waste water into the Shiranui Sea, creating more victims.

The total numbers of victims is unknown. The birth of stillborn babies and miscarriages were treated secretly; many died before official identification. A large number of people are still unrecognised by the government. Soshisha (the supporting centre for Minamata Disease) estimates over 100,000 victims, excluding approximately 40,000 deaths that occurred in the past (Soshisha, 2017). As of 2013, the government has only recognised 2,977 applicants from this total, as victims who are eligible for official relief measurement (Ministry of the Environment, 2013, p. 7). An unknown, large number of people are still struggling in sickness, prejudice, discrimination and poverty.

In Minamata, economic growth was prioritised over anything else. The government supported the Chisso Corporation to continue their industrial activities, which contributed to the country's economic growth in the post-WWII period, and ignored the voices of victims for ten years. Shiranui Sea, once described by a local villager as the bountiful sea overflowing with fish (Ishimure, 2003), was polluted with 4 meters of sludge containing 500ppm mercury. The local society sustained by cultural and economic systems based on fishing, collapsed. The poor became poorer and more marginalised. The word, 'disease', refers to the 'sick' social and economic structure that has been created by the development, and the knowledge, value and belief systems that underpin it (Ui, 1968).

Fig. 4.1 Minamata disease in Japan

marginalised people have experienced psychologically, physically, economically and socially (Kitoh, 2007, 2009; Ui, 1971).

The policy systemic view picks up only what it is able to perceive and wants to know and understand, based on the limitations of modern knowledge, while simultaneously dismissing a significant part of the victims, marginalising and forcing them to be silent about their problems. Hence, with the policy systemic view, researchers and the government officials neither understand the overall picture of the problems faced by marginalised people, nor establish the research and policy to fundamentally solve them (Kitoh, 2009, p. 164). This is the epistemological oppression of the experiences, knowledges and problems of the marginalised people.

The official recognition process of the Minamata disease victims since 1969 demonstrates how epistemological oppression occurs. The government and experts have defined and recognised whom they believe the victims are. Unrecognised victims are forced to live with undiagnosed symptoms and in prejudice within local communities. Others have already passed away without recognition (e.g. Harada, 1985; Ishimure, 2003; Oiwa et al., 2001; Saishu, 1984). The one-sided classification of marginalised people exacerbates this discriminatory effect and causes further social injustice (Kitoh, 2009, p. 164).

Epistemological oppression occurs in any form of research, including positivism, interpretivism and critical theory. This is because critical theory 'emerged and flourished within the same system of knowledge production as modern thought' (Morris-Suzuki, 2011, p. 17). On this point, critical theory is no different from positivism and interpretivism, despite its strong criticism on the injustice and power disparity created by them.

The issues faced by marginalised people are identified in critical theory, however, they are not understood at the level of truly knowing and understanding the marginalised people. Their problems tend to be understood in a way that is acceptable within the modern knowledge production system. This method of understanding in critical theory is entrenched *within* modern knowledge which re-interprets the problems of the marginalised people and marginalises them even further.

4.2.2 Schooling Focus of Critical EE

The second factor that could make critical EE utilitarian in a community development context is the schooling focus of critical EE, or more precisely, the 'framework' that schooling provides. Schooling provides a conditioned, formal education. As (Illich, 1973) argues, schooling sets a framework onto a social reality to enclose a particular type of knowledge that fits within it. This framework is socially and physically conditioned; the curriculum guidelines, educational policies, school cultures, and teaching contents provide social conditions, while the space, facility, and target groups provide the physical conditions. These conditions all come together and enable educators to conduct their activities.

Critical EE is predominantly theorised in the formal education setting. Critical EE has challenged this schooling framework, aiming to re-direct the education system to facilitate social change (see Chap. 2). Critical EE may be able to stretch the schooling framework or even change its shape or the size, however, it cannot remove it. This is because schooling is the foundation upon which critical EE is based.

The framework that schooling provides can be problematic when critical EE is applied to ESD in a community development context. The framework imposes limitations upon teachers who wish to teach beyond the schooling boundary. At the same time, however, it allows the teacher to choose how to contribute within this context, such as selecting a resource person, teaching content, targeting a group of people or defining aims. The actions of the teacher can enhance the modern knowledge-based approach so that application of critical EE to ESD does not sufficiently reflect local community problems. Activities within the schooling framework enhance the 'homogenous' view in critical theory because of the modern knowledge upon which the modern education is based.

4.2.3 Critical Theory in Critical EE

The schooling focus of critical EE and the homogenous view of critical theory negatively synergise in a community development context. This negative synergy can be explained by unpacking how critical EE draws upon critical theory and how it explains the process of social change through school education.

Most theorising in critical EE, EfS and ESD draws on critical theory (Huckle, 1993) or post-modernism (Sauvé, 1999) in school education contexts. The communicative discursive action theory of Habermas becomes the central feature of praxis in EE, EfS and ESD (Huckle, 1993, 1996). The approach is based on critical EE in practice, including multi-stakeholder approaches, participatory and inclusive approaches, as well as action-oriented learning (UNESCO, 2014, p. 174).

Habermas's discursive communicative action has the following four points:

1. Universal moral consensus is inherent in the nature and use of human language;
2. All human communication can be an ideal speech situation in which all participants have equal power to defend their contributions as meaningful, true, justified and sincere;
3. Claims to truth and justification to public scrutiny is revealed; and
4. The rational consensus is made based on an open argument, which undermines the false consensus (Huckle, 1993, p. 61).

Discursive communicative action believes that careful discussions can reach a rational consensus among a diverse group of people, providing people can express themselves safely and freely. This concept is based on the belief that words can explain everything and can bring consensus among multiple stakeholders. It dismisses, however, any other knowledge that cannot be expressed in words.

Teacher's challenge for social change

In critical EE, educators such as Fien (1995) and Edwards (2015) draw upon the theory of structuration by (Giddens, 1984) to explain the process where teachers try to take critical approaches in the teaching activities at their schools. Structuration

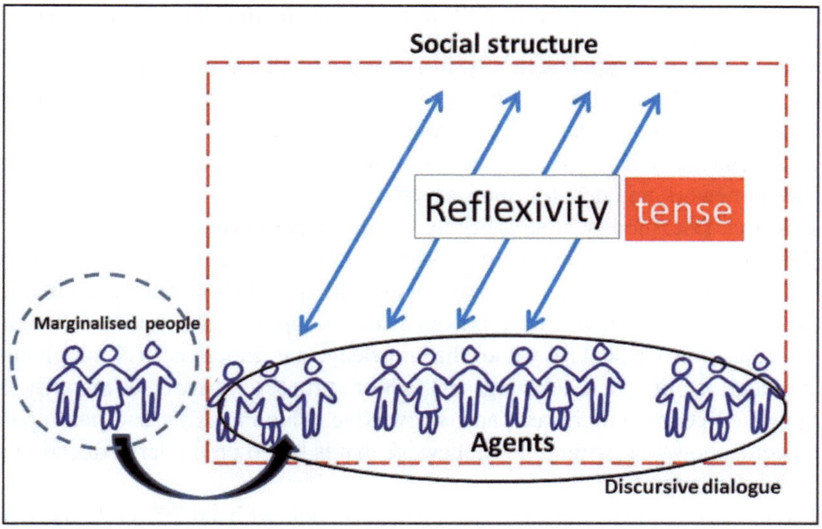

Fig. 4.2 Educational challenging process for sustainable development in critical EE. *Source* Adopted from Fien (1995)

theory conceptualised the relationship between social structure and the agent as the driving force of human action. Unlike Marxism that observes how social structure determines human acts, structuration theory considers that the social structure and the agent are mutually constructed and that its relationship is interactive and dialectic. The social structure provides the rule and resources for the agent. At the same time, the agent retains the ability to understand the surrounding environment and to reproduce the social structure. Hence, the social structure and the agent can both constrain and enable.

In a schooling context, teachers act as agents who bring the environmental paradigm, and their struggles and resistance in challenging the dominant social paradigms, particularly school education system. Figure 4.2 illustrates the process of achieving sustainable development in education, drawing on social theories of Habermas and Giddens. In this figure, the schooling context provides the framework, within which the individuals participate in the learning, discussions and activities. The challenging against the framework is not easy. However, critical EE finds the possibility of reproduction, confirmation and entrenchment of existing structures for school education and through school education (Fien, 1995). Hence, the process of critical environmental education is 'counter-hegemonic', where the resistance and conflict accompany with their efforts. Therein, teachers are viewed as capable of enacting themselves with educational and environmental belief as an agent for social change (Fien, 1995).

Applicability of critical EE to ESD in a community development context

When critical EE is applied to ESD in a community development context, it comes with a concept of schooling that frames a particular aspect of the local community, such as community members and their knowledge, based on the educators' intention for social change. The schooling focus of critical EE allows community educators to set the framework and decides upon which activities fit within the framework. The educators choose, modify or simplify the diverse experiences and knowledge of the local community, to fit within the framework, influencing the time, space, resources dedicated to these learnings, and whatever else the educators decide the local needs.

Critical EE is sensitive to the power disparity and marginalisation inherent in formal education. Critical EE values the knowledge and experiences of marginalised people and facilitates a learning and action process where the majority and marginalised people co-create a new knowledge. This inclusion and participation only occurs, however, within the framework that is based on modern education and modern knowledge.

There is an unknown number of marginalised people with unidentified experiences and knowledge that resides outside the framework. A significant issue, however, is that education within the framework dismisses what is outside the framework. Selected individuals engaging in these educational activities may not fully represent the marginalised group, as they may not have any functioning social ties, or a system for consensus building, like the Ainu people in Japan (see Chap. 2). New knowledge, however, is created based on discussions with these marginalised people within the framework. Stakeholders within the framework then re-interpret the problems of marginalised people based on the newly created knowledge.

Kitoh warns about the policy systemic view in environmental education.

> The response toward the environmental problems from the global perspectives seems to be an unarguable logic to everyone. Such EE expects everyone to see the Earth as if each one of them were a policy maker, supervise each other, raise the awareness of the individuals and establish each environmental ethics for the solution of these problems. Such EE certainly can contribute to solving a part of problems and sounds valid. However, there are the problems that become covered and invisible in such overwhelming understanding of the problem from the policy systemic view. (Kitoh, 2007, pp. 139–140)

To this point, Harako (2013) argued that the views, scope and orientation of critical EE are 'too systemic, gigantic and extroverted' (p. 2). These indicate some aspect of the problem in critical EE, which looks utilitarian when critical EE is applied to ESD in a community development context.

The above arguments imply that there might have been an epistemological problem in the ESD approaches applied to the MSN. The socially-critical approach to ESD created an inclusive and participatory process for the learning and social actions by both Ainu and non-Ainu people. This openness was only possible, however, because the MSN became an 'invisible framework' of schooling. There, the educators were able to decide who should be there, what needed to be discussed and how to facilitate participatory discussion among the 'multi-stakeholders'. Such intentions may have deflected the focus from the diverse and complex issues, and contradicted the reality of the entire Ainu group, including the power disparities within their group and the broader local community. This was the cause of patchy empowerment.

4.3 A Way Out: Decoloniality

The crisis encountered during research with the MSN implied that there was no way forward while a solution was sought within an understanding of modern knowledge. To this point, Agrawal (2005) argues that the oppression that modern knowledge imposes on others is a 'catch-22 situation' (p. 73). A catch-22 also occurred in the knowledge production process that appeared in Minamata disease research in Japan. As Tsurumi argues:

> The problems in Minamata are the ones of those who were forced to endure extreme harm during the modern industrial civilisation. In that case, our analytical tools for research are the languages that have been developed within the framework of modern industrial civilisation. As long as we use these, the most objective and scientific assumption that we could get in breakthroughs of Minamata disease could be 'no way out'. Any research with such an approach cannot make any change in Minamata disease problems. (Irokawa et al., 1983, p. 501)

The only possible way to change course was to adopt a decoloniality methodology (Mignolo, 2007, 2011, 2014; Ndlovu-Gatsuheni, 2013; Smith, 1999). With the decoloniality methodology, the a priori theory was set aside and the epistemological activity was given to a few Ainu members, particularly, Hatakeyama.

Although its conceptual linkage has not yet been discussed, 'outsider methodology' by Kitoh (2007, 2009), which is proposed for research on the development-environment conflict, provides practical insights in understanding the decoloniality methodology. The outsider methodology is described as follows:

> The 'outsider' methodology begins with leaving intentionally the methodological objectivity. Instead of taking the stance of 'third party' as a researcher, with this methodology, the researcher 'listen' to the victims by standing on the 'view of the resisting individuals' and analyse their words from not the objective but the outsider's views, and weave the universal language (for the research). This does not mean that the researcher should stand on the same political ground as the victims. Rather, the researcher should attempt to stand on the victim's views in terms of epistemology. The approach premises that a researcher engages with the research participants in the field and mutually transform through the intellectual and academic acts. (Kitoh, 2009, p. 168)

The 'outsider' methodology shares many characteristics of the critical ethnography method, in particular, retaining a critical view of the disparity and seeking mutual transformation through the research. It differs from the critical ethnography method however, in the point that it stands on the perspectives of the marginalised, establishes their epistemology and understands the problem of the environment-development disputes through the views of established epistemology. This part echoes with the decoloniality methodology and takes much wider theoretical perspectives than critical theory.

In an attempt to obtain an in-depth understanding of patchy empowerment, the field of Mombetsu was revisited in December 2014 with the decoloniality methodology. The process of engaging a decoloniality approach adopted the following four principles:

1. Observing the everyday life situation of Hatakeyama and other key MSN members, through living and working with them in their everyday life context;
2. Setting aside or 'bracket out', the guiding theories and research;
3. Trying to understand the learning and knowledge creation process of Hatakeyama, from his views and perspectives obtained from their everyday life context;
4. Re-engaging with critical EE based on key findings using the decoloniality methodology and contributing to the current understanding of critical EE if needed.

4.4 Summary

Patchy empowerment, which was highlighted from the analysis in the previous chapter, created a critical situation in the practice and research of the MSN's ESD. This chapter reported on the self-reflection process during the time of crisis, where the literature was revisited within and beyond critical EE to investigate 'patchy empowerment'. In particular, the utilitarian aspect of critical EE that was assumed through the discussions in the previous chapter was thoroughly examined. The literature review beyond critical EE involved an investigation on the struggles of marginalised individuals in the conflict between development and environment. The literature of Minamata disease in Japan in particular guided the identification of two factors that could make critical EE utilitarian and could cause patchy empowerment in a local community context.

The first factor was that critical theory could cause epistemological oppression in the understanding and knowing of marginalised people and their problems, despite its strong focus on the marginalisation and the power issues that cause it. Modern knowledge overpowers other types of knowledge; it *scientises* the knowledge of marginalised people for the sake of reproducing modern knowledge. Critical theory can identify marginalised people and the power problems that cause marginalisation, but cannot go beyond what the modern knowledge system understand regarding language, and local/indigenous knowledge that is often embodied and hardly verbalised. The oppression problem is inherent in the knowing and understanding of modern knowledge, that is, epistemology. Epistemological oppression can occur in all forms of critical research, including positivism, interpretivism and critical theory.

The second factor was that the schooling focus of critical EE negatively reacts with a homogenous view of critical theory, when it is applied to ESD in a local community development context. Critical EE enlarges the problem of epistemological limitation and oppression of critical theory. Particularly, the 'frame', which schooling could set, gives educators the 'authority' to choose who to be in the frame, such as the resource person, as well as the curriculum and the teaching aims. The educators can take a part of the diverse marginalised people, their knowledge and dynamic learning processes that are inextricably connected with community development process, to fit within the frame of schooling. Such authority makes educators focus on what happens within the frame, but deflects their attention away from the complex reality of marginalised people that exist outside of the frame. This includes people, their knowledge and their complex power relationship within the group and with the majority.

Critical EE is insufficient in a community development context. This finding necessitated modification of the methodological approach applied to the rest of the research. The decoloniality methodology was chosen to get closer to the learning process of the few marginalised people who were not empowered by the MSN's ESD, particularly Hatakeyama. There, the a priori theory was set aside for a certain period and Mombetsu was revisited to observe key MSN members in their everyday life context. This helped establish Hatakeyama's epistemology and to understand the learning and knowledge creation process of Hatakeyama based on his epistemology.

References

Agrawal, A. (2002). Indigenous knowledge and the politics of classification. *International Social Science Journal, 54*(173), 287–297.

Agrawal, A. (2005). The politics of indigenous knowledge. *Australian Academic & Research Libraries, 36*(2), 71–81.

Edwards, J. (2015). *Socially-critical environmental education in primary classrooms: The dance of structure and agency*. Springer International.

Fien, J. (1995). *Education for the environment: Critical curriculum theorising and environmental education*. Deakin University.

Giddens, A. (1984). *The constitution of society: Outline of the theory of structuration*. Polity Press.

Harada, M. (1985). *水俣病に学ぶ旅: 水俣病の前に水俣病はなかった* [A journey to learn from Minamata Disease: No Minamata Disease existed before Minamata Disease]. Nippon Hyoron Sha Co. Ltd.

Harako, E. (2013). *ESD は教育を考え直し、その向きを変えることである。とするならば、それをどのように着手するか?* [ESD is all about re-thinking and re-orienting education. If so, how can it be done?]. Paper presented at the Japan Society of Environmental Education 24th Conference, Shiga, Japan.

Huckle, J. (1993). Environmental education and sustainability: A view from critical theory. In J. Fien (Ed.), *Environmental Education: A pathway to sustainability*. Deakin University Press.

Huckle, J. (1996). Teacher education. In J. Huckle & S. Sterling (Eds.), *Education for sustainability*. Earthscan.

Illich, I. (1973). *Deschooling society*. Penguin Books.

Irokawa, D., Uchiyama, H., Sakurai, T., Tsuchimoto, N., Tsurumi, K., Hidaka, R., Munakata, I., & Watanuki, R. (1983). 座談会:「水俣調査の課題をめぐって」 [Round table talk on issues of the research in Minamata]. In D. Irokawa, (Eds.), *水俣の啓示—不知火海総合調査報告 (下)* [A relveration of Minamata: Shiranui Sea comprehensive research report (II)]. Chikuma Shobo.

Ishimure, M. (2003). *Paradise in the Sea of Sorrow: Our Minamata disease*. University of Michigan Press.

Kitoh, S. (2007). 水俣と抵抗の原理としての環境倫理学 [Minamata and environmental ethics as principle of resistance]. In S. Saishu & H. Tamba (Eds.), *水俣五〇年: ひろがる「水俣」の思い* [Minamata 50 years: Expanding thoughts on 'Minamata'] (pp. 131–164). Sakuhinsha Publisher.

Kitoh, S. (2009). 環境破壊をめぐる言説の現場から [Critical review on the discourse sites over the environmental problems]. In T. Iida, K. Ito, T. Inoue, T. Kawamoto, S. Kumano, M. Shinohara, T. Simizu, F. Sueki, N. Nakaoka, M. Nakahata, K. Noe, & J. Murata (Eds.), *岩波講座8 生命/環境の哲学* [Iwanami Lectures 8: Philosophy of Life/Environment] (pp. 151–170). Iwanami Shoten.

Mignolo, W. (2007). Delinking. *Cultural Studies, 21*(2–3), 449–514.

Mignolo, W. (2011). Epistemic disobedience and the decolonial option: A manifesto. *Transmodernity: Journal of Peripheral Cultural Production of the Luso-Hispanic World, 1*(2), 44–66.

Mignolo, W. (2014). Spirit out of bounds returns to the East: The closing of the social sciences and the opening of independent thoughts. *Current Sociology, 62*(4), 584–602.

Ministry of the Environment, Japan. (2013). *Lessons from Minamata disease and mercury management in Japan.* Ministry of the Environment, Japan.

Morris-Suzuki, T. (2011). A conversation with Minoru Hokari. In M. Hokari (Ed.), *Gurinji Journey: A Japanese historian in the outback* (pp. 12–29). University of Hawai'i Press.

Ndlovu-Gatsuheni, S. (2013). Why decoloniality in the 21st century? *The Thinker, 48*, 10–15.

NIMD. (2001). *In the hope of avoiding repetition of the tragedy of Minamata disease—What we have learned from the experience.* Social Scientific Study Group on Minamata Disease, National Institute for Minamata Disease.

Oiwa, K., Ogata, M., & Colligan-Taylor, K. (2001). *Rowing the Eternal Sea: The story of a Minamata Fisherman.* Rowman & Littlefield Publishers.

Saishu, S. (1984). *生あるものは皆この海に染まり* [All who live are dyed in this sea]. Sinyosha.

Sauvé, L. (1999). Environmental education between modernity and postmodernity: Searching for an integrating educational framework. *Canadian Journal of Environmental Education, 4*(Summer), 9–35.

Smith, L. (1999). *Decolonising methodologies.* Zed Books.

Soshisha. (2017). *水俣病のしつもんばこ* [Minamata disease Q&A]. http://www.soshisha.org/jp/about_md/for_child/%E6%B0%B4%E4%BF%A3%E7%97%85%E3%81%AE%E3%81%97%E3%81%A4%E3%82%82%E3%82%93%E3%81%B0%E3%81%93#patients

Ui, J. (1968). *公害の政治学: 水俣病を追って* [Politics of industrial pollution: Investigating Minamata disease]. Sanseido.

Ui, J. (1971). *公害原論 I* [Principles of industrial pollution I]. Aki Shobo publisher.

Ui, J. (Ed.). (1992). *Industrial pollution in Japan.* The United Nations University.

UNESCO. (2014). *Shaping the future we want: UN decade of education for sustainable development (2005–2014)* (Final Report). UNESCO.

Chapter 5
Rethinking ESD from the Perspective of a Socially-Marginalised Individual

The experiences of socially-marginalised individuals with Minamata disease provide clues to understand Hatakeyama's puzzling behaviours with the MSN. In particular, it is the life experience of one fisherman with Minamata disease, Masato Ogata (b. 1953), that provides the strongest insights to explain those (Ogata, 2001; Ogata & Oiwa, 1996; Oiwa et al., 2001).

Despite several differences between Hatakeyama and Ogata (such as the nature of issues with which they struggled, and ethnic background—Ogata as a Wajin), both had gone through similar experiences. Ogata was a fisherman from a poor village and had gone through struggles of discrimination. He had also fought for the rights of victims suffering from Minamata disease. Ogata's experiences provide clues to understand the causes behind Hatakeyama's Swing.

5.1 Ogata, a Minamata Disease Victim Fisherman

Ogata was born into the *Amimoto* (The head of fishermen's group in Japanese) family, in a small fishing village of Minamata, Japan. Around that time, the outbreak of the symptoms of methylmercury poisoning began spreading (Ogata, 2000). This was diagnosed as Minamata disease and life for Ogata's family changed drastically. Ogata lost his father when he was six from acute mercury poisoning (which was not identified as a cause of the sickness at that time). 'His [father's] hands and legs shook. He could no longer stand and walk. He drooled, went into fits of madness, and finally died' (Oiwa et al., 2001, p. 113). This new disease took the lives of his brothers, sisters, nieces and nephews almost at the same time.

F. Noguchi, *Rethinking Education for Sustainable Development in a Local Community Context*, Education for Sustainability 6,
https://doi.org/10.1007/978-981-16-9464-6_5

It took over ten years for the Nippon Chisso Company (NCC)[1] and the government to finally admit that there was methylmercury in NCC's wastewater. It was determined that a sub-chemical product from the production of acetaldehyde[2] caused the disease.[3] During that time, Ogata's family was subjected to discrimination by the residents in their small village. They were cast as having 'the strange disease' or 'the contentious disease' (Ogata, 2000, p. 184). Fishermen, in general, were looked upon as 'lower than beggars in Minamata' (Oiwa et al., 2001, p. 54), and the discrimination towards victims and their families multiplied.

Having experienced tragic deaths of close family members, discrimination and poverty, Ogata grew with anger and held a grudge against the NCC and society in general. 'Fighting among school kids was an everyday occurrence' (Oiwa et al., 2001, p. 55). Ogata's anger drove him to social activism when he was 15 years old. He searched for a way to 'avenge his late father' (Ogata, 2000, p. 187). In his own 'swing', as he changed his political stances from right to left—similar to Hatakeyama.

Ogata took a philosophical right-wing position in his teens (although later he switched to the left in his 20–30s). After leaving home at the age of fifteen, he joined an organisation which was a front for criminal *yakuza* operations in Kumamoto City. He spent a few years fighting against left-wing organisations and selling amphetamines (Oiwa et al., 2001, p. 67) and was arrested in 1971. After that experience, he decided to go back to his hometown to live as a fisherman. During this time, he was influenced by the leftist students in his community, who supported the Minamata disease movement. Within a few years, Ogata joined the Minamata Disease Certification Applicants' Council (MDCAC) to support the lawsuit for the official recognition of Minamata disease victims in 1974. He became the president of MDCAC in 1975 (Fig. 5.1).

He spent ten years arguing and fighting with government officials, police officers and doctors. He became notorious—'if they ignored me, I showered them with verbal abuse, kick them or threw ashtrays' (Oiwa et al., 2001, pp. 79–81). However, one day in 1985, he suddenly resigned as the president of MDCAC and withdrew himself from all social activism and his application for official recognition as a Minamata disease victim.

His decision came from his realisation of the contradiction in the dominant approaches to social transformation, including both political left or right activism. He noticed that Minamata disease victims had to stand on the very same ground and understanding that was held or understood by modern society. However, to fight against modern society, which kept producing problems like Minamata disease, contributed in maintaining the modern society (Oiwa et al., 2001). Ogata saw that social activism was entrapped in this understanding of modern society. Social

[1] NCC changed the company name to JNC Corporation in 2011 (JNC, 2017).

[2] Acetaldehyde is used as the agent to produce plastic material.

[3] The University of Kumamoto found that the methyl mercury in the NCC's waste water caused Minamata disease in 1959. However, this finding was concealed by the Kumamoto Municipal government and NCC until 1968 (Harada, 1995).

Fig. 5.1 Banners used by MDCAC. *Note* *怨 represents grudge in Japanese. *Source* Photo taken by the researcher in 2013 at Soshisha

activism only looked at the nation as a whole. It hardly recognised whose responsibility the Minamata issue was and did not do anything with the symptoms that the victims experienced through their suffering in their everyday life at the local community level.

Social activism did not give back what Minamata disease had destroyed. Ogata stated:

> There is something, which could be described as a problem of 'un-savable' souls in Minamata disease, which could not be saved by institutionalisation or by compensation money. (Ogata, 2001, p. 137)

Compensation and lawsuits were insufficient to save all the people and animals that had lost their lives or lived the suffering from Minamata disease in the past and present. Minatama disease destroyed the whole ecosystem around the Shiranui Sea. This ecosystem supported complex life cycles created through the interaction of the sea, rivers and mountains—including the lives of humans who subsisted on that environment (Ogata, 2001).

This realisation pushed Ogata to choose to live as a local fisherman, wishing to reconnect his broken social ties, spiritual connection with the spirits of the dead victims, and broken ties between humans and nature. For Ogata, the ideological right or left was not the final goal. These were just present there when he was desperately searching for any possibility of relieving them from the situation where the problems unreasonably kept occurring in every aspect of his community's lives.

5.2 Hatakeyama's Ainu World

The life of Ogata guided me to the assumption that Hatakeyama might not be 'swinging' like a pendulum between Group A and B, because of his weakness or a defect in his personality. Like Ogata, Hatakeyama might have desperately searched for a solution to the unreasonable problems that he had faced in his life—one where the political thoughts of 'left' or 'right' could not really give a clear answer. I began investigating this assumption by asking Hatakeyama what 'rights' recovery meant to him.

'Rights recovery of the Ainu is to get back what the Ainu used to have' (S. Hatakeyama, personal communication, December 13, 2013). I assumed that 'what the Ainu used to have' could be akin to Ogata's 'unsavable souls'—where compensation would not help.

If Hatakeyama was not able to describe this 'something' that the arbitration or the international legal framework could not solve, then what? I tentatively labelled this 'something' as 'Hatakeyama's Ainu world' and explored it by focusing on Hatakeyama's words of 'whale' to find clues to define and understand it.

What 'whale' represents to Hatakeyama

For Hatakeyama, 'whale' had more meanings beyond just catching and consuming one. When asked why he wanted to catch one, Hatakeyama's answers provided insight into how he understood the word, 'whale':

> I do not intend to make a profit out of it [hunting a whale] at all. This is my rights claim, as an indigenous person. Challenging the largest [animal] and top [sic] of the ecosystem on the globe would be just a full privilege of being born as a man... I always perceived myself as a loser. I put on a brave face at work. However, it was only at work. I am always carrying a feeling of inferiority. I really want to tell Wajin who have insulted Ainu until now. Even Ainu can do. We can do, because we are Ainu. I don't want to end my life as a loser. (S. Hatakeyama, personal communication, December 13, 2013)

Three words in his remark struck me; *the largest and top* [sic] *of ecosystem... a full privilege of being born as a man*, and *I really want to tell Wajin*. These statements gave me an insight of what 'whale' really meant to Hatakeyama. For Hatakeyama, catching the largest animal on the globe might represent his revenge against Wajin. It would demand attention given that it was the top of the ecosystem for a fisherman. It would be the biggest catch. 'Whale' might have also represented himself and his people. And now, as a fisherman, his power of catching such a mighty beast had been taken away from him and his Ainu people. The rights now controlled by a bigger power than he—the nation of Japan.

Hatakeyama saw an association between the unfairness and unreasonableness of the government of Japan in their control over whaling rights with the control of him and his people through assimilation and modernisation policies. He viewed them as ignoring his peoples' history in return for national growth instead.

For him, regaining control of whale hunting could have two implications. The Ainu rights to access natural resources based on his and his people's decisions could be reinstituted. This point would be congruent between Hatakeyama and other MSN members.

The other implication could be the emancipation of him and his people. The Ainu people traditionally believed in the spirits of all living creatures, plants and commodities that they related to in their everyday life. In their belief, *Kamuy* (spiritual being) appears in the Ainu (human) world in the outer form of animals (such as bears, owls, and salmon), plants (such as monkshood), diseases (such as smallpox) and natural phenomena such as fire and lightning (Utagawa, 1992). The Ainu people understand that killing, consuming or using these things meant freeing their spirits from their outer forms and sending them back to the place where their ancestral spirits dwelled (Fujimura, 1982; Utagawa, 1992). The Ainu people conduct a ceremony to express gratitude towards the spirits for these things that they believe have been bestowed upon mankind, and this may be seen as a 'respectful return gift from humanity to the heavens' (Utagawa, 1992, p. 255). This Ainu belief in the 'spiritual sending-back' (Utagawa, 1992, p. 255) is 'a different notion of sacrifice in Christian belief' (Fujimura, 1982, p. 177).

The second implication could make Hatakeyama's words of 'catching whale' much more than the indigenous rights as understood in the Western or Japanese modern context. Hatakeyama could see the spiritual connection between humans and whales, like Ogata had with his experience in Minamata. Hatakeyama had a memory of his *fuchi*, who told him not to mess with a particular area near the local mountain because the ancestral local Ainu people enshrined the head bone of a whale there for their ceremony purposes (S. Hatakeyama, personal communication, December 22, 2015). Hatakeyama might one day wish to return to this place, his people and connect with his ancestor's spirits through catching a whale. Hence, the underlying meaning of 'full Ainu as human' could be the emancipation of him and his people. This understanding of what Hatakeyama means by 'whaling' might be the best way he can express, using his limited vocabulary that had been shaped by his life as a fisherman and colonial history.

The researcher conducted an interview with an MSN key member (Member B) who offered an interpretation of Hatakeyama's meaning of 'whale' and 'whaling':

> It is very easy to understand that 'whaling' symbolises something about what Japan has done to Ainu, such as losing Ainu culture and its oppressive history. Many unreasonable problems have always been around Hatakeyama's life. Hatakeyama had fought against these, but he cannot see and express the entity that has always caused him problems. Considering his age, Hatakeyama is of the generation that cannot express their thoughts and feelings in words well. This is very different from the Ainu younger generation who are educated and can express their thoughts in straightforward and sophisticated Japanese words – this helps Japanese people understand them more easily. Such young Ainu people have hardly had unreasonable experiences such as those that Hatakeyama experienced. So, even the young Ainu, just like the Japanese people, are never going to be able to understand what Hatakeyama symbolically meant by his use of the word 'whaling'. When the words 'whaling rights' or 'indigenous rights' are spoken by these Ainu youth, these lose the very important meaning that Hatakeyama wanted to express. (MSN Member B, December 20, 2013)

It would be interesting whether or not Hatakeyama still wanted to seek whaling rights, if he was well-educated and not a fisherman. It was apparent that Hatakeyama used a specific language in his daily life and in his Ainu world so that when he tried to express ideas, such as through the words 'indigenous whaling rights', it was understood differently by others. Hatakeyama speaks Japanese, and specifically, the dialect of the Mombetsu fishermen. Just like most of the Ainu in his generation, he had little opportunity to study in modern educational systems in Japan. He was not familiar with particular Japanese words currently spoken in specific contexts, such as in the arbitration process, and even at MSN meetings. It was difficult for him to express and present his ideas logically and meaningfully to his audience.

On the other hand, the words 'indigenous whaling rights' also meant more to him than ideals. Hatakeyama had long dreamed of hunting a whale as a fisherman, as he had worked in the environment where fellow fishermen envied whaling as a profitable business and he understood the political and economic power surrounding it; and he had detested the Japanese government's attitude towards whaling. Hatakeyama's feelings, experiences and concerns had a depth of complexity that meant to describe them to others was a difficult challenge, yet it would be important to do so, so that everyone, including those at the MSN meetings could really understand what Hatakeyama stood for in regard to the emancipation of his people.

5.3 Embodied Local and Indigenous Knowledge

Hatakeyama could not express the meaning embodied in his local knowledge when he appeared to advocate 'whaling' in his beliefs. Berger and Luckmann (1985) explained that the process of forming identity occurred in 'the period during which the human develops towards its completion in interrelationship with its environment is also the period during which the human self is formed' (pp. 67–70). Drawing on their explanation, the reason why he could neither verbalise nor recognise his Ainu world as different from modern understandings by others can be assumed that his identity and knowledge was developed from his childhood through his particular life experiences.

Hatakeyama was born in the 1940s when the Ainu culture had already been decimated. The values, social ties, traditional ceremonies, materials and languages that had supported Ainu society were vanishing. The Ainu adults belittled their culture and convinced Hatakeyama to believe in the superiority of the Japanese people and their culture over the Ainu's ways. Hatakeyama grew up hardly having opportunities to learn traditional Ainu culture.

At the age of fifty, when he came out as identifying as Ainu for the first time, he began to explore what his Ainu identity meant. Hatakeyama had to confront memories that he had wanted to deny and forget for a long time. Then, he had to weave pieces of memories of Ainu ways into a firm and stable cultural ground upon which he could stand for his rights claim. However, this process was not easy as his Ainu memories were fragmented.

Some memories were clear though. He often told stories of his early childhood days in conversations with MSN members. Hatakeyama spoke about the drunken Ainu fishermen of his *kotan* (village), who had spent days drinking whenever the sea was rough. Hatakeyama, as a child, had to run to the town to buy *saké* for them. Their drinking always ended up with a fight among them. He also often talked about his grandmother who had a traditional Ainu tattoo around her mouth. His grandmother told him the stories of the Ainu gods who lived in all the natural creations (MSN, 2011). In my own listening to these stories, they were not coherently linked to each other, but distinct from each other without relation.

To fill in missing pieces of his memories, Hatakeyama drew on his life experiences as a fisherman. Wind, temperature, swell, humidity, smell, the colour of the ocean and sky, flying seabirds, fish running in waves, fishing techniques, business, values, trust relationship and ethics—he has experienced these and expressed them through his daily practice as a fisherman. Pálsson (1997) described that fishermen's knowledge about fishing was mainly the result of practical engagement with the environment, based on his participant observation on the Iceland fishermen. This statement indicates that fishermen's knowledge covered not only technical fishing information but also a comprehensive knowledge of trust and relationship with the local community people and was constructed through the interaction with local nature and cultural influences.

Hatakeyama also obtained the knowledge to be a fisherman from his local social environment. He filled in the gaps of his fragmented Ainu memories with his embodied local fishing knowledge and his imagination of what life was like for his Ainu fisherman ancestors. Hatakeyama's Ainu world was understood now by this type of distinct knowledge—a knowledge which could be characterised as tacit, practical, embodied and locally and historically contextualised. This knowledge can also be referred to as 'embodied local and indigenous knowledge'.

5.4 Epistemological Oppression

There was a power differential between modern knowledge and Hatakeyama's embodied local and indigenous knowledge. This did not surface in the MSN's arbitration process. It can be assumed that the power differential created epistemological oppression, without any of MSN members' and even Hatakeyama's being aware of this oppression.

The epistemological oppression that Hatakeyama experienced can be explained by the work of Berger and Luckmann (1985), which explored how social interaction with others affects the process of one's knowledge creation.

> Only a small part of the totality of human experience is retained in consciousness. The experiences that are so retained become sedimented, that is, they congeal in recollection as recognizable and memorable entities... Intersubjective sedimentation also takes place when several individuals share a common biography, experiences of which become incorporated in a common stock of knowledge. Intersubjective sedimentation can be called truly social only when it has been objectivated in a sign system of one kind or another, that is when the possibility of reiterated objectification of the shared experiences arises. (Berger & Luckmann, 1985, p. 67)

One can identify a part of his/her life experiences and store it as his/her knowledge while he/she repeats the interaction back and forth with surrounding people. In this process, the values, thoughts, the way of understanding and knowledge of the surrounding people significantly affect one's understanding and knowing of a part of his/her life experiences as 'knowledge'.

This process of social interaction and knowledge creation also happened to Hatakeyama in the MSN's ESD process. Hatakeyama tried to recognise a part of his life experience in the conversation with the people around him in regard to his rights claim. He did this, in particular, through meetings, workshops and seminars. Hatakeyama interacted back and forth with the MSN members and the participants at the events. He tried to recognise, verbalise and socialise his Ainu world. Hatakeyama recalled his life and talked about his concerns at the meetings, seminars and workshops in, and outside, of Mombetsu and at international conferences. The conversations with other participants and the documents that recorded his talks might have helped him to re-develop his Ainu identity.

In this process, unfortunately, there was a mismatch between two parties—Hatakeyama and most MSN members. The reasons behind this mismatch can be categorised into four obstacles: place, language, knowledge and a feeling of inferiority.

Place

The first obstacle was the place where the social interactions happened. These included the locations of the meetings, workshops and seminars. These settings physically cut Hatakeyama from his connection with his life as an Ainu and a fisherman. Hatakeyama had to recognise that was locally contextualised and he needed to identify it as knowledge in an entirely different context. It could be argued that Ainu communication methods, like drawing and singing, could be incorporated in these meetings. However, these options would be able to represent only a part of his Ainu world. Because of its local and historically contextualised nature, Hatakeyama could hardly verbalise, or even conceptualise, in a narrow and closed meeting room his arguments for indigenous rights in a place that was foreign to him.

Language

The second obstacle was the language used for the communication at the meetings (Japanese, more specifically, modern Japanese—the language of the coloniser). In the discussions at MSN, the following Japanese words were often used, such as, 権利 (*kenri*; rights), 先住民族 (*senjyu-minzoku*; indigenous people), 捕鯨 (*hogei*; whaling), 鯨 (*kujira*; whale) and 鮭 (*saké*; salmon) to represent his Ainu rights claim. However, these words relate highly to the cultural and political contexts of Japan, which colonised the Ainu people. Hatakeyama did not know the Ainu language so he had to use Japanese words to describe things that did not exist in Japanese society or were subjugated by the Japanese. Thus, these key Japanese words used for Hatakeyama's rights claim did not fully represent Hatakeyama's Ainu world.

Further those words inherited the oppressive relationship between the colonisers and the colonised, without anyone being aware of it, including Hatakeyama.

Knowledge

The third obstacle was the knowledge that predominantly underpinned the communication, thoughts and the language used for the discussions of the MSN meetings, workshops and seminars. The members mostly had some modern background, in terms of their education, lifestyles and career. Many of them were not the subject of this activism and were without direct experience of discrimination or working in the primary industries like Hatakeyama. They were concerned with environmental and human rights issues largely based on their learning at schools, seminars, media, documents or observing someone else's life experience. It was difficult for MSN members to fully know and understand the life experiences of Hatakeyama. Hatakeyama's words tended to be understood literally through the lens of modern Japanese, which meant Hatakeyama could not accurately express his Ainu world.

Feeling of inferiority

The last obstacle was Hatakeyama own outlook—that he felt inferior towards the Japanese people and their modern knowledge backgrounds. Hatakeyama grew up receiving physical and verbal abuse which imprinted on him and contributed to his feeling of inferiority. He did not complete his compulsory education due to the discrimination. Remembering multiple and ongoing experiences of discrimination in the school and local community resulted in his feeling of inferiority towards the Japanese people and those with modern educational backgrounds. Even after a few decades since he publicly claimed his Ainu identity, the feeling of inferiority still rankled Hatakeyama:

> I never have the right words to describe my concerns because I do not have an education. It does not matter how many years have gone by after telling the world I am Ainu. This thought of 'I am stupid' keeps haunting me, even after shaking it off again and again. (S. Hatakeyama, personal communication, December 13, 2013)

His feeling of inferiority obstructed him from recognising and expressing what he felt through his body. Despite the strong confidence that he obtained through his hard work in his fishing business, Hatakeyama felt inferior to Wajin. He felt fear and anxiety in relation to the Japanese experts who live their lives by using the skills and knowledge obtained through the modern educational system.

The four obstacles above blended together, creating an epistemological oppression between those with modern knowledge and those without it in the MSN. At the MSN meeting in Mombetsu, during the process of arbitration, Hatakeyama murmured that he felt 'threatened' when he was discussing issues with Group A members (MSN, 2012). He did not say any more about how he felt about Group B but he told me later that he had a similar feeling with both groups (S. Hatakeyama, personal communication, December 13, 2013). None of the MSN members had any intention to threaten him at all; rather, what was present was each member's sincerity, and all of them did their best to try to help Hatakeyama from their own sense of justice.

It seems reasonable that it was more his fear and inferiority in relation to modern knowledge and the Japanese (who control this modern knowledge) that made him feel threatened.

> I am such a dumb person. My emotion always comes first before the words.... (S. Hatakeyama, personal communication, December 13, 2013)

I often observed Hatakeyama putting himself down in his everyday life. However, his claims were not true. Hatakeyama could not put his concerns into articulate statements not because of his lack of an academic background. He was engaging with a very local and historically contextualised knowledge, which was far beyond the understanding, thoughts and languages of modern knowledge. Furthermore, the power of modern knowledge placed most MSN members' knowledge and their epistemology superior to Hatakeyama's knowledge and his epistemology. In so doing, it dismissed a large part of Hatakeyama's Ainu world and even redefined it by the understanding obtained through discussions at the MSN. As a result, the MSN discussions were sometimes oppressive to Hatakeyama, even though it was organised in a 'participatory' and inclusive way. This view of the discussions might be because he felt that something in him was oppressed silently in an unexplained way.

5.5 Rethinking Hatakeyama's 'Puzzling' Behaviour

Hatakeyama's 'irrational' behaviour emerged while he was struggling to deal with the power differential between two knowledges and epistemologies. In the conversations with MSN members, without most MSN members' and even Hatakeyama himself knowing, Hatakeyama had to cross over the different knowledges and different epistemologies; between modern knowledge and embodied local and indigenous knowledge. He was trying to recognise what he never recognised before, and to verbalise his recognition that he never verbalised, by looking for the words of the coloniser that underpinned the modern knowledge of the Japanese people. At the same time, however, he resisted the power that could drag him back into the modern and colonial understanding.

MSN members with modern educational backgrounds and expertise knowledge interpreted Hatakeyama's concerns and provided advice (drawing on the concepts and approaches within the modern knowledge system, such as the Japanese legal system or the UNDRIP). Their suggestions did not fully represent Hatakeyama's true concerns. Hatakeyama even tried to make every effort to fit into their perspectives—motivated by the nature of his knowledge and his feeling of inferiority. After a while, he began to feel unsettled because he felt somewhere in his body that none of the advice fully addressed what he wanted. It was at this juncture that he would meet yet another expert. His behaviour and conflicted thinking made him look like a pendulum in motion.

Hatakeyama's 'irrational' behaviour was not a one-time phenomenon that happened only in the MSN process. It happened in his activism, even as early as the 1980s. One time, he approached politicians and researchers who were renowned for their conservative opinions to lobby and research possible activities related to his activism. Another time, he worked with activists in the field of environment and human rights who committed to their efforts for social change. One day, a journalist pointed out a lack of clarity in Hatakeyama's ideological standpoints, half blithering: 'Hatakeyama-san, are you right or left?' (MSN, 2010). Like Ogata, Hatakeyama looked for whatever he could to improve his outcomes but he could not find it in either ideological camp of right or left. Hatakeyama had struggled with the power differential between these knowledge paradigms for a long time.

There was no intention to disempower Hatakeyama at all. There was only the 'good' intention for social justice and attempts to stop the modernisation process of Japan by working with marginalised people. But all this occurred without going beyond the understanding of modern knowledge.

Close friend A said:

> I may be able to call it 'overcoming of modernity'. Both Hatakeyama and I are carrying plenty of dirty modernisation stuff. The possible way to go beyond modernity is, I always think, that I, 'shamo' [another way of calling Japanese in Ainu, in a slightly discriminative way], as a being charged with the responsibility for the Ainu issues, could stand on the same ground with the Ainu people for us to work together. (Close friend A, personal communication, December 16, 2013)

'Translation was never possible' (Atwood, 1986, p. 5), even in the 'participatory' and 'inclusive' MSN process. None of MSN members, even Hatakeyama, realised that there was something that could go far beyond the words in their conversations. Ideas and *Weltanschauungen* (worldviews) are only part of the sum of what passes for knowledge (Berger & Luckmann, 1985, pp. 26–27). Hatakeyama could express only a part of his 'Ainu world' that arose from the unverbalised daily environment in which he lived. And even then, Hatakeyama's words were interpreted into a coloniser's modern Japanese language and their true meaning lost their accuracy.

As pointed out before, Hatakeyama's 'puzzling' behaviour was the result of him being torn between two types of knowledge. His Swing behaviour represented his struggles in expressing his knowledge when the power of modern knowledge excluded his knowledge from its understanding. He showed his irritation, anger and desperation when he struggled to express his Ainu world—one that he could not articulate or verbalise.

From my experience, critical theory-based approaches could be effective only for those who share the same languages, ways of communicating and approaches to social change within modern knowledge. This could be an effective approach with most MSN members who possessed the modern knowledge and lived in urban cities. But, unfortunately, it was not effective for the few Ainu people, like Hatakeyama, who were contextualised in their own Ainu world.

5.6 New Beginning

After withdrawing from the rights claim for official recognition of Minamata disease victims, Ogata in Minamata, decided to live as a fisherman on the Shiranui Sea of Minamata. He stepped away from the social activism that challenged the nation because it was the modern knowledge and the same system of modernisation in which he would need to fight that was also producing problems, such as Minamata disease. His word, '*moyai* (tying two ships together in Japanese)' (Ogata, 2001), symbolically represented his decision to return to a simple life:

> I would like to rejuvenate the values [in Minamata] that we lost by reconnecting and strengthening the weakened moyai. (p. 213)

> I will really have a feeling of 'I am living' when I could be a part of the world where our sea, mountains and islands of Shiranui are ranging. (p. 71)

For Ogata, reviving his traditional way of living through simply living as a fisherman in Minamata was the only way to save his spiritual and cultural beliefs.

The amount of the social impact that Ogata's change actually brought was very little. However, he internally made a large paradigm shift. He had left the social context that someone else had created and suppressed him for many years. He overturned the understandings about 'rights' and the approach to obtain the rights, which were taken for granted by those who live in the modern Japanese society. He began to establish his own context based on his understanding and his words, to solve the Minamata disease problem. His struggles through his life enabled him to see its internalised contradictions when he attempted to enact major social change. This was, in fact, the process of Ogata's spiritual emancipation and his learning for his growth.

In an interview with Hatakeyama, I noticed that there were a few words that indicated the new beginning of his own personal paradigm shift, which appeared similar to Ogata's experience (S. Hatakeyama, personal communication, December 13, 2013). In our conversation, Hatakeyama talked about his dream to create a locally based enterprise, as well as a space to connect socially-marginalised people in Mombetsu. He told me that he had visited a few organic farms and food processing factories for disabled people to explore his interests.

Hatakeyama told me his dream to build his own *chisé* (Ainu traditional house) on his land where his house and his warehouse were formerly. From this land, about 300 Ainu people' remains were excavated when his house was built in the late 1990s (Hayasaka Komuten and Takanaka Consultant, 1998). In 2012, his land needed reimagining due to the fire that burnt his house. He was thinking about what to do about his land:

> The Ainu used to not only catch salmon and trout but also traded these with the Wajin and Russians. I think that I should revive our trading culture in this modern context –producing and selling the fishery products, with a label that tells you about Ainu rights. In this production work, I want to create the work for those who are struggling to live, such as the youth, the disabled and the elderly. I want to give these people work to obtain skills. This land should not be used for building a house or a warehouse. Developing such people will console the ancestral spirits who sleep here. There, we can get together and talk about the problems that

> we face. This is my humble dream. (S. Hatakeyama, personal communication, December 13, 2013)

He believed that creating a space for sustainable fishing, and for socially-marginalised people to get together, would comfort his ancestral spirits' sleep. Then, I asked him:

> For most MSN members, the indigenous fishing rights are about whether or not the Ainu people would catch something, such as salmon and whales. However, what you said to me that it is more than that. Your indigenous rights are about re-connecting people and creating a new sustainable livelihood. The Ainu used to enjoy very rich 'human to nature' relationships regarding salmon and whales before. Yes, the government still does not give you the rights to catch these, but, doesn't it mean there has already been some indigenous rights recovery? Especially, if you are launching some efforts to regain such a rich human-nature relationship, before obtaining the actual fishing rights? (S. Hatakeyama, personal communication, December 13, 2013)

Hatakeyama became silent for a moment, staring at me for a while. Then he replied:

> Oh, yes. It does. (S. Hatakeyama, personal communication, December 13, 2013)

and added:

> The meaning of indigenous right recovery includes the realisation of a society where the socially-marginalised can live together. I had such a kind of idea but I could not get the right words. (S. Hatakeyama, personal communication, December 13, 2013)

After the arbitration, most MSN members and the media regarded the recognition of Ainu as a local stakeholder as a success. This result might have a socially transformative impact on the knowledge and social framework that the majority of Japanese supported. However, I question what was meant by 'success', and for whom. This success belittled Hatakeyama's Ainu world, and reinterpreted it to fit into the knowledge and social framework of the majority.

The conversation above with Hatakeyama points towards the idea that he was at the beginning of his own paradigm shift. Hatakeyama expressed his thoughts about his indigenous rights in more diverse and richer words than what I had heard in my early involvement with the MSN in 2010. These words were not given to him by the experts. Years of struggling and 'swing' finally brought him to the landing point at which he is now at. And this is neither a right nor left ideological camp. He began to localise himself; to find the right words to articulate and even to realise a glimpse of his true Ainu world.

5.7 Summary

Hatakeyama's paradigm shift and his 'irrational' behaviour formed a significant part of his learning and knowledge creation process—one that could not be understood with critical theory. Decoloniality in this research allowed an understanding of his struggles and dis-empowerment process that modern knowledge overlooked. Hatakeyama also took his own decoloniality approach where he de-contextualised himself from thoughts and approaches that were taken for granted in modern society; and he began finding his own words and approaches based on his local Ainu identity.

Ogata in Minamata and Hatakeyama in Mombetsu made very little social impact. However, their individual internal paradigm shifts could be the essential learning step to achieve sustainable community development. If the challenge for social change of marginalised people was understood through modern knowledge, could their epistemological oppression actually be changed? It would be necessary for socially-critical ESD to re-establish the knowledge and the epistemologies of the socially-marginalised people so that they would be enabled to engage in a real dialogue between the modern knowledge holders and other indigenous knowledge holders.

The next chapter presents a critical reflection and conclusion to this book. It theoretically summarises the experiences of MSN's ESD, including Hatakeyama, MSN members and myself as an educator. It also presents the theoretical implication of these on the gap between critical EE and socially-critical ESD. The chapter will then offer a praxis framework for ESD in a community development context based on the critical reflection of this research. The framework could then provide guidance for educators, socially-marginalised people and wider community members who work in sustainable community development.

References

Atwood, M. (1986). Greenfield Review. *Canadian Poetry Issue, 13*(3 & 4), 5.

Berger, P., & Luckmann, T. (1985). *The social construction of reality*. Doubleday.

Fujimura, H. (1982). *アイヌの霊の世界* [The Ainu's spiritual world]. Shogakukan.

Harada, M. (1995). Minamata disease: Methylmercury poisoning in Japan caused by environmental pollution. *Critical Reviews in Toxicology, 25*(1), 1–24.

Hayasaka Komuten and Takanaka Consultant. (1998). *紋別市旧元紋別墓地移転改葬事業発掘調査報告書* [Mombetsu City Old Moto-Mombetsu Ainu grave relocation project: Archaeological study report]. Hayasaka Komuten and Tanaka Consultant.

JNC. (2017). *Historical Overview*. http://www.jnc-corp.co.jp/english/company/time-line/time-line.html

MSN. (2010, 20–21 June). *Mopet Sanctuary Network meeting report*. Mopet Sanctuary Network.

MSN. (2011, November 12–14). *Mopet Sanctuary Network meeting report*. Mopet Sanctuary Network.

MSN. (2012, February 18). *Mopet Sanctuary Network Okhotsk Mombetsu ESD Seminar report*. Mopet Sanctuary Network.

Ogata, M. (2000). *魂のゆくえ* [Whereabouts of the spilit]. In A. Kurihara (Ed.), *証言 水俣病* [Testimony: Minamata disease] (pp. 182–202). Iwanami Shoten.

Ogata, M. (2001). *チッソは、わたしであった!* [Chisso, It was me!]. Ashi shobō.

Ogata, M., & Oiwa, K. (1996). *Tokoyo no fune wo kogite* [Rowing the Eternal Sea: The story of a Minamata Fisherman]. Seori Shobo.

Oiwa, K., Ogata, M., & Colligan-Taylor, K. (2001). *Rowing the Eternal Sea: The story of a Minamata Fisherman*. Rowman & Littlefield Publishers.

Pálsson, G. (1997). Enskilment at Sea. *Man: Journal of Royal Anthropological Insititute, 29*(4), 901–927.

Utagawa, H. (1992). The "sending-back" rite in Ainu culture. *Japanese Journal of Religious Studies, 19*(2–3), 255–270.

Chapter 6
Within and *Beyond*: A Praxis Framework for ESD in a Community Development Context

The previous chapters looked at a tacit part of ESD that I observed through my practical experiences of twenty years. The research focused on informal education that sought to empower local community members in a development process for achieving sustainability. In particular, a tacit gap between two fields was identified: ESD and community development. This research assumed that the underpinning conceptual framework of ESD, which was part of critical EE, might not be efficacious to the wider and broader scope of, and settings for, ESD. This assumption went beyond the dominant assumption by critical educators who identified political, socio-, and economic pressures as the cause of the rhetoric-reality gap in ESD.

Therefore, this research sought how ESD might contribute to (or be integrated within) community development, and vice versa; and how a community development practice might enrich ESD discussions. The main aim was summarised as:

> To develop a praxis framework for integrating ESD and community development as mutually supporting to strength the practices in both ESD and community development field.

The relevance of critical EE to socially-critical approaches to ESD in a community development context was also explored. Critical EE had provided a theoretical framework for policies and research on ESD and had been the guiding theory for my practices with the MSN.

The following three subset research questions were developed to explore informal ESD in a community development context more fully:

1. How useful is critical EE in understanding ESD in a community development context? Answers to this question might provide an understanding of the relevance and effectiveness of critical EE to ESD in a community development context.
2. What are the key elements of ESD that can facilitate the empowerment of marginalised community members in efforts to achieve sustainable community development? Answers to this question might contribute to the development of a praxis framework for ESD in a community development context.

F. Noguchi, *Rethinking Education for Sustainable Development in a Local Community Context*, Education for Sustainability 6,
https://doi.org/10.1007/978-981-16-9464-6_6

3. How might this praxis framework be validated and how might it add new insights to current critical EE? Answers to this question might lend validity to a praxis framework for ESD in a community development context.

To address these subset aims, this research conducted two critical ethnographic studies of MSN, presented as separate parts: Part I—ESD *within* socially-critical Approach; and, Part II—ESD *beyond* socially-critical Approach. This research began with an investigation of the effectiveness of socially-critical approaches to ESD in relation to local community empowerment, particularly marginalised community members. The research in this section was informed by critical theory (Part I). However, the results of Part I made it evident that critical EE (guiding theory) and critical theory (methodology) were insufficient to understand the learning process and knowledge construction of the few Ainu people (including Hatakeyama). This finding necessitated a methodological shift of this research to decoloniality (Part II). This resulted in the findings of the two parts to be contrastive; one could not explain particular data but the other one could, and vice versa.

Reflecting on the key findings from the research, this chapter concludes with critical reflections and a conclusion. These are presented in three sections: (i) proposing 'a praxis framework for ESD in a community development context'; (ii) an analysis of the significance of the study; and, (iii) the way forward.

6.1 Proposing a Praxis Framework

Praxis integrates theory and practice, or reflection and action, for the consicentisation and the emancipatory empowerment of the learners for the transformation of themselves and the society. A praxis framework in this research comprised of a theoretical lens and a practice framework. The theoretical framework (that informed the praxis framework) was developed based on four key findings of this research.

The four key findings that this research identified are:

- Key finding 1: Insufficiency of critical EE due to epistemological limitation of critical theory;
- Key finding 2: 'Schooling' in critical EE as the enhancer of epistemological limitation;
- Key finding 3: Necessity of a decoloniality lens to surface what 'critical' overlooks; and,
- Key finding 4: Silencing of different knowledges and different learnings for ESD in a community development context

The practice framework, in turn, operationalises the theoretical framework in four steps. These four key findings became the theoretical lens that supported each of these steps:

Step 1: 'Conscientising' the limitation of understanding local community problems within an understanding of critical EE;

Step 2: 'Stepping out' from the dominant frame of views and knowledge, which is supported by modern knowledge;
Step 3: 'Establishing the epistemology' of marginalised people from their perspectives; and,
Step 4: 'Re-engaging' back with dialogue about social change with majority members.

My experiences as an educator are also incorporated into the praxis framework. This included the struggles I had in finding a better methodological approach and my pursuit of understanding the real meaning of knowledge and learning of the Ainu community.

Based on the four key findings and four steps, a praxis framework for ESD in a community development context is proposed. This framework is summarised in Table 6.1. This praxis framework has three elements, including: (i) a practice framework; (ii) a theoretical framework and, (iii) a role of educator. These three elements can involve four steps in practice.

This framework can be used by anyone who is involved in seeking solutions for community problems and to support mutual learning among the stakeholders (which might, e.g. include researchers, practitioners, local residents, marginalised people and government officials). This framework encourages a mutual learning and reflection process where the diverse stakeholders have a chance to take a leadership role and to participate in actions for social change.

Theoretically, a **praxis framework** takes the integrated approach of decoloniality into critical EE. It concerns both modern knowledge and other knowledges of marginalised people. This framework acknowledges the importance of critical EE in understanding the dominant and powerful modern knowledge of a society and its oppression of other knowledge types. But rather than criticising this as the march

Table 6.1 A praxis framework and its three pillars (summary)

	Theoretical framework	Practice framework	Role of the educator
Step 1	Key finding 1: Critical theory and decoloniality integrated	***Conscientising*** the limitation of understanding in local community problems	In addition to the roles of the educator as facilitator and coordinator, this research describes additional roles as a ***cultural broker*** and ***escort runner***
Step 2	Key finding 2: Decoloniality	***Stepping out*** from the dominant frame of views and knowledge	
Step 3	Key finding 2: Decoloniality	**Establishing** the epistemology of the marginalised	
Step 4	Key finding 3: Critical theory and decoloniality integrated	***Re-engaging back*** with the multi-stakeholder dialogue with the reconstructed epistemology from the below	

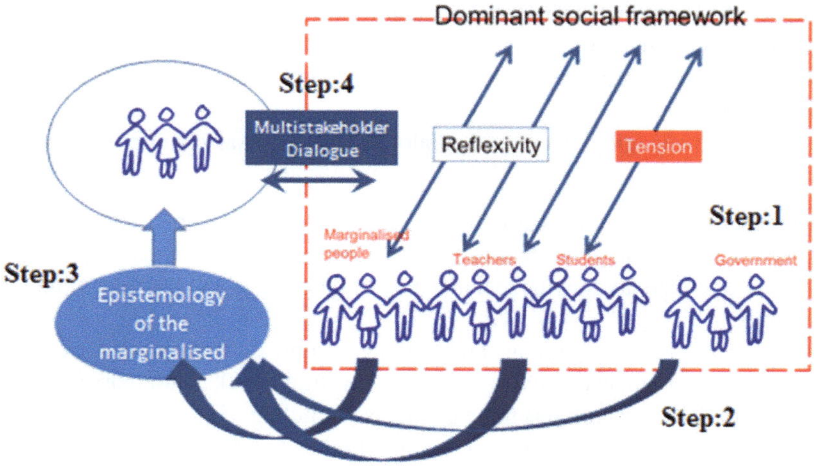

Fig. 6.1 A praxis framework for ESD in a community development context: Four steps in practice

of modernity, it integrates a decoloniality lens. This understands the modern knowledge, including its benefits to, and problems of, marginalised people by shifting the positionality of knowing, and establishing a new epistemology—as discussed below.

Learning and knowledge creation can occur through the four steps, when the participants and educators attempt to transcend the boundary of a dominant social framework, and allow themselves to be immersed in the different context of others (Fig. 6.1).

This section presents the four steps (in their own subsection from 6.1.1, to 6.1.4) and the role of educator in the process of going through the four steps (subsection 6.1.5).

6.1.1 Step 1: Conscientisation

This step encourages stakeholders who engage in the process of community development to consider three aspects of the knowledge paradigm upon which the majority people stand (Fig. 6.2). Firstly, it encourages them to understand the oppression and limitations of modern knowledge that causes the marginalisation of particular groups of people, their views and indigenous knowledge. Secondly, it raises an understanding that this modern knowledge (that supports the majority, critical EE and critical theory) has epistemological limitations for understanding the knowledges and learning processes of marginalised people. Thirdly, applying modern knowledge to know and understand the problems of marginalised people can oppose the marginalised people even further.

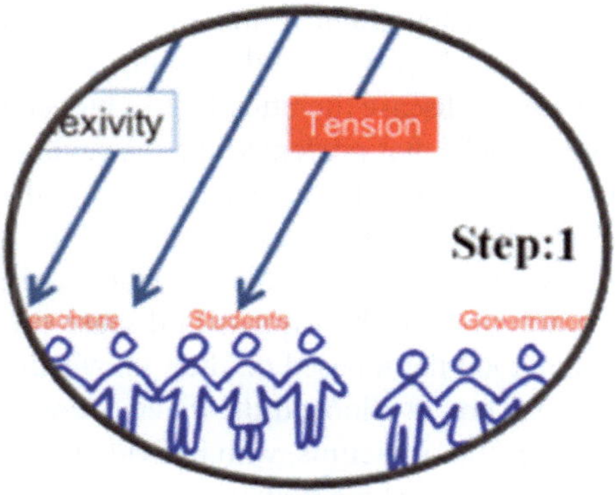

Fig. 6.2 Step 1

6.1.1.1 Theoretical Framework

The theoretical framework of this step helps the stakeholder to understand the epistemological limitation of modern knowledge, including through critical theory. The step is informed by Key finding 1 of this research. Methodologically, though, this process is informed by the integrated approach of decoloniality and critical theory.

Key finding 1: Insufficiency of critical EE due to epistemological limitation of critical theory

This research identified that critical EE was insufficient when it was applied to socially-critical approaches to ESD in a community development context. This finding was determined because of the epistemological limitations of critical theory. The insight about the potential for this epistemological limitation arose from the review of literature in Chap. 2. It became clearer when this research confronted the problems of 'patchy empowerment' and Hatakeyama's 'irrational' behaviour that were portrayed in Chap. 3. 'Patchy empowerment' meant that there was a presence of a few disempowered people among the larger numbers of community members who *were* effectively empowered by the inclusive and participatory learning and actions of MSN. These large numbers of community members included both Japanese and Ainu people. They were mostly urbanised, had a modern education background up to a higher education level, and were not engaged in primary industry. They took part in many local learning activities and undertook a range of actions on national and international issues. On the other hand, the same activities resulted in less-empowerment or disempowerment of a few Ainu members, including the MSN founder, Hatakeyama. Guiding theory (critical EE and critical theory) could not explain the insufficiency of critical EE in the MSN.

The epistemological limitation of critical theory was elaborated in the literature review in Chap. 4 when discussing the impact of Minamata disease in Japan.[1] The Minamata disease literature highlighted the issue of a 'policy systemic view' (Kitoh, 2007, 2009) that prevented the research, practices and policies to provide a fundamental solution for Minamata disease, and instead, caused epistemological problems. The policy systemic view understood the problems of marginalised people systemically with a bird's eye like 'a policy maker'. With this view, those who search for the solutions to the Minamata disease problems saw the victims as one mass and understood them based on their knowledge (mostly scientific and universal knowledge). They overlooked the diverse, complex and even contradictory reality of the same group of victims, who individually are burdened and experience the problems through their whole body and through their everyday life at the bottom of society. This view creates a new knowledge for solutions that 'particularises, verifies and generalises (Agrawal, 2002)' the totality of the victim's experiences. In the power relationship between those who hold the agency of knowing and the marginalised people, the newly created knowledge defined who the victims were and the problems and could be applied to solutions. The victims were forced to fit into this new definition and solutions for the problems were decided by others. As a result, problems with Minamata disease were never solved. The Minamata disease literature provided an internal understanding about why critical theory was problematic in a local community context.

Critical theory concerns who, whose voices, what perspectives are missing in a society, and attempts to bring marginalised people into a space for discussion with diverse stakeholders (Habermas, 1972, 1979). However, as shown in Fig. 6.3, it has three problems.

> Firstly, critical theory does not concern itself about marginalised people's view. While it is true that critical theory can decide who is to be in the discursive dialogue space, it can, however, overlook marginalised people and leave them. It treats marginalised people as a mass and it is not mindful of their diversity, complexity and contradictions within their group and in the relationships they have with the majority.
>
> Secondly, critical theory does not question their viewpoints or the ground upon which they stand. Whereas, the stance of the majority is highly supported by their modern knowledge, leaving marginalised people to conform (by fitting into the modern languages, concepts and knowledge used in the modern knowledge paradigm). The act of bringing even part of a marginalised people's group to this paradigm could distort their own understanding of their experiences, relationships, knowledge and epistemology.
>
> Despite its strong criticism of modernity, critical theory also emerged from, and was developed, based on the same knowledge production system that supported the modern knowledge paradigm (Morris-Suzuki, 2011). It produces newly

[1] At this time, the opportunity to study at the University of Tokyo in 2013–14 as an exchange PhD fellow allowed me to study the causes and impacts of Minamata disease after 1950s, where extensive studies had already been conducted.

Fig. 6.3 Epistemological limitation of critical theory

created knowledge with some of marginalised people. It reintegrates this into the current modern knowledge and uses it for redefining the problems of marginalised people. However, the power imbalance between modernity and the marginalised people still remains.

Thirdly, critical theory does not question the 'good intentions' of those who engaged with activism for social justice, environmental problems and solutions to those problems. Part II portrayed that many participants of the MSN believed their approaches or tools for liberation and emancipation of the marginalised people were still problematic in terms of knowing and understanding of the true nature of the problems of the marginalised people. Such approaches/tools included participatory and inclusive workshops, seminars, facilitation, rallies, petitions, lobbying and participatory research.

These approaches/tools for liberation and emancipation were still the products of modern knowledge. In terms of learning and knowledge creation, such approaches still oppress marginalised people. The power of modern knowledge in these tools tended to dismiss the epistemologies of marginalised people and became stronger when it was connected with social status, class, race and gender of the modern knowledge holders. This majority could not understand that there were different ways of knowing and expressing the problems of marginalised people.

But also the power of modern knowledge reproduces the modern knowledge by focusing on only the part of marginalised people's knowledge that the modern knowledge can understand and integrating it into the modern knowledge. Such reproduction of the knowledge does not challenge the epistemological oppression of the modern knowledge over the knowledge of the marginalised people.

6.1.1.2 Practice Framework

The theoretical framework is applied in the practice framework of Step 1. Considering the epistemological limitation of critical theory involves the process of *consicentisation* (Freire, 1972). Individuals within the dominant framework need to recognise the epistemological limitations of the current critical methodological and theoretical frameworks. These frameworks may guide practitioners and researchers in their engagement with marginalised people in terms of sustainability. In this process, individuals might acknowledge that knowledge paradigms exist outside the dominant framework and cannot be fully known and understood solely by remaining within the lens of the dominant framework.

6.1.2 Step 2: Stepping Out

This step encourages the stakeholders to *step out* from the knowledge framework that they are familiar with, in terms of the way of knowing and learning the knowledge of marginalised people. Individuals educated within the dominant framework need to set aside their guiding theories and thoughts and step out from the dominant social framework to engage with marginalised people (Fig. 6.4). The people from the majority group should attempt to hand over their agency of knowing and understanding into the hands of the marginalised people. The experiences in this step can help the modern knowledge holders to re-capture and re-identify problems of the marginalised people. In this step, the marginalised people also need to step out from their own boundaries (such as beliefs of negativity and inferiority of their own values, images and knowledges) that were borne out of the oppressive relationship with the majority.

Fig. 6.4 Step 2

6.1.2.1 Theoretical Framework

The theoretical framework of this step helps the stakeholders to understand the need to step out from their existing knowledge framework to understand marginalised people from theirs. The theoretical framework of this step was informed by Key finding 2 of this research. Methodologically, this represents the bridging process between critical theory and decoloniality.

Key finding 2: 'Schooling' focus of critical EE enhances epistemological limitation

The second key finding was that schooling (which is the dominant focus of most research in critical EE) enhances the epistemological limitation of critical theory, when critical EE is applied to community development context. As Chap. 2 shows, critical EE has grown mostly in formal education settings based on the premises of curricula, learning goals and schedules, pedagogical approaches, educational materials, roles of teacher and learners. The adaptation of critical EE to non-formal and informal education settings was often discussed by looking at the part that could be understood within a particular schooling environment, rather than from the broad and dynamic learning processes in a local community.

This schooling focus sets a frame for a clear perspective, the aims, the role of educator and the learners. When a schooling concept is applied to a community development process, it creates a setting where a practitioner may associate their role with a teacher in a formal education setting or a school. Therefore, a practitioner attempts to set a semi-structured learning process in the community development process, such as seminars, workshops and participatory citizen research. (Often, only these parts are highlighted and named as ESD in the literature.) Such semi-structured learning process becomes an invisible framework that functions more like a school. In this framework, the practitioner may think that he/she holds the agency of knowing. They may choose who should be in the learning frame, who the marginalised people are, what their problems are and what the goal of learning is, how the problem can be solved, and whom the local community people can work with.

The practitioner may apply participatory and inclusive approaches to the whole learning process. But, once again, he/she may be unaware of the knowledge paradigm that produced these approaches. As seen in the arbitration process of the MSN, the participatory workshops, seminars, field surveys and policy advocacies—all of these provided learning opportunities for only those who were familiar with the way of learning and knowledge that schooling could provide. These approaches may not be relevant to those who live based on the embodied local/indigenous knowledge, such as Hatakeyama, who struggled at the MSN meetings.

Because of its strong focus based on schooling, it limited the community learning process and may have even oppressed different knowledges and ways of learning from becoming explicit. As discussed in Chap. 4, while critical EE tends to 'particularise', 'validate' and generalise, diverse, complex and even contradicted marginalised people within the schooling frame, it does not see what exists outside of what modern knowledge currently understands. Community learning processes need to be explored beyond just a schooling way of understanding.

In a local community development context, critical EE needs to expand its understanding of learning and knowledge which often narrows the settings of ESD to a schooling context. To make ESD more socially-critical, ESD practitioners in a local community development context may need to understand the process of sustainable development (ESD = SD), where the dynamic learnings and actions are inextricably embedded in everyday life experiences in a local community.

In a local community development context, the stakeholders need to be aware of the particular framework that is imposed on them. The framework can include the knowledge framework, social framework and curriculum framework. It is important for stakeholders to step out from the way of understanding and knowing that they are familiar with and to step into the context of the marginalised people. This is the decolonising process that was discussed in Part II.

6.1.2.2 Practice Framework

This step encourages both the educators and the participants to focus on what is overlooked in the understanding of modern knowledge. It suggests that stakeholders set aside their dominant knowledge, values and ways of knowing and instead immense themselves in the very real context of the marginalised people. They should seek to experience what the marginalised people tacitly experienced in their day to day lives, if the situation allows.

The approaches taken here may include living in the local community context and actually experiencing the life of the marginalised people as one. They should seek to understand and listen to the knowledge of the marginalised people from their perspective. Through this, they will come to understand the totality and complexity of their issues that the marginalised people experience in their everyday life.

6.1.3 Step 3: Establishing the Epistemology of the Marginalised

This step encourages the stakeholders to immerse themselves in the context of the marginalised people (Fig. 6.5). It is required for them to be apart from the modern knowledge for a certain period and provide them with an opportunity to learn the knowledges and way of learning of the marginalised people.

Fig. 6.5 Step 3

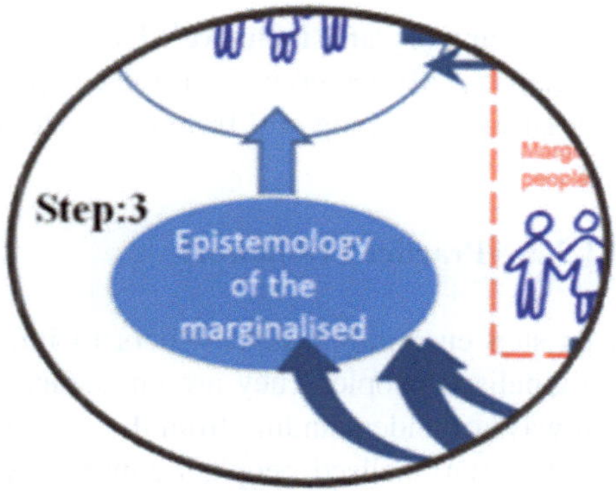

6.1.3.1 Theoretical Framework

The theoretical framework of this step facilitates the stakeholders in identifying the knowledge and the learning process of the marginalised people. The theoretical framework of this step is informed by Key finding 3 of this research. Methodologically, this process is informed by decoloniality.

Key finding 3: Necessity of establishing the epistemology of the marginalised people

The third finding reveals the necessity of establishing the epistemology of the marginalised people. This provides the stakeholder with a decoloniality lens that allows them to surface the knowledge and the learning processes of the marginalised people. This is often overlooked in the modern knowledge framework, and it also helps to the stakeholder understand why and how this overlooking occurred.

The idea of establishing the epistemology of the marginalised people was developed from the Minamata disease experience in Japan, as discussed in Chap. 5. It was asserted that it would be the 'only way' to get close to the real problems of the marginalised people. This was to know and understand the problems of the marginalised people from their way of understanding and knowing, or establishing epistemology of the marginalised people (Kitoh, 2007, 2009). This approach was similar to decoloniality methodology in the Western research literature (Ndlovu-Gatsuheni, 2013, 2015).

The assumption of epistemological limitation in critical EE required a methodological shift to decoloniality for Part II. Theoretically, I set my guiding theory and methodology aside by handing over my agency of knowing to Hatakeyama, who was the most marginalised Ainu member in MSN. In so doing, I immersed myself in the Mombetsu local community to understand the meaning of knowledge and learning process of Hatakeyama and other MSN local community members.

Decoloniality helped to establish Hatakeyama's way of knowing and learning—or his epistemology—which brought to the surface his embodied local/indigenous knowledge and previously unrevealed oppression that he experienced in the process of 'participatory and inclusive' discussion process of the MSN (see this analysis in Chap. 5). My experience of a decoloniality shift in this research highlights the necessity of 'stepping out' from the modern knowledge frame.

6.1.3.2 Practice Framework

This step encourages stakeholders to immerse themselves in the context of the marginalised people. They are encouraged to learn the knowledge, the problems and ways of understanding from the marginalised people by immersing themselves into the marginalised people's community context. In this step, the stakeholders might come to better conceptualise and understand the plight and perspectives of the marginalised people.

6.1.4 Step 4: Re-Engaging Back with the Multi-Stakeholder Dialogue

Step 4 facilitates the marginalised people to re-engage back into dialogue with modern knowledge holders. This is based on the established epistemology of the marginalised people (see Fig. 6.6).

6.1.4.1 Theoretical Lens

The theoretical framework of this step facilitates the marginalised people to re-engage back into dialogue with the majority people. The theoretical framework of this step is informed by Key finding 4 of this research. Methodologically, this process is informed by the integrated approach of decoloniality and critical theory.

Fig. 6.6 Step 4

Key finding 4: Silencing of different knowledges and different learnings

A decoloniality lens helps to bring to light the different knowledges that have been overlooked and oppressed by modern knowledge. Gaining insights from the life story of Ogata (Ogata, 2000, 2001; Oiwa et al., 2001), presented in Sect. 5.1, helped to analyse Hatakeyama's thinking based on his words of 'whale' and 'whaling' and the assumed existence of 'Hatakeyama's Ainu world'(see Sect. 5.2).

Hatakeyama's embodied local/indigenous knowledge provided the base for his Ainu world. This knowledge significantly contributed to Hatakeyama's identity as an Ainu. In this process, he drew on his experiences as a fisherman, which were embedded in Hatakeyama's body movement, actions and senses in an everyday, local community context, together with his emotional struggles from targeted discrimination. This research identified that Hatakeyama's knowledge was tacit, locally contextualised and embodied in nature. It contrasted with the modern knowledge that was verbal, conceptual, universal and rational.

In the MSN process, the power of modern knowledge oppressed his embodied local/indigenous knowledge. The discrimination, assimilation and oppression he faced resulted in the feeling of inferiority of himself and for his Ainu people. Three factors ('place', 'language' and 'knowledge') impacted on the way he communicated with the MSN members, and a fourth, Hatakeyama's feeling of 'inferiority', oppressed him at the workshops, seminars and in the participatory citizen's research. These factors work like a 'frame' that set the boundary in a community context, wherein modern knowledge dominated. While this frame allowed the members to discuss freely within the understanding of modern knowledge, it separated Hatakeyama from his own context and his epistemology.

Through a decoloniality lens, the real issues behind Hatakeyama's Swing came to be understood. His 'swing' symbolically represented his struggles and resistances that he experienced when his embodied local/indigenous knowledge was excluded and alienated from the understanding of modern knowledge. However, this allowed Hatakeyama to obtain his own words to describe Ainu rights and to re-engage back into dialogue with the modern knowledge holders using his own words and knowledge (see Chap. 5).

6.1.4.2 Practice Framework

In Step 4, the marginalised people are encouraged to re-engage back with the modern knowledge holders in the dominant social paradigm. Given the modern knowledge stakeholders now have a better understanding of the marginalised peoples' plight, both parties should be able to re-engage in dialogue within the modern knowledge paradigm. This should lead to outcomes and solutions to the problems of the marginalised people.

6.1.5 Role of Educator: Cultural Broker and Escort Runner

Throughout the four steps of this praxis, the role of the educator goes beyond what has been recognised in the critical EE literature, where the educator acts more as facilitator and coordinator (see Sect. 2.1). In these new roles, linked to the praxis framework, they could be described as a *cultural broker* and or an *escort runner*. Hereafter, these roles are briefly explained based on my personal and research experiences and supported by relevant academic literature.

During this research, I, as the educator and the researcher, experienced crossing between two knowledge systems of modern knowledge and the local knowledge of Hatakeyama. This experience allowed me to discover the role of the educator to deal with these different knowledges. This role of crossing between different knowledge paradigms can be related to the concept of the cultural broker which has been recognised in the field of community development and social work. Particularly, this term describes a person who deals with people from multiple cultural backgrounds and multiple knowledges (see, e.g. Escobar (1991) and Jenkins (2015)). The term is used to describe educators who are willing to cross over different knowledges, including both dominant modern knowledge and the knowledge of the marginalised people. They immerse themselves in the knowledge of the marginalised people to understand their epistemology and to reflect this back to the modern knowledge paradigms, but from the perspective of the marginalised people. They create the space for the dialogue between the majority people and the marginalised people. They facilitate the discussions during multi-stakeholder dialogues, with the epistemology of marginalised people. The role of the educator as described in the praxis framework, as a cultural broker could be further examined in the literature and investigated in the future research.

However, the research also helped me to identify that the educator needs to go beyond the role of dealing with different knowledges. In the process of exploring different knowledge paradigms, educators also act as what I can best describe as an *escort runner*. The idea of an escort runner was gained from my personal experience when I was attending a conference in early 2015. I was connecting between flights, on my way from India to Australia. The flight from India was delayed, and I had only five minutes to transit in the airport in Singapore. A conference co-participant from Japan was on the same flight from India with me but was connecting to a different flight, headed for Japan. She saw my confusion and panic, and said, 'OK, I will run with you to the boarding gate'. Running with her gave me the encouragement I needed to overcome what was otherwise a very confusing and panicked feeling. This experience illustrated for me the important role of the escort runners, who guide and assist blind people in running competitions.[2]

Escort runners need to have analytical eyes because they are seeing on behalf of someone else and have to be able to communicate instructions to the runner.

[2] The role of escort runner in a running competition is well-explained in (The Japan Times, 2016): '…running with eyes covered while being guided by someone else, in order to experience what it feels like for blind people to run'.

Therefore, they must have knowledge of the runner, their preferred language and so on. This is similar to the role that I played in the journey with Hatakeyama. Despite the conflict between the two groups of the MSN and Hatakeyama's 'irrational behaviour', I attempted to go through the process with Hatakeyama, all through my engagement with MSN. Based on my experience, I have described the term escort runner in this research to mean a person who crosses the different knowledges, shares the experience of the 'swing' in crossing different knowledge paradigms with marginalised people, but who maintains an analytical view to see what is really behind his disempowerment. The role of escort runner may include elements of cultural broker in terms of dealing with multiple knowledges. However, the role of escort runner is different from the role of cultural broker, in the point that it attempts to understand the learning and knowledge creation process of the marginalised people from the perspectives of the marginalised people. While the role of cultural broker may concern the sensitivity of dealing with different knowledges, however, it still stands on the modern knowledge to understand the problem of the marginalised people (Escobar, 1991; Jenkins, 2015). This research indicated that both roles were required for the educator.

In the praxis framework, the two roles of cultural broker and escort runner are integrated throughout the four steps. The degree of how these two roles are integrated may vary depending on the stages of practices. It is also worth to explore the role of the educators as an escort runner in the future researches.

6.2 Reflection on the Significance of the Research

This section reflects on: (i) the validity of the research process; and, (ii) the contributions it has for the research community. This section responds to the third sub-research question of this book.

6.2.1 Validity of Research Process

The validity of the analyses of data and theoretical discussions are discussed in the following six categories.

(i) Validity of the critical ethnography method

The critical ethnography method created a mutual learning process between the research participants and me, as the researcher. This process contributed to the empowerment and emancipation for both Hatakeyama and for me.

Throughout the research process, I shared all the transcribed data and analyses with the key MSN members who participated in this research. These communications created the opportunities for us to critically reflect on what the MSN had or had not achieved and what the obstacles were. After the arbitration process was complete and the construction plan for the final industrial waste management facility was finalised, I shared all collected communication with the MSN members. This raw data and its analyses allowed MSN members and I to reflect what we had done and what were the actual factors behind Hatakeyama's disempowerment.

The communication with Hatakeyama also brought me countless learning opportunities. These often challenged my pattern of thinking and my understanding of my research discipline. It encouraged me to hand over my epistemological agency into his hands. Hatakeyama came to see his words and behaviour from a different perspective than that he had held until the end of the arbitration process. The analyses on the power differential between modern knowledge and his embodied local/indigenous knowledge helped Hatakeyama to move away from his feeling of inferiority both of himself and his view of the Ainu people. Hatakeyama's new knowledge that arose from the analyses, provided the strength for me to re-engage back into the conversation and reconsider my theoretical stance.

The following words of Hatakeyama[3] indicate some of our mutual learning:

> You came to see me a number of times. Then, you drew a picture [see Fig. 6.1] to make 'what Hatakeyama is thinking of, and what he is aiming at' concrete. Well, Noguchi-san, you also, kind of, went through huge struggles in your heart, just like me. (S. Hatakeyama, personal communication, December 22–24, 2015).

These words confirmed the value of the framework. He was aware that he could not change the power differential between modern knowledge and his embodied local/indigenous knowledge in the short term. But he stated that he was now in a better place. He could engage with different knowledge and perspectives from his own, and he could better understand the limitation of modern knowledge. It was an inspiring moment for me as a researcher and as a practitioner when I heard his words. I felt that this research, through sharing someone's life's burdens and emancipation, validated the methodological framework of this book by giving a new, empowered voice to the marginalised.

(ii) Validity of the data analyses with local community people: What do theoretical discussions mean to local community people?

The verification of the data and analyses was made through circulating the drafts of two book chapters in Japanese (Noguchi, 2014a, b). These publications helped the participants to understand how their words were analysed for the purpose of the research and how it would be used in any publications. I communicated with the participants via post, telephone and fax message between Melbourne and Japan, as I found that they did not use email or social media. The continual communications with them after the data collection in the field helped me to maintain a trusting relationship with the key participants. This also provided both participants and myself the confidence to deeply reflect and provide rich detail on the events and experiences of all in this book.

---

[3] These words were from an interview with Hatakeyama when I went back to Mombetsu in December, 2015. I went back to share my preliminary conclusions with Hatakeyama and a few key members of the MSN.

(iii) Validity of the analysis in the Japanese research context

To ensure the relevance of my research in the theoretical discussions on ESD and community development in Japan, I presented my research progress at ESD-related conferences of the Japan Society of Environmental Education[4] and shared the manuscripts of the publications of critical ethnographies with researchers in the field of ESD and community development. These researchers worked for the University of Tokyo, Tokyo University of Agriculture and Technology, Tokyo Gakugei University and Kyoto University. The opportunity given to be a Specially Appointed Research Fellow at the University of Tokyo (2013–14) allowed me to obtain consistent and critical feedbacks on my analyses of Part I and II, the key discussions around the epistemological limitation of critical EE and the need for decoloniality. Further discussions with my supervisor and colleagues who were familiar with the ESD in Japan and the issue of marginalisation in the environment-development problems like Minamata disease further acted to increase the reliability of the interpretation and findings of this research.

(iv) Validity of the analysis in English-speaking, Western research context

It was also necessary for this research to be valid in terms of the theoretical discussions of the Western English-speaking research community where this PhD research was conducted. In so doing, the research process was presented at conferences for EE, EfS and ESD. Particularly, the analyses of Part I and II were presented at the Australia Association for Environmental Education (AAEE) Biannual Conference in 2012, 2014 and 2016 and the Contemporary Approaches to Research Symposium at Deakin University in 2015 for their comments.

(v) Validity of the analysis in practical context in Asia

This research also considered the validity of the analyses with the NGO practitioners in ESD and with those involved in community development fields in Asia. The analyses and key discussions of this research, particularly, the epistemological limitation of critical EE and the praxis framework, were presented at the ESDGs International Conference in 2015 for their comments.

(vi) Validity of the data translation from Japanese into English

Some of the literature used in this research, and almost all of the interview data were in Japanese. The interviews were all transcribed in Japanese characters initially, and the parts that I quoted for the book were translated by me into English. To keep the accuracy of the original language, a professional translator, who had a 20 year translation and interpretation career in social science (including many works in EE, EfS and ESD), proof-checked the translated texts presented in this book.

[4] Presentations were made at JSOEE conference in 2013 and 2016, Tokyo University of Agriculture and Technology in 2016, University of Kyoto in 2017.

6.2.2 Contributions of This Research

This research presents two major contributions that might enrich current theory and practices of ESD and the theoretical grounding of critical EE.

(i) Re-affirming the value of critical ethnography method

This research re-affirmed the value of a critical ethnography methodology in terms of challenging against the dominant knowledge paradigm. The key findings from the critical ethnographies challenged my guiding theory and methodological frameworks that were supposed to influence the way of understanding and knowing in the research. These resulted in a methodological shift in this research where critical ethnography was replaced by a decolonisation methodology as being more appropriate for the research questions.

In this research, the finding from the analyses based on a critical ethnography methodology indicated the epistemological insufficiency of critical theory. The need for a methodological shift became apparent during data collection. The decolonisation methodology reverses the understanding of critical EE that methodology decides a research method (Fien & Hillcoat, 1996). This research highlights that critical ethnography, in itself, can keep hidden the oppression of the dominant social and knowledge paradigms. It was through the decolonisation methodology (including the joint efforts made by the research participants and the researcher), that the process of 'unlearning' and re-learning between the participants and the researcher occurred more profoundly, and that it enhanced the understanding of modern knowledge holders with the perspectives held by marginalised people.

(ii) Decoloniality gives an unwavering perspective to theoretical and policy discourses on ESD

In the middle of this research, the UN Decade of Education for Sustainable Development (UNDESD) ended in 2014. The global education community had been searching for a direction in education for sustainable development (ESD) towards new Sustainable Development Goals by 2030. Currently, the new educational concept, GCED, is being added to the post-UNDESD policy discourses for sustainability-related education by UNESCO (UNESCO, 2015a). This responds to the call for GCED that would address sustainability problems in everyday life context that ESD could not do during the UNDESD (Huckle & Wals, 2015).

EE, EfS, ESD, and now, GCED, all have differing mantras that can confuse research into this area. This is similar to when ESD became the key educational framework at the start of the UNDESD in 2005. While the ongoing conceptual confusion over sustainability-related education, UNESCO focuses on 'local community' as one of the five key priority action areas for the *GAP on ESD* (UNESCO, 2013) and *ESD for 2030* (UNESCO, 2019). Can, then, GCED solve local community problems that ESD could not solve during the UNDESD?

Unfortunately, the situation around community-based approaches to ESD appears not to have changed much during this research. Theoretical frameworks that might support community-based ESD is still lacking and a formal education and schooling approach still dominate in the sustainability-related education field. This research gives a firm perspective from a decoloniality perspective to practitioners who are searching for ways to move ESD forward in their everyday context in local communities.

This research strongly supports decoloniality as an unwavering approach to overcome the ongoing confusions around sustainability-related education, including EE, EfS, ESD and GCED. It could enhance the local community-based ESD to confront severe realities at a local community level. Recently, Lotz-Sistika (2017) advocated decolonisation as a future frame for sustainability education. She contended, 'hearing those that have been silenced and marginalised would appear to be vital to the project of more socially just, sustainable societies characterised by a renewed commitment to the common good' (p. 14). This research aims to move forward decolonisation as an appropriate methodology. ESD (and also EE and EfS) could not face the local community reality during the UNDESD because it was unaware of the epistemology of the marginalised people and pushed ESD into a schooling frame. The changing of the labels of in sustainability education will not be effective unless ESD decolonises its understanding and steps out from its epistemological boundaries.

Political and economic pressures remain strong and have been making the ground of sustainability-related education 'shaky' (Selby, 2006, p. 355). This research confirms that decoloniality could truthfully, authentically and carefully help to understand and articulate local community problems, such as those who are marginalised. The praxis framework suggested in this research could provide a firm and stable ground for those who are in search of sustainability-related education at a local community level.

6.3 The Way Forward

This final section of the book offers implications for practice and further research arising from the findings of this book. A praxis framework has potential applicability to other areas, not just ESD. It is hoped that it would especially encourage fellow practitioners in the field of ESD and community development to further their work on the emancipation and empowerment of local communities, particularly marginalised people.

During this research, I often thought how my thinking and a praxis framework could be relevant to different problems in a different context, and I have not explored its applicability yet. Like the MSN situation presented in this book, similar oppression and marginalisation seem to be occurring all around the world, even when the efforts might be believed to be 'good'. For example, I foresee the potential of a praxis framework for practices and research on topics such as community resilience in a post-disaster period, gender issues and the livelihood of Australian indigenous people.

In the first example, of community resilience in a post-disaster experience, I immediately think of a symbolic incident that happened at the start of this research in 2011. It was the 3.11 Earthquake and Fukushima nuclear power plant accident. I was living in Tokyo and experienced this earthquake and its aftershocks for over a month. I lived in fear of nuclear radiation poisoning. Since then, Japan has experienced numerous natural disasters, more earthquakes, typhoons and storms, floods and bushfires. The situation is very similar to the rest of the world, including Australia.

A praxis framework could be applied to understand the process of redevelopment in the post-natural disaster process. Local community people, particularly who engage in primary industries in rural areas of Japan, hold so much embodied local/indigenous knowledge. In the redevelopment process, they often find themselves struggling to express their claims and concerns in the discussions with the governments and experts. This situation is no different from the struggles of Hatakeyama. In the redevelopment process of 3.11 Earthquake, there were issues around the 'Giant Sea Wall' construction project by the Japanese government.[5] These need to be re-thought to be more inclusive and understanding of the local indigenous people of that area.

The second example is one of gender. This research was initially based on critical EE, which has its theoretical root in critical feminist theory. I would like to see how this research might contribute to critical feminism studies. I also have observed the mismatch in understanding gender-related problems—those between what women experienced tacitly and what Western, modern and male dominant knowledge understands as a problem. For example, through my experiences of natural birthing and the home birth of my two sons in Australia, I have observed that what a mother experiences through my body in my prenatal and postnatal period were often neglected, ignored and silenced by the power of modern scientific Western medical knowledge. In particular, when I had my second son in Darwin, I often saw Australian indigenous pregnant women loitering outside the hospital. They had been transported to the hospital in advance of their due date because of Northern Territory government policy which viewed the high risk of complications in childbirth of indigenous women (Carson et al., 2013). The issue was that they did not have a choice to homebirth. I wondered how a praxis framework might inform the government and change policy. Based on Hatakeyama's experience, I assume that these mothers may lose their opportunities to learn and embody their indigenous knowledge to be a mother in their own local context and may be forced to fit into the frame of Western scientific maternity care set by the government.

What does such experience really mean to those indigenous women in relation to the power differential between their embodied indigenous knowledge and the modern knowledge? A praxis framework could provide key perspectives in understanding the epistemological problems of women in childbirth. Such study might contribute to new concepts and new words to describe their problems from their own epistemology and

[5] Japanese government has been building 400 km-long, four storey-high walls on coastal lines of Tohoku region to stop tsunami (Stone, 2015).

re-engage them back into discourses around the dominant Western medical science and the better birth choices for the Australian indigenous women.

The last example, relates to the rights of the livelihood of the Australian indigenous people. Based on my work experience, attending seminars and my life in the Northern Territory, I have observed the epistemological mismatch between those with good will (those who intends to 'help' the Aboriginal people) and the Aboriginal people. The situation is similar to the MSN. A praxis framework could be used in search of solutions for the problems associated with sustainable development in Australia and the Aboriginal people. Likewise, the indigenous recognition in the Constitution and the rights of the indigenous people are debated and argued in English, and in the meeting rooms of big cities. This discussion happens in a framework based on the majority of Australians who are coloniser of the land, rather than the indigenous Australian people. This situation can be appreciated in the reports on Aboriginal fishing rights:

> Indigenous people have a culture that relates to the land and sea in a holistic way that also includes connections to powerful and significant places. However, the emphasis that is now put on the management of discrete sites can overlook and diminish Indigenous connections to the environment as a whole. (National Oceans Office, 2002, p. 1)

In discussion spaces for indigenous rights recovery, the Aboriginal people could share only a part of their entire knowledge by borrowing the words of the coloniser's language. On the other hand, efforts have been made towards a solution of indigenous problems with the Aboriginal people in a local community context. One such example is the Outback Pride, a small-scale enterprise that promotes and sells bush food cultivated and produced by Aboriginal people (Outback Pride, 2017). Despite the potential of these small-scale influences, indigenous rights recovery (based on local, sustainable community development) have not moved beyond its epistemological boundary, and are not yet at the interface with the rights recovery arguments that happen in a modern, English-speaking context. My passion now is to develop comparative critical ethnographic studies between the Ainu people and the Australian Aboriginal people. By so doing, it might facilitate mutual learning and provide the basis for empowering marginalised people the world over.

References

Agrawal, A. (2002). Indigenous knowledge and the politics of classification. *International Social Science Journal, 54*(173), 287–297.

Carson, D., Berger, V., & Taylor, A. (2013). Where are the babies?: The spatial distribution and mobility of indigenous infants in the Northern territory. *Charles Darwin University: Demography and Growth Planning,* (201306), 1–13.

Escobar, A. (1991). Anthropology and the development encounter: The making and marketing of development anthropology. *American Ethnologist, 18*(4), 658–682.

Fien, J., & Hillcoat, J. (1996). The critical tradition in research in geographical and environmental education. In M. William (Ed.), *Understanding geographical and environmental education: The Role of Research* (pp. 16–40). Cassell Education.

Freire, P. (1972). *Pedagogy of the oppressed*. Penguin Books.
Habermas, J. (1972). *Knowledge and human interests* (2nd ed.). Beacon Press.
Habermas, J. (1979). *Communication and the evolution of society*. Beacon Press.
Huckle, J., & Wals, A. (2015). The UN decade of education for sustainable development: Business as usual in the end. *Environmental Education Research, 21*(3), 491–505.
Jenkins, S. (2015). Rehabilitating psychology in Australia: The journey from colonising agent to cultural broker. *Psychotherapy and Politics International, 13*(2), 115–128.
Kitoh, S. (2007). 水俣と抵抗の原理としての環境倫理学 (Minamata and environmental ethics as principle of resistance). In S. Saishu & H. Tamba (Eds.), *水俣五〇年: ひろがる「水俣」の思い (Minamata 50 years: Expanding thoughts on 'Minamata')* (pp. 131–164). Sakuhinsha Publisher.
Kitoh, S. (2009). 環境破壊をめぐる言説の現場から (Critical review on the discourse sites over the environmental problems). In T. Iida, K. Ito, T. Inoue, T. Kawamoto, S. Kumano, M. Shinohara, T. Simizu, F. Sueki, N. Nakaoka, M. Nakahata, K. Noe, & J. Murata (Eds.), *岩波講座8 生命/環境の哲学 (Iwanami Lectures 8: Philosophy of Life/Environment)* (pp. 151–170). Iwanami Shoten.
Lotz-Sistika, H. (2017). Decolonisation as future frame for environmental and sustainability education: embracing the commons with absence... (Semi-final version). In P. Corcoran & J. Weakland (Eds.), *Envisioning Futures for environment and sustainability education* (pp. 45–62). Wageningen Academic Publishers.
Morris-Suzuki, T. (2011). A conversation with Minoru Hokari. In M. Hokari (Ed.), *Gurinji Journey: A Japanese historian in the outback* (pp. 12–29). University of Hawai'i Press.
National Oceans Office. (2002). *Sea Country—An Indigenous perspective: The South-east Regional Marine plan assessment reports*. The Commonwealth Government of Australia.
Ndlovu-Gatsuheni, S. (2013). Why decoloniality in the 21st century? *The Thinker, 48*, 10–15.
Ndlovu-Gatsuheni, S. (2015). The decolonial Mandela: Embodiment of peace, justice and humanism. *Journal of Developing Societies, 31*(3), 305–332.
Noguchi, F. (2014a). ESD のラディカルアプローチ-モペッ・サンクチュアリーネットワークの活動 (Radical Approach to ESD: Efforts by Mopet Sanctuary Network). In Japan Society of Environmental Education (Ed.), *日本の環境教育(Environmental Education in Japan)*. Toyokan Publisher.
Noguchi, F. (2014b). 身体化された地域知とアイヌ民族の権利回復: 社会的被排除者の〈生〉の個別性からESDを捉えなおす (Embodied local knowledge and right recovery of Ainu: Rethinking ESD from the individuality of a socially marginalized). In Japan Society for the Study of Adult and Community Education (Ed.), *アイヌ民族・先住民族教育の現在(Current Research on the Ainu and Indigenous People's Education)* (Vol. 58, pp. 94–108). Toyokan Publisher.
Outback Pride. (2017). *About outback pride*. http://www.outbackpride.com.au/about
Ogata, M. (2000). 魂のゆくえ (Whereabouts of the spilit). In A. Kurihara (Ed.), *証言 水俣病 (Testimony: Minamata disease)* (pp. 182–202). Iwanami Shoten.
Ogata, M. (2001). *チッソは、わたしであった!Chisso, It was me!* Ashi shobō.
Oiwa, K., Ogata, M., & Colligan-Taylor, K. (2001). *Rowing the Eternal Sea: The story of a Minamata fisherman*. Rowman & Littlefield Publishers.
Stone, J. (2015). *Japan to build 250-mile-long, four storey-high walls to stop tsunamis*. http://www.independent.co.uk/news/world/asia/japan-to-build-250-mile-long-four-storey-high-wall-to-stop-tsunamis-10131013.html
Selby, D. (2006). The firm and shaky ground of education for sustainable development. *Journal of Geography in Higher Education, 30*(2), 351–365.
The Japan Times. (2016, December 20). *Escorts for blind runners keeping pace amid Japan's marathon boom*. https://www.japantimes.co.jp/news/2016/12/20/national/escorts-blind-runners-keeping-pace-amid-japans-marathon-boom/#.WiTqAFWWaUl

UNESCO. (2013). *Proposal for a global action programme on education for sustainable development as follow-up to the United Nations Decade of Education for Sustainable Development (DESD) after 2014*. UNESCO.

UNESCO. (2019). *Framework for the Implementation of Education for Sustainable Development (ESD) Beyond 2019* (40 C/23), UNESCO. https://unesdoc.unesco.org/ark:/48223/pf0000370215.locale=en

MIX
Papier aus verantwortungsvollen Quellen
Paper from responsible sources
FSC® C105338

If you have any concerns about our products,
you can contact us on
ProductSafety@springernature.com

In case Publisher is established outside the EU,
the EU authorized representative is:
Springer Nature Customer Service Center GmbH
Europaplatz 3, 69115 Heidelberg, Germany

Printed by Libri Plureos GmbH
in Hamburg, Germany